AUTHOR'S NOTE

This book is based upon interviews conducted in 2024 and 2025. I also rely on newspaper and magazine articles, personal correspondence, biographies, commentary tracks, and other archival sources. If a subject "says" something, it was during the course of my original reporting. If he or she "said" something, it came from an archival source.

HANNIBAL LECTER

A LIFE

BRIAN RAFTERY

SIMON & SCHUSTER

New York Amsterdam/Antwerp London
Toronto Sydney/Melbourne New Delhi

Simon & Schuster
1230 Avenue of the Americas
New York, NY 10020

First Simon & Schuster hardcover edition February 2026

SIMON & SCHUSTER and colophon are registered trademarks of Simon & Schuster, LLC

Simon & Schuster strongly believes in freedom of expression and stands against censorship in all its forms. For more information, visit BooksBelong.com.

For information about special discounts for bulk purchases, please contact Simon & Schuster Special Sales at 1-866-506-1949 or business@simonandschuster.com.

The Simon & Schuster Speakers Bureau can bring authors to your live event. For more information or to book an event, contact the Simon & Schuster Speakers Bureau at 1-866-248-3049 or visit our website at www.simonspeakers.com.

Interior design by Lewelin Polanco

Manufactured in the United States of America

10 9 8 7 6 5 4 3 2 1

Library of Congress Control Number has been applied for.

ISBN 978-1-6680-7058-1
ISBN 978-1-6680-7060-4 (ebook)

 Let's stay in touch! Scan here to get book recommendations, exclusive offers, and more delivered to your inbox.

To my mom, Kay Raftery—
always my favorite writer.

CONTENTS

"Hannibal Lecter! Anybody ever heard of the wonderful Hannibal Lecter?"

It was November 2023, and Donald Trump was speaking to a crowd of more than a thousand spectators in Houston, Texas. The presidential candidate had spent the last several weeks name-dropping Lecter, whom he would go on to hail as "lovely" and "legendary." Trump's praise of Lecter—and of a movie he sometimes called "Silence of the Lamb"—grew more emphatic as his campaign went on. During an event in Wildwood, New Jersey, in May 2024, he even appeared to address Lecter directly. "Congratulations," he said, "the late, great Hannibal Lecter."

By then most Americans had become used to Trump's verbal digressions: In that same New Jersey appearance, he told an inconclusive semi-story involving Frank Sinatra, Luciano Pavarotti, and a "very good" hot dog he'd recently eaten. Yet his repeated shout-outs to Lecter confused critics and supporters alike. The "wonderful" Lecter he was praising was, in fact, Dr. Hannibal Lecter, aka "Hannibal the Cannibal," the hyper-intelligent, world-famous fictional serial killer.

Lecter's wicked nature has been known to millions since 1991, when the big-screen thriller *The Silence of the Lambs* became a global phenomenon. The film starred Anthony Hopkins as the wild-eyed Lecter and Jodie Foster as the wide-eyed FBI trainee Clarice Starling, who seeks the doctor's help in catching an on-the-loose murderer. *The Silence of the Lambs* went on to win five Academy Awards, including Best Picture, and sent the 1988 novel upon which it was based to the top of the bestseller lists. It also turned Lecter, whose scenes make up barely half an hour of screen time, into a marquee murderer, one whose heinous crimes have since been chronicled in movies, novels, and even a prime-time network TV series. In 1999, no less a horror authority than Stephen King declared

Lecter to be "the great fictional monster of our time," a title he still holds today. As modern pop culture menaces go, Lecter's as recognizable as *Harry Potter*'s Voldemort, as imitated as *Halloween*'s Michael Myers, and as quotable as *The Social Network*'s Mark Zuckerberg.

All of which made Trump's public displays of affection toward Lecter, whom the president once described as a "nice gentleman," so bizarre. At one point during the campaign, the candidate even implied that Lecter—or perhaps Hopkins—was a Trump fan himself. "Hannibal Lecter, how great an actor was he?" he exclaimed. "He said on television 'I love Donald Trump.' So, I love him. I love him. I love him."

Each nod to Hannibal the Cannibal raised new questions: Why would a law-and-order-loving candidate fawn over a guy who had once sliced off a police sergeant's face and used it as a mask? Did Trump not realize that in addition to not being real, "the late, great Hannibal Lecter" was (presumably) still very much alive? And how many times would Lecter's most vocal fan keep referring to the doctor's breakout film as *Silence of the Lamb*?

Even some of those attending Trump's rallies struggled to explain why the candidate kept bringing up Lecter. "I think he's just trying to portray a character that's pretty divisive and needed a lot of help," explained a man who watched the president speak in Atlanta, Georgia, in 2024, "and I think America needs a lot of help."

As the campaign went on, a hazily logical reason emerged for Trump's Lecter fixation. One of his go-to claims was that foreign countries were sending violent offenders across America's borders. "They're emptying out their insane asylums," he said. By invoking Lecter, Trump was apparently trying to connect the "insane asylum" in which Hannibal the Cannibal had dwelled in *The Silence of the Lambs* with the asylum some immigrants seek in the United States.

But there are perhaps deeper reasons for Trump's admiration of Lecter—who, truth be told, is not without estimable qualities. Granted, he's a cannibal with a double-digit body count. But he's also fiercely intelligent, as familiar with the musings of Marcus Aurelius as he is with the book *Joy of Cooking*. And he *is* rather gentlemanly, signing his personal correspondence with a cheerful "Ta" and flinching at public displays of rudeness: When a grotesque fellow inmate hurls semen at Starling in *The Silence of the Lambs*, Lecter responds by convincing the man to commit suicide by swallowing his own tongue. ("Discourtesy," he explains afterward, "is unspeakably ugly to me.") Lecter's also a man of refined tastes, with a fondness for Ducati motorcycles, Steuben chandeliers, and $1,100 cases of Bâtard-Montrachet. They're just some of the luxury items Hannibal the Cannibal seeks out when he's on the loose, and on the town.

"Lecter looks only for the fun," a character notes in *The Silence of the Lambs*. It's one of the many cravings he and Trump have in common. They both long for glitzy goods, as well as grandly emotive music: Trump's rallies are sometimes accompanied by tunes from such Andrew Lloyd Webber musicals as *Cats* and *Phantom of the Opera*, while Lecter soothes himself postkill with the strains of Bach's *Goldberg Variations*. And both men embrace opportune disorder. In the 1999 hit novel *Hannibal*, a character asks, "What does [Lecter] believe in?" The answer is simple: "Chaos." That sentiment was shared by Trump, who in 2018—in the middle of an exodus of White House staffers—noted how comfortable he felt surrounded by tumult: "I like chaos. It really is good."

Perhaps most notably, both are unapologetically id-driven, pursuing their desires without hesitation or guilt. It's a trait that only makes them all the more beloved by their admirers.

"Lecter is so nakedly what he is—he doesn't pretend to be anything else," notes Brian Cox, who played Hannibal the Cannibal in the 1986 neon noir film *Manhunter*. "And there's no qualifying whether he's guilty or not, which makes audiences think, 'What's he going to do *now*?'" (As Trump put it in 2025, in the middle of escalating tensions between the United States and Iran, "Nobody knows what I'm going to do.")

Lecter and Trump are even contemporaries in a way, their celebrity growing around the same time. They both became notorious in the 1980s, thanks in part to a pair of hit books—*The Silence of the Lambs* and Trump's *Trump: The Art of the Deal*—that solidified their respective bad-boy reputations. By the 1990s, Trump and Lecter were competing for space in the same celebrity gossip columns (in one 1995 article, an update on the next Lecter film was followed by an item about Trump's new Pizza Hut commercial). And in 2001, the two even crossed paths, as it were, with Trump showing up at the New York City premiere of the film *Hannibal*, during which the future president covered his eyes as Lecter dined on an enemy's brain.

By the time Trump began commending Hannibal the Cannibal in interviews and speeches, both men had been infamous for decades—so much so that they'd managed to reinvent themselves. Trump, despite his history of bankruptcies and inflammatory statements, was now a mainstream politico, cruising toward his second presidential term. And Lecter, a man who thinks nothing of biting off and swallowing a nurse's tongue—and doing it so calmly that his pulse stays under eighty-five beats per minute—had evolved into a root-worthy antihero, one whose name elicited cheers and applause on the campaign trail. Stick around long enough, it turns out, and Americans will either forgive your past transgressions or forget them altogether.

Still, the bond between the leader of the free world and an imaginary serial killer rattled those who were familiar with Lecter. Hopkins, who had played Hannibal the Cannibal in three hit films—and who'd spent decades talking and thinking about the character—couldn't believe that Trump had willingly aligned himself with Lecter. "I'm shocked and appalled," the actor said.

How had a flesh-eating killer become so acceptable, so name-dropworthy, so *beloved*? There was only one man who could possibly explain it—and he wasn't talking. In fact, despite selling tens of millions of books, the author of such Lecter novels as *The Silence of the Lambs*, *Red Dragon*, and *Hannibal* was as elusive as Hannibal the Cannibal himself. He was a writer who, for decades, had refused the schmoozy stations of the cross his best-selling contemporaries found irresistible. You'd never spot him taking a turn on the *Tonight Show* couch, or subjecting himself to the cozy glare of a *Playboy* Q&A. Most readers didn't even know what he looked like.

Yet his books are among the most culturally and critically successful of all time, mixing pulpy thrills with gilded prose. In 1994, the novelist David Foster Wallace included *The Silence of the Lambs* in the syllabus for a fiction-writing class he was teaching. Anyone thinking they were in for a dumbed-down serial killer story was in for a surprise. "WARNING," he wrote to his students. "Don't let any potential lightweightish-looking qualities of the texts delude you into thinking that this will be a blow-off-type class."

It's unclear if Wallace's enthusiasm for *The Silence of the Lambs*—or Trump's affinity for Hannibal the Cannibal—ever reached the man who created Lecter. Though perhaps "created" isn't the right word, as Lecter wasn't invented so much as he was conjured up. He was part of a long lineage of flesh-and-blood killers, the heir to a violent history that stretched back decades, long before anybody had heard of the late, great Hannibal Lecter.

PART 1
BIRTH

CHAPTER 1

"I JUST HAD AN IMPULSE TO KILL SOMEBODY."

He had many fathers, all of them killers. But this may have been the first: In the early hours of March 5, 1935, a group of onlookers gathered in the rain outside a four-story jailhouse in Bolivar County, Mississippi. The crowd included curious spectators, cautious lawmen, and more than two hundred National Guard troops. Some of the soldiers held machine guns; others stood with bayonets. They'd been waiting in the dark all night, their eyes trained on the muddy roadway leading to the jailhouse.

Finally, around 3:45 a.m., a pair of buses approached, carrying dozens of armed escorts. They'd been tasked with watching over the most infamous murderer in the South—one whose violent behavior had been chronicled in newspapers nationwide.

"Cannibal Killer Admits Carving Woman Victim," declared a front-page headline in Illinois's *Decatur Daily Review*. The accompanying story laid out the details of a gruesome crime: In December 1934, Mr. and Mrs. Aurelius B. Turner of Cleveland, Mississippi, had been mutilated and killed in their home. News of their deaths had quickly spread across the state, and police had questioned several suspects before arresting Alonzo Robinson, a Black military veteran and apparent drifter who'd changed his name to James H. Coyner. Authorities claimed to have found two damning bits of evidence in Coyner's possession: a wristwatch belonging to Mr. Turner and portions of flesh belonging to Mrs. Turner.

According to articles from the time, which were crude and often conflicting, the woman's remains had been "salted and cured" before being preserved in alcohol and pocked by what appeared to be teeth marks. That was all the proof the press needed. Within days, Coyner would be condemned as a "cannibal slayer," one who had "an insatiable desire for human flesh and bones." As evidence, reporters chronicled Coyner's unsavory past. He'd recently spent time in an Indiana prison for stealing a corpse. And he'd once been questioned for murder in Michigan after the heads of four women had been found in a trunk he owned.

Coyner denied having killed anyone, and told police that the only reason he'd excavated the Michigan women's bodies was to "get the bones." But during one interrogation, he *did* admit to being an expert on why and how men kill. "I could tell yous lots of things that you'd like to know—a lot of things about murders and murderers," Coyner said. "But I won't talk. I'll die first."

His expertise wasn't limited to criminal acts. Reporters took note of Coyner's intelligence, the way he easily discussed religion and history. He could even be somewhat philosophical at times. "What is to be, will be," he said while on the bus to Bolivar County, casually smoking a hand-rolled cigarette. And during an interview with a district attorney, Coyner noted: "Everything we do or say is predestined, and we have no control over it."

Coyner was so self-assured, so seemingly *reasonable*, that many were shocked when, weeks after his arrest, he changed his story and confessed to killing the Turners in Mississippi. His motive, he said, was simple: "I just had an impulse to kill somebody." And while he insisted that he was no cannibal, he acknowledged cutting off a few pieces of Mrs. Turner's flesh—"just to see how the skin felt."

A one-day trial followed, during which jurors examined the woman's wretched remains up close. It took less than five minutes for Coyner to be found guilty. He was immediately sentenced to death.

By that point, the so-called cannibal slayer had become an object of public fascination and scorn across the region—as evidenced by the crowd outside the Bolivar County jailhouse on that late-winter night.

Some of those gathered in the rain no doubt wanted to kill Coyner themselves. He was a Black man accused of murdering a white couple in the post-Reconstruction South. To many, he had been guilty from the moment the word "Negro" had first appeared in headlines.

Several of the onlookers, however, simply wanted to witness that notorious alleged cannibal in the flesh. What they saw emerging from the bus in the predawn hours was no monster. Instead, he was a tall and tired-looking thirty-nine-year-old man wearing a collarless blue shirt, old pants, and beat-up shoes. After being hustled into a courtroom, Coyner was taken to the building's gallows, where he was to be hanged.

According to one eyewitness, Coyner wasn't nervous about dying: "He just seemed to be sort of matter-of-fact about the whole thing." The condemned man declined to give any final words—*I won't talk; I'll die first*—and a muted smile passed over his face right before his head was covered with a dark hood. At 3:58 a.m., the trapdoor was sprung, and Coyner dropped to his death.

Afterward, the crowd scrambled for souvenirs, grabbing anything that proved they'd seen the now-infamous convicted killer: a swatch of fabric from his hood, a cigarette from his pocket.

Other attendees left the courthouse that night carrying something even more valuable: a story. As soon as he died, Coyner became a local legend to generations of kids around the Delta region. "He was someone that was talked about," remembers librarian and historian Ronnie Wise, who spent three decades in Bolivar County. "He was almost like a bogeyman figure."

Stories about the insightful cannibal who knew the ways of murders and murderers would be whispered across playgrounds and campfires for decades. Such tales would twist and shift like a breeze, and one day, they'd finally drift toward a young boy living in Rich, Mississippi.

"There's a tradition of storytelling in the South," Thomas Harris said quietly. "You sit on the front porch, and you listen to people tell stories to amuse each other. That is a coveted skill down there."

It's the summer of 2019, and Harris is being interviewed for *Conversations*, an East Hampton, New York, local television show. Sitting on an all-black stage, he is wearing dark-rimmed glasses, a white button-down shirt with a flattened collar, and suspenders. His voice is cotton soft, his demeanor as gentle as a chuckle. At seventy-eight years old, Harris—always "Tom" to his friends and colleagues—looks almost serenely plump, the result of a lifelong devotion to fine cuisine.

It's hard to say what's more unusual about Harris's *Conversations* appearance: the fact that a best-selling novelist has agreed to talk to a public access TV program with a tiny audience or the fact that he has agreed to talk *at all*. Throughout his decades-long career, the author of such blockbusters as *Red Dragon*, *The Silence of the Lambs*, and *Hannibal* has remained happily invisible. He has spoken to the press just a handful of times, and aside from a few author headshots—all of which feature graying variations on the same fuzzy-faced, vaguely beatific look—not many images of him exist. As far as anyone knows, before *Conversations*, he'd never appeared on TV.

But Harris, despite his need for privacy, hadn't spent that time in hiding; he'd been sitting on the front porch of the world, listening.

Harris grew up in the Mississippi Delta less than sixty miles from where Coyner met his late-night fate. As a young boy, he no doubt heard the killer's legend as it spread in the 1940s and '50s. "In casual conversation, we did talk about Coyner," recalls Wise, the librarian, who socialized with the author in his later years.

Harris would eventually leave Mississippi to begin his writing career, working as a newspaperman and freelance journalist in Waco, Texas, where he covered the police beat. "I got sort of interested in crime," he said on *Conversations*. "You meet every sort of person on Earth."

That included an array of accused killers. In the 1960s, Harris visited a small town in Mexico, where murderous sisters had left a trail of bodies buried in their backyard furnace. Around that same time, he interviewed a man suspected of wiping out nearly an entire family. He also had an unnerving run-in with a chilling doctor—a man with "a sort of gravity about him," Harris said—who'd chopped up his lover and stuffed the body parts into a box before calmly hailing a cab so he could ditch the remains elsewhere. That crime, and the man who committed it, would stay with Harris for years afterward.

Harris studied all sorts of outlaws. But murderers, especially serial killers, held a particular fascination for him. "He collected everything on them," noted one of Harris's former newspaper colleagues. "He followed them, wrote about them, and studied all about them."

For Harris, those years in Texas marked the beginning of a lifelong study of violence. In the late 1960s, he became a crime reporter in New York City, where he was plunged into a world of robberies and riots—a world that let him see human nature "at its worst," he said. And after becoming a best-selling novelist in the 1970s, Harris traveled the world, learning all he could about abhorrent behavior. He hung out with homicide detectives, attended the trial of a high-profile serial killer, and went all the way to the FBI, to meet with the agents who'd stared down infamous mass murderers such as Ted Bundy. Over time, those findings bled into his fiction. "You write about what you know," he said on *Conversations*. "You don't have to make anything up."

CHAPTER 2

"SOMETHING TERRIBLE IS WATCHING YOU OUT OF THE DARKNESS."

The kids were sitting at the cafeteria table, waiting for Tom Harris to finish his story—to find out who would live and who would die.

That was in 1949. Or maybe it was in 1950; as with most stories from Harris's past, the exact details are either foggy or forgotten. At the time, he was a nine-year-old living in Rich, Mississippi, a scratch of a town about sixty miles outside Memphis. "You drive through it, and a minute or two later, you're out of it," notes Wise. Harris's father worked as a farmer, his mother worked as a teacher, and Harris himself worked in the cafeteria of his small country school. "I earned my lunch by busing tables," he remembered. "By the time I got through, lunch was over. And there was no time to go to the playground."

One day, while finishing his food so he could get to cleaning, Harris began spinning a tale for a few friends. It was a wartime adventure, set in the South Pacific, about a submarine being pummeled by depth charges. The vessel was flooded, and the water was rising high, almost covering the faces of the hapless crew members. Their deaths seemed certain.

Harris's story ended in an abrupt cliff-hanger. "I said, 'Uh, hey, look, I gotta go. I gotta go bus these tables,'" he remembered. But his friends couldn't wait to hear the conclusion of his made-up submarine adventure.

They offered Harris a deal: "If we help you," one of them asked, "will you tell us the rest?"

Harris continued his story of the water-filled submarine and the boys helped with his cleanup. He finished his tale, and for once, there was enough time left over for him to go outside and play.

Harris would tell more of those cafeteria-time adventures in the months ahead. Finally, he said, "a dim little light went on in my brain." A good storyteller, he realized, always kept his audience in suspense and his characters in danger. "The water had better be [high] when you need help busing," he realized, "or everybody's gone."

For a writer who adores vivid details—he can devote entire passages to, say, the proper way to cook and serve human brain—Harris has kept the particulars of his life as obscure as possible. He gave his first official interview upon the release of his 1975 debut novel, *Black Sunday*, and didn't formally speak to a journalist again for more than four decades. In the decades between, his missives to the public were limited to a few short press statements and the occasional foreword or author's note. He is the rarest of species: a writer who doesn't want attention. "I just work and I try to put things in my books that I want to say," he told a reporter during a brief phone chat in 1991. "And really that's about the size of it."

On that point, he was polite but firm. In 1999, the year *Hannibal* became his fourth consecutive bestseller, a newspaper writer who'd socialized with Harris wrote him a letter, requesting an interview. Harris's response, left on an answering machine, was equal parts gracious and taunting: "Good luck getting information for your story."

It's not just Harris who's kept quiet over the years; his friends, family members, and colleagues—many now deceased—have either dodged the press or spoken of him with caution. ("Do not use our names—he cannot know we talked to you," a former neighbor said to a journalist, threatening to sue if her identity was revealed.) And what people *have* said on the record about Harris has often been innocuous: They note the author's unassuming demeanor—that he's "plain as an old shoe" (an uncle). They recount Harris's longing for adventure, his "Ernest Hemingway bent" (a classmate). And they mention his limitless desire for books—that, even as a child, he "read all day and all night" (his mother).

These are benign observations. And they provide scant material for anyone trying to work up a psychological profile, however rough, of the man who helped bring Hannibal Lecter to life. "If you've read his books, he's unexpected," noted one of Harris's friends. "He's polite, civilized, reticent . . . he doesn't give much away."

Yet Harris did leave behind a few clues about his past. They're scattered among his interviews and tucked into his writing. They tell the story, however frustratingly incomplete, of a man who refused to let his modest means thwart his grand ambitions, and whose old-shoe disposition belied a thrill-seeking nature. "Dr. Lecter likes his fun," a character once remarked of Hannibal the Cannibal. So did Harris. It was what helped get him out of a small southern town with a brief, troubled history and a sometimes cruel-seeming name.

They started pouring into the Delta in the mid–nineteenth century: fortune seekers looking to tame the fertile terrain of Coahoma County, Mississippi. Despite the region's hazards—polluted water, biting mosquitoes—the settlers believed that they could turn the county's forests into farmland. They began buying up property, and by the late 1800s, new towns were being established around the squiggly Mississippi River, including a small cluster of lots and streets that would eventually be christened Rich, Mississippi.

As a new century began, the town was thriving, with sawmills, stores, churches, and a two-story hotel populated by transients and traveling salesmen. The future looked good for Rich—which was likely what drew Tom Harris's grandfather to the area. Dr. William Thomas Harris had just started his medical career when he arrived in 1900 and set up a private practice. In the years ahead, he and his wife, Daisy, had two children, including his only son, William Thomas, Jr.

Dr. Harris and his family would become mainstays in Rich—and bear witness to the town's unexpected and uncontrollable decline in the 1910s and 1920s. Businesses began to shutter, including the local sawmills, and a series of fires ravaged several buildings. By the 1940s, Rich's railroad stop and local hotel were gone, and its population was dwindling.

That was the town—hollowed out, ground down, isolated—in which Tom Harris would grow up. He was born William Thomas Harris III on September 22, 1940, in Jackson, Tennessee, where his father was working as an electrical engineer. But the elder Harris would soon return to Rich, along with his young son and his wife, a Delta native named Pauline "Polly" Coleman. She was curious and clearly brilliant. A 2011 obituary for Coleman, presumably written by Harris, cataloged her many passions, which included:

> the history of Native Americans; life among indigenous Alaskans; the work of Charles Darwin and Mother Teresa; advances in medical technology; anything concerning the natural sciences; and country and western music. She was also a natural critic and student of narrative film, wore hats to great effect, and followed the worlds of men and women's fashions religiously.

W.T. and Polly had big plans for their future in Rich: He would abandon engineering and take up farming, while she'd become a public school teacher. The family soon settled into a three-bedroom home sitting on a shade-covered lot, and Tom Harris became one of about a hundred students enrolled at the nearby Lula-Rich Consolidated School.

One day during recess at Lula-Rich, Harris noticed a commotion among his classmates. Looking up, he saw a massive bloblike shape slowly approaching the playground. "It's a spaceship!" exclaimed one kid. In fact, the object was something nearly as alien, at least in the Delta: a blimp. As it passed over the school, tiny objects began raining down from its underbelly, landing all over the playground. They were Baby Ruth bars. "It took two hours to round up all the student body," Harris later recalled, "because they were running across like mad catching the candy."

For Harris, who couldn't have been older than eight or nine, the moment was a brief glimpse of life beyond Rich—a town he'd seemingly already outgrown. And if that blimp had dropped down a ladder, there's a good chance he would have grabbed hold and been borne away.

Harris was a restless, unassuming kid who didn't always connect with others. One high school friend would later note that compared to his fellow students, Harris was "smarter, more quick-witted, with a larger view of the world"—traits that don't always help win popularity contests. And while Harris never spoke about his childhood in detail, he'd later write of adolescence in damning terms: "By the time we reach the ninth grade, we've seen a lot of cruelty and brutish behavior and willful ignorance. It's hard to fashion a life that can stand the weather."

Some of the childhood cruelty he witnessed—and possibly endured—would later be filtered through his 1975 debut novel, *Black Sunday*. The book's troubled antagonist, a would-be terrorist named Michael Lander, comes of age in the rural south in the 1940s—just as Harris did. In *Black Sunday*, young Lander is bullied for being too smart, and is unable to fit in with his peers. He struggles to adopt what Harris described as "the Code"—a set of rules by which all tough southern boys were supposed to live. According to *Black Sunday*, young men like Lander were expected to fight, hunt, play sports, and talk crudely about girls: "When you are a child, the Code without the equipment will kill you."

Growing up, Harris lacked the equipment. "He was a very quiet kid," noted a relative, "probably the most nonviolent man I've ever known." Though Harris sometimes trekked into the woods with a .22, looking for turtles and snakes, he didn't like hunting. One outdoors expedition would trouble him for decades afterward. "As a small boy playing cowboy by myself I shot a sparrow," he recalled in his seventies. "I stood in the weeds looking at the bird, warm in my hand, tears hot on my cheeks." And Harris didn't fare much better when it came to sports. "He did not want to play ball," Harris's mother said. "Oh, I guess he did play, but he did it half-heartedly."

Shut out of Rich's most popular pastimes, Harris spent his early years living by his own solitary Code. Some days, he simply wandered about.

"My companions when I was a small child," he later said, "were mostly turkeys." Much of the time, he could be found at the Carnegie Public Library, a modest-sized redbrick refuge in nearby Clarksdale. "Thomas wore out Carnegie Library," his mother said. "He read everything in it."

Harris's literary diet would include the naval adventures of C. S. Forester; the arch satire of Jonathan Swift; the world-beating swagger of Ernest Hemingway; and the poetry of Carl Sandburg. Those were all works of exotic pursuits and passions (as was D. H. Lawrence's *Lady Chatterley's Lover*, which Harris discovered at the age of fourteen). To an only child living in the 1940s and '50s, those stories must have been teleportative. Harris's family wasn't well off. His father grew soybeans, wheat, and cotton, but the crops were apparently modest in size: "They were never 'big' farmers, like most of us," one former neighbor told a reporter. There was no television in the family home, no movie theater within walking distance. Books were Harris's ticket out of Rich, even if the trip lasted no longer than a few hundred pages.

Yet despite his intelligence, or perhaps because of it, school was a constant struggle for Harris. "I wish I had never attended," he once wrote, "but had only been shown where the books are." His early dreams of becoming an aeronautical engineer, inspired in part by that glimpse of the blimp, were abandoned after he repeatedly failed trigonometry. His other classes didn't go any easier. "It was just dull, you know," he said. "And I wasn't too hot at getting out my homework."

As he grew older, though, Harris managed to rework his Code. He started attending dances, joined the school chorus, and cruised around in a buddy's 1954 red Ford convertible, blasting Elvis Presley's "That's All Right" and other current hits on the radio. And while he didn't have a steady girlfriend, he did date around. "In high school, Tom blossomed," recalled a friend. "Sometimes, the things that make you an outcast as a kid make you cool when you get older."

Even if Harris had adapted to his surroundings, he had no plans to make them permanent. By the time he graduated from high school in the late 1950s, he was ready to leave his hometown behind—to drift away like the blimp he'd seen so many years before, toward unknown horizons.

Decades later, some of Harris's former neighbors would reflect on his childhood in Rich. "One of the things we love about Tom," an anonymous resident said, "is that he is so gracious, we know he has forgiven everyone."

"But Tom got revenge in another way," said another. "He left and got wealthy and famous."

It's known as Cuesta de Los Muertos, Spanish for "Pass of the Dead." Made up of cutbacks and hairpin curves, Cuesta de Los Muertos is an assaultive stretch of road in northern Mexico. Harris would find himself on that fast-moving highway one night in 1963, guiding his tiny Yamaha motorcycle toward his destination: Monterrey, Mexico.

He and his traveling companion, a buddy named Johnny Myers, had begun their no-budget, multicity adventure in Waco, Texas. The trip had gone fairly smoothly until they hit the Pass of the Dead, where their bikes were surrounded by massive trucks decorated with light-up crucifixes. "One of the most harrowing experiences of [my life]," Harris later wrote in the pages of *Cycle World* magazine.

The danger was all part of the fun, of course. At the time of the trip, Harris was in his early twenties, an age when young men are primed for exploration and unconvinced of their own mortality. He and Myers had brought just a few supplies for their trip through Mexico, including a compass, a Spanish-English dictionary, and a chocolate cake. Over the course of a week, they encountered wild wolves and frigid temperatures, pushing their bikes—which Harris described as "skinny 250cc workhorses"—to their limits. When the journey was over, Harris roared back home at 3:00 a.m. He was "dog-tired, sunbaked and grinning."

The road trek was just the latest outside-world exploit for the indoor kid from Rich. By then his personal and professional lives had been transformed. After graduating from high school, he had enrolled in Baylor University in Waco, Texas, to pursue an English degree. He was still a student when, in the summer of 1961, he married Harriet Anne Haley, a biology student at the University of Texas at Austin. He had also picked up a part-time gig at two daily papers: the *Waco News-Tribune* and the *Waco Tribune-Herald*.

Harris studied during the day and hung around the newsroom at night. In photos from that time, he's a skinny workhorse with short hair, dark-rimmed glasses, and a confident semismirk. "He was already pretty set on being a writer," remembered Dallas Lee, a classmate at Baylor and fellow reporter. "[He] wanted to cover the bulls running in Spain, things like that."

Such adventurous assignments would have to wait. As the new kid in the office, Harris took whatever stories he could get. One of the first articles to feature his byline, Tom Harris, was an earnest write-up of *Cavalcade of Song and Dance*, a 1961 stage show held at a Waco military base ("a sparkling musical revue," he wrote, that had earned "a well deserved standing ovation.")

It was the kind of unsexy, bare-bones reportage most editors demanded of their young staffers. But in October 1962, he threw himself into one of the most incendiary stories in the country. The all-white University of Mississippi had been ordered by a federal court to admit a Black air force veteran named James Meredith. The state's governor, Ross Barnett, vowed to fight the order, and after Meredith showed up to register for classes, swarms of segregationists clashed with government troops in what would become known as the Ole Miss riot.

As the fighting escalated, Harris, who'd been raised not far from the university, made a middle-of-the-night pilgrimage to the school's Oxford campus. "I thought the lid was going to blow off and I felt I should be there," he said at the time.

The resulting dispatch, headlined "Little Conversation in Ole Miss Hangouts," ran a few days later in the *News-Tribune*. It was compact but powerful. Harris wrote of freshly dug foxholes along the campus grounds; random gunfire sounds in the distance; rattled college kids unsure what to do with themselves. "The students ate without conversation and no one fed the jukebox," the story noted.

Harris's article was fast moving and finely observed, the kind of reporting that got a young journalist noticed in the newsroom. When he graduated from Baylor, full-time work was waiting for him at the *News-Tribune*. By then, he and Harriet had a daughter, Elizabeth Anne, and the young reporter felt pressure to start bringing in money. "The wages were very, very low," he said decades later, "and I was feeding a baby."

Though his salary wasn't great, the gig let Harris embark upon a series of far-flung reporting escapades. Throughout the mid-1960s, he covered everything from a double-death car-train collision to a hostage standoff to a drowning in Lake Waco. He also spent time in the local courts, listening to firsthand tales of vicious assaults and high-speed car chases. At one point, he even got to fly in an F-4C fighter-bomber. "He was game to look into anything," Lee remembered. "He was fascinated with gathering facts, information, and angles."

To his coworkers, Harris came off as tight-lipped and a bit high strung. They didn't always know what to make of the kid who drove his Yamaha motorcycle to work, wore an old gray hat around the office, and spent long late-night hours obsessing over the copy coming out of his Royal Standard typewriter. "Sometimes he got a little off the beaten track and I had to calm him down, like most young reporters," recalled a former editor.

Over time, Harris would ingratiate himself into the newsroom, occasionally meeting up with coworkers for after-work drinks. "He was not a talkative member of the writing group," recalled one colleague. "He'd sit around listening to what other people were talking about."

In 1965, Harris was among the staffers spotlighted in a full-page *Tribune-Herald* ad celebrating the "best bunch of newspaper employees any newspaper could have." But he was still struggling to get by on his reporter's salary. To make ends meet, he'd need some freelance-writing gigs. And so, not long after he and his buddy Johnny Myers took that first motorcycle trip to Mexico, Harris returned there, on the hunt for the one commodity he knew he could peddle back home: murder.

Throughout the mid–twentieth century, American newsstands were awash in tales of sex, violence, and revenge. Cheapo magazines such as *Front Page Detective* and *Inside Detective* featured racy covers and schlock-teasing headlines such as "Who Iced the Red Hot Mama?" and "Find the Strip-Tease Killer!" By the late 1950s, it seemed as though the number of murder-obsessed publications was multiplying every week, their titles interchangeable. It was an epidemic, one that some parents and educators wanted contained. "Mothers Launch Drive on Lurid Sex Books" declared a 1958 Oklahoma City newspaper story. It was about parents who planned to scour "every magazine rack in the metropolitan area" to rid the town of the "cheap crime, sex and prurience which has flooded the market."

Such crackdown attempts were useless. By that point, Americans had lived through the back-to-back nightmares of World War II and the Korean War. They'd seen the worst of humanity—in some cases, up close—and many had become shockproof. The new crime rags weren't going away. Soon, even respectable publications were looking for stories that were ripped from the headlines and soaked in blood. In December 1957, *Life* magazine ran a gruesome eight-page package on Ed Gein, a farmer from Plainfield, Wisconsin, who'd recently been arrested for a series of appalling murders. One story recounted what officers had discovered upon entering Gein's "house of horrors": "Hanging by the feet in Gein's summer kitchen the sheriff found [a] body, headless and eviscerated. That was not all. There were 10 other human heads . . . some neatly wrapped in cellophane, and a chair upholstered in human skin."

Life's coverage of the Gein murders was deeply reported, highly detailed, and unapologetically sensational. "NEIGHBORS RECALL GEIN'S TALK OF WOMEN, MURDER—AND EMBALMING" read one headline. The articles were accompanied by photos of Gein's neighbors peeping into his filth-ridden farmhouse, where the killer had left spare body parts lying on the stove (the only neat area of the house, according to *Life*, was the room that had once belonged to his beloved late mother). It was all tactfully trashy stuff, and proof that one of the most mainstream magazines in America—at that point, *Life* was hitting more than 5 million mailboxes every week—was now competing with the true-crime rags.

The details of the Gein case were so titillating and so widespread that looky-loos began making pilgrimages to Wisconsin, to get a glimpse at

Gein's home. His notoriety was further cemented by the release of Robert Bloch's grody 1959 novel *Psycho*, which follows a mom-obsessed, murderous motel operator named Norman Bates. Bloch would deny that Gein had directly inspired *Psycho*—as would Alfred Hitchcock, the director of the 1960 film adaptation. But Bloch's novel and the upscale slasher flick it inspired would turn Gein into a nationally known killer, one whose acts would continue to make front-page news throughout the fifties and sixties.

By then, the true-crime genre—once seen as lightweight or lewd—was slowly becoming acceptable, perhaps even respectable. In the fall of 1965, *The New Yorker* debuted Truman Capote's multipart investigation into the 1959 killings of four family members in rural Kansas. Capote had spent years digging into their deaths, and his reporting was eventually collected in the "nonfiction novel" *In Cold Blood*, which became an instant hit upon its release in 1966. Bookshelves and bestseller lists would soon crowd with vivid accounts of real-life violence—an evergreen subject, according to Capote. "The human heart being what it is," he wrote, "murder [is] a theme not likely to darken and yellow with time."

For a young, hungry writer like Harris, the mass embrace of gnarly crime tales was more than just a norm-bending cultural shift; it was a business opportunity. And while a prestigious magazine such as *The New Yorker* wasn't exactly desperate for freelance pitches, there were plenty of publications interested in dark stories. That included the long-running *Argosy*, a monthly men's magazine that had recently published stories with salacious headlines such as "Murder! It Keeps Tijuana Alive!" and "Homicide on the High Seas?" *Argosy* may not have been as sexy as *Playboy*, but its editors were always on the lookout for stories that would appeal to its alpha-male readers.

Though Harris was still working full-time for the Waco papers, he began pitching freelance ideas to the *Argosy* staff. "They paid, like, you know, a couple of hundred bucks," he said. "Buys a lot of baby food." His first assignment for the magazine, in 1964, sent him on a grim pilgrimage to Mexico. According to his reporting, police there had recently arrested three sisters for their roles in a widespread kidnapping and sex work operation in the small town of Lagos de Moreno. The siblings were accused of luring girls to work in brothels, then forcing them to live in squalor in a building Harris described as "a prep school for prostitutes." Some of the women had died, and their remains had been burned in a furnace. They weren't the sisters' only victims: Authorities believed that they'd robbed and killed as many as twenty American men, burying their bodies in a pit underneath a bathroom toilet.

It was a horrific story, but a tantalizing one. While reporting the *Argosy* piece, Harris visited Lagos de Moreno, describing it as "the headquarters of the largest white-slave ring on the North American continent." He interviewed police officers and examined crime scenes, and, while attending a trial in the city of San Francisco del Rincón, even came face-to-face with one of the sisters in her cell. "When she looks directly at you," he wrote, "you feel that something terrible is watching you out of the darkness."

That was just one of several haunting lines in Harris's account of the murders, which ran in *Argosy*'s July 1964 issue under the title "Sisters in Slaughter." Untethered from the restraints of the Waco papers, Harris delighted in dark details from the very first page: "When the investigators found the man's hat and his underwear in Guadalajara de Noche, he was not in either." Throughout "Sisters in Slaughter," Harris acted as a sort of wry tour guide for the reader, punctuating the story with disbelieving asides—as when he described a male victim having been "robbed, rolled and dropped piecemeal down the john."

It was nasty material, rendered cleanly and clearly—a writing style Harris would perfect in the decades ahead. The story's violence and inhumanity might have turned off other reporters. But not Harris. He had "an appetite to examine the horrors of existence," remembered Dallas Lee, "and a curiosity to know about these things without any moralizing about it."

"Sisters in Slaughter" evidently pleased the editors at *Argosy*, who quickly handed Harris another across-the-border assignment. This time, he was asked to meet with Dykes Askew Simmons Jr., an American crane operator and former mental patient whom Harris described as having "the eyes of a fierce turtle." Simmons had been arrested in Mexico in 1959 on suspicion of murdering three young siblings in a brutal roadside slaying. By the time Harris met with Simmons, the accused killer was in a jail cell at the Nuevo León state prison in Monterrey. Working on the story would be an eye-opener for Harris. He was slowly familiarizing himself with modern crime-fighting tools—lie detectors, paraffin, and blood testing—and learning the day-by-day workings of the criminal justice system. "I was twenty-three years old," he later wrote, "and I thought that covering a police beat in Texas had taught me all about the world."

That belief would soon be challenged by a man Harris encountered in Monterrey, a calm, keenly intelligent doctor working in the prison. "Dr. Salazar," as Harris called him, had treated Simmons for a wound. When Harris went to interview Dr. Salazar, he found him standing still in his cell, surrounded by little more than jars of medical equipment and stools for his patients. He was "a small, lithe man," Harris recalled, with maroon-colored eyes. But what impressed Harris the most was the doctor's elegance: "This man was very, very smart. And he had a sort of gravity about him. Very courteous, very quick."

After answering a few questions about Simmons and his injury, Dr. Salazar folded his fingers under his chin, steeplelike, and began interrogating Harris. "Do you have sunglasses with you, Mr. Harris?" he asked.

"Yes," Harris said.

"May I suggest that when you question [Simmons], you do not wear them?"

Dr. Salazar then proposed a theory. He believed that Simmons had likely been mocked as a child for a few scars he had on his head and face. He theorized that the prisoner had come to loathe his own appearance—and that seeing the reflection of his face in Harris's eyewear could set him off. "Early torment makes torment easily . . . imagined," he said coolly. At that point, Harris later wrote, "he looked up at me and his countenance changed, seemed to pop wider, like a moth flashing the owl face printed on its wings."

After their meeting ended, Harris asked the warden how long Dr. Salazar had worked in the prison. *"Hombre!"* the official replied. "You don't know who that is?" Dr. Salazar, the warden explained, wasn't an employee; he was an *inmate*. "The doctor is a murderer," Harris was told. "As a surgeon, he could package his victim in a surprisingly small box. He will never leave this place. He is insane."

In 2013 a reporter for *Vice*, after corresponding with Harris, identified "Dr. Salazar" as Alfredo Ballí Treviño, who in 1959 had confessed to the murder of a young Mexican man named Jesús Castillo Rangel. One newspaper account claimed that the two men, who'd been "friends on a homosexual level," had clashed after Castillo had ended their relationship. Ballí, a trained surgeon, had responded by injecting his lover with a tranquilizer, slitting his throat, and placing the corpse on an operating table, where he had cut it into eight segments. Ballí had then stuffed the pieces into a carton and hailed a taxi. Once he felt he was far away from the murder scene, he had buried Castillo's remains in the ground. That may not have been Ballí's only crime; according to accounts from the time, police also suspected that he might also have been involved in a 1958 incident in which a "neatly carved" body had been discovered jammed into a box and placed in a trash can.

Ballí's confession in the Castillo case had been enough to send him to the Monterrey prison. While there, he took care of fellow prisoners, as well as local residents unable to afford health care. "He is not insane with the poor," the prison warden explained to Harris.

The writer didn't mention Ballí in his *Argosy* story about Simmons. But Harris never forgot the chilly, talkative, maroon-eyed prisoner he'd met in that small cell in Mexico—the killer with a keen insight into the ways of murders and murderers.

CHAPTER 3

"I CAN'T WRITE IT UNTIL I BELIEVE IT."

B y the late 1960s, Harris had managed to land a handful of crime stories for *Argosy*, including a profile of an infamous 1930s bank robber whose legacy Harris summarized with a pithy eulogy: "Clyde Barrow started out stupid, and ended up dead." Eventually he got a call from one of the magazine's editors, telling him that there was even more work awaiting him in New York City: "You could compete up here—why don't you come on up?"

The invitation was well-timed. Harris had been with the Waco papers since 1960, and his journalism work had sharpened his writing—much as it had for his hero Hemingway. But he didn't want to stay on the Waco crime beat for the rest of his career. And his marriage to Harriet was coming to an end.[*] So in the late 1960s, Harris decided to relocate to New York City—a decision some colleagues believed he'd regret. "In six months," a Waco editor warned Harris, "you'll be coming back here with your tail between your legs, asking for your old job back."

That prediction nearly came true. As Harris quickly learned, New York City had its *own* Code—one far more punishing than the one he'd

---

[*] According to records maintained by the state of Texas, the couple divorced in 1968.

known growing up in Rich. "The first year in New York, I made $1,700," he reflected. "[I thought I'd] starve to death."

Before that could happen, he landed a job as a reporter with the Associated Press, where he started working in 1968, spending long hours at the news service's offices at 50 Rockefeller Plaza in Manhattan. "It was cops and fifty-dollar stickups and stuff for a long time," Harris remembered. He covered everything from a "Wild West–style" bank robbery shootout in Harlem to a protest at Columbia University, where he got a taste of tear gas. "There was a lot of civil unrest in New York in '67 and '68," he said. "We combed a good bit of glass out of our hair, you know? It was exciting."

Not all of Harris's assignments were potentially life threatening: He once wrote an article about caterpillars that were falling from Brooklyn trees, giving kids terrible rashes. But for him and his colleagues, the AP job was an immersive experience—a way to study the behavior of crooks and cops alike. "Most of the stories would be murders, society slayings, fires— we had a lot of fires back then," says the author Nicholas Pileggi, a fellow AP crime-beat veteran whose later work inspired the films *Goodfellas* and *Casino*. Yet despite the up-close thrills that came with the job, working the police beat was hardly glamorous. "I can't tell you how low we were on AP's talent scale," Pileggi remembered. "They thought of us as the garbage pail."

Harris eventually moved up the ranks, landing a stint as a night editor, where he reshaped other writers' copy. "He understood precision in language," said an AP colleague, "and how to get a piece to move." After his late shift finished, Harris sometimes rode his motorcycle to W. M. Tweeds, an Upper West Side bar where the AP gang would meet for beers. Yet he still didn't socialize easily. While his AP colleagues would forever praise his smarts and geniality, Harris kept them at a distance. "He is just naturally shy," noted another former coworker. "He doesn't seek the limelight."

By the early 1970s, Harris was no longer worried about surviving New York City. But he'd become frustrated and restless at his AP job. "I had to put up with the details of the news *forever*, and I was sick of it," he complained. One day at the Rockefeller Plaza office, Harris and two colleagues, reporters Sam Maull and Dick Riley, were hanging around with their feet on their desks, daydreaming of ways to leave their jobs for good.

"We were prisoners of war there at the AP," said Harris. "We were going to bust out of the place, [and] tunnel out of having to spend our lives in an office, being told what to do."

As they talked, Harris and his two coworkers came up with an escape plan: They'd collaborate on a novel, one they could write and sell quickly. The idea of jamming out a cheapo bestseller wasn't too far-fetched. In the late 1960s, more than two dozen *Newsday* journalists had worked together to write *Naked Came the Stranger*, a fake sex memoir—purportedly written by a Long Island housewife—that became an instant bestseller.

Harris and his colleagues figured they could write their *own* hit book; all they needed was a juicy plot. The three men made a list of hot-topic current events and looked for ways to fictionalize them. One of their initial ideas was a complicated thriller in which the Mafia took on a lesbian cult. After that concept was abandoned, Harris finally threw out a winning story pitch: "What about blowing up the Super Bowl?"

The notion had been inspired by a pair of recent headline-making events—one diverting, the other devastating. In 1969, President Richard Nixon had made a grinning appearance at a game between the Miami Dolphins and the Oakland Raiders, where he'd sat in open view of more than thirty-five thousand fans. Three years later, in 1972, members of a Palestinian militant group known as Black September had raided the Olympic Village in Munich, Germany, where they had killed eleven Israeli athletes—an event that had played out on live television.

Harris's Super Bowl story would merge the two incidents, focusing on a jaded American veteran who teams up with Black September to kill thousands of spectators (and the sitting US president) at the biggest sporting event in the country. It was an absurd premise—but not *too* absurd. After years of international turmoil, terrorist attacks, and political assassinations, a high-profile attack on American soil seemed scarily plausible. "People would never believe how simple it is," Harris wrote to his agent.

To suss out the finer points of their story, Harris, Maull, and Riley began holding brainstorming sessions at the back of Teacher's, another Upper West Side bar. "We were going to do it in—bang!—two weeks," Harris said.

That timeline proved to be optimistic. But the trio quickly worked up an outline for their novel, which would be titled *Black Sunday*. The story follows an embittered southerner, Michael Lander, struggling to adjust to life back home after spending time as a prisoner of war in Vietnam. Feeling abandoned by both his wife and his country, he decides to exact revenge by teaming up with Black September and detonating 1,200 pounds of explosives from a blimp over New Orleans' Tulane Stadium. The blast will send high-velocity .177 caliber rifle darts into the crowd of more than eighty thousand spectators below.

That's a rather slimmed-down synopsis. *Black Sunday* was a complex global thriller, taking place across multiple continents—exactly the kind of overstuffed potboiler the publishing industry wanted in the mid-1970s. Tautly written novels such as Frederick Forsyth's *The Odessa File* and *The Day of the Jackal* had become essential beach reads, and editors were looking for high-metabolism tales of conspiracy and cover-ups. It was the perfect moment for Harris, Maull, and Riley to shop around *Black Sunday*, which they'd end up selling to the publisher G. P. Putnam's Sons for $320,000, splitting the advance three ways. After the deal closed, Harris celebrated with a champagne-fueled dinner at a ritzy Manhattan restaurant.

That money would help finance the daunting amount of research required to make *Black Sunday* feel as authentic as possible. Harris began studying weaponry and terrorism techniques, and familiarized himself with maps of the book's numerous locales. Then he hit the road, scouting locations in New Orleans and even traveling to an airfield in Montauk, Long Island, where he talked his way into the cockpit of a Goodyear blimp. "They let me fly that baby," he said. "It's a lot of work."

Harris approached his first novel the same way he'd approached his newspaper stories: with a near-fanatical curiosity and a seemingly inexhaustible capacity for detail. "I can't write it until I believe it," he'd tell a colleague decades later.

Because Harris knew how to manage workloads and deadlines, he soon realized that he'd be unable to continue working for the AP while writing *Black Sunday*. So he came to an agreement with his coauthors: They'd continue to handle research for the book, and he'd head back to Mississippi to finish the manuscript. "The idea was to share the writing," Maull recalled. "But after 50 pages, Tom took over, which was obviously a good thing."

Leaving the distractions of New York City and returning to the stillness of Rich energized Harris. He spent his days writing by hand, piecing together *Black Sunday* on a series of Big Chief-brand writing pads, which featured an illustration of a proud Native American on the cover. The work was painfully slow going: For the first several months, Harris filled barely two pages a day. "I felt like a man who was erecting a tent from the inside," he said of writing *Black Sunday*. "It was dark in there and I put up the poles and stretched out the ropes, but I had no idea what it looked like from the inside."

Though he remained in touch with Maull and Riley, Harris would later claim sole authorship of *Black Sunday*: "We passed it around for the first chapter or two, and then I redid the whole thing, pretty much." And when the finished novel was sent to critics in late 1974, just before its official release date, it was Harris's name that was on the cover—right below an illustration of a blimp-covered football field and a teasing tagline: "Do not begin this novel unless you are prepared to finish it in one sitting."

As it turned out, readers wouldn't need too much convincing to pick up *Black Sunday*. From its opening chapter featuring a daring assassination in Lebanon to its ticktocking finale above Tulane Stadium, Harris's 312-page debut was brisk and precise. His paragraphs were high-velocity darts all their own, flying with precision and landing with force. His unfussy style is evident in Harris's description of Dahlia Iyad, a Black September operative who helps Lander in his mission: "Dahlia had helped train the three Japanese terrorists who struck at Lod Airport in Tel Aviv, slaying at random. Originally there had been four Japanese terrorists. One lost his nerve in training and, with the other three watching, Dahlia blew his head off with a Schmeisser machine pistol."

After years of covering the news, Harris had finally been liberated from the tyranny of objectivity. In fiction, he could write whatever he wanted—no matter how violent, outrageous, or clumsily pervy ("The stadium spread its sides open to the sky, labial, passive, waiting."). And thanks to his reporting skills, *Black Sunday* was packed with small but effective journalistic minutiae. In one passage, he outlined the process of rigging a bomb to a refrigerator light bulb socket; in another, he wrote of the acrid scent of plastic explosives, describing the smell as that of "a garden hose left in the sun."

In *Black Sunday*, Harris occasionally even reported on his own life. When the novel flashes back to Michael Lander's first sighting of a blimp as a young child, it's inspired by Harris's experience decades earlier on his Mississippi schoolyard: "Silver, wearing for a reach across the wind, [the blimp] floated over the schoolyard, scattering in the air behind it tiny objects that floated down—Baby Ruth candy bars on small parachutes."

Before *Black Sunday* hit stores, G. P. Putnam's sons embarked upon an enthusiastic public relations blitz, positioning it as the first must-read novel of 1975. "What's the hottest book-publishing story today?" asked one syndicated gossip columnist. "We'd say it's the coming thriller *Black Sunday*."

When the book finally arrived in January—the same month the Pittsburgh Steelers and Minnesota Vikings arrived at Tulane for Super Bowl IX—it was met by critics with a combination of enthusiasm and concern: "Could it really happen?" wondered the *Chicago Daily News*. "This is the question you continually ask yourself as you tiptoe through this thriller." In *The New York Times*, Christopher Lehmann-Haupt praised *Black Sunday*'s high-tech details and *Realpolitik* verisimilitude: "Given Mr. Harris's ability to keep the plot boiling," he wrote, "he could have thrown Godzilla and King Kong into his Super Bowl and I still would have bought it."

Though the *Times* review noted Maull and Riley's involvement with the book, Harris received most of the praise. If that rankled his former AP colleagues, they never mentioned it publicly. Decades after the novel's release, Maull acknowledged that Harris deserved full credit: "In the final analysis, he was the one who whipped it into shape."

Black Sunday's strong reviews and scary real-life implications proved irresistible to readers. In early 1975, while visiting his parents in Mississippi, Harris got a phone call informing him that the book had hit the *New York Times* bestseller list. He and his father celebrated the success by immediately going out and buying a brand-new Ford Ranchero pickup truck. "I don't think I've ever been happier," Harris remembered decades later.

The good news kept coming. *Black Sunday* would also be named the main selection of the prestigious Book-of-the Month Club—a designation that held huge sway over book readers and retailers. The novel was an unorthodox choice for the club, which tended to favor highbrow pop novels and bulky biographies (recent selections had included *Einstein: The Life and Times* and *Khrushchev Remembers*, neither of which seemed likely to contain the word *labial*). A letter to Book-of-the-Month Club subscribers asked readers not to judge Harris's book by its cover. *"Black Sunday,"* it noted, "belongs to a special genre of our time: sub-literature, if you care to be sniffy." The letter compared Harris's novel to Mary Shelley's *Frankenstein* and the detective tales of Dashiell Hammett—all of them examples of "sophisticated popular writing [that's] worthy of serious attention."

Some members of the literati might not have known quite what to make of *Black Sunday*, but in Hollywood, "sub-literature" wasn't an insult; it was a come-on. Studio executives were hungry for propulsive, grown-up novels that could be translated to the screen—Peter Benchley's 1974 best-seller *Jaws* would soon become 1975's biggest film—and the movie rights to *Black Sunday* were soon scooped up by Robert Evans, the hotshot producer behind such hits as *The Godfather* and *Chinatown*.

Between the book deal, the movie rights sale, and the all-but-assured steady stream of residuals and royalties to come, Harris was about to become quite rich. Having already left his job at the AP, he vowed to take a break from reading the papers altogether: "I'm free of the news," he declared. Yet even he must have been aware that throughout 1975, many of the year's biggest headlines would reflect the agitations and anxieties of *Black Sunday*. The nightly news reports were filled with tales of political bombings, including a blast in Jerusalem that featured a bomb-rigged refrigerator similar to the one in Harris's book. And in September, President Gerald Ford survived two separate assassination attempts in a single month, with a third effort being thwarted before the gunman could pull the trigger. *Black Sunday* had become the year's timeliest book. It wouldn't be the first time Harris's work took on an eerie prescience.

The more popular *Black Sunday* became, the more Harris retreated from view. He stuck around Mississippi, where he spent time with his boat on a lake near his parents' home. He also began cutting ties with some of his old friends and colleagues from his newspaper days. "After he sold the film rights for *Black Sunday*, he told me he wasn't going to talk to anybody anymore," remembered one former coworker. "I hadn't realized when he said *anybody*, he really meant *everybody*."

Yet before Harris could retreat from view, he consented to a single on-the-record interview—the first of his career, and his last for many decades. In late 1974, the New York City–based writer Linda Kuehl headed to Mississippi to profile Harris for the *Book-of-the-Month Club News*. She sat down with the Harris family for Sunday lunch, during which Harris's mother expressed surprise regarding her son's success. "I always did know that Tom could write *true* stories," Polly said, "but I never did imagine that he could make them up."

Her son was in his midthirties now, and the clean-cut look he'd favored in his Waco days was long gone, replaced by a bee's nest of a beard and a bushy riot of hair. He was still wrapping his brain around the reception to *Black Sunday*. In just a few years, he'd gone from midtier newspaper reporter to respected novelist—an unexpected career shift. "My feathers aren't dried yet," Harris told Kuehl. "I feel like I just hatched out." His only immediate plans, he said, was to grab a banana boat and ride from New Orleans through the Panama Canal with his father. After that, Harris would start working on his next book—a "fast-paced" adventure tale in the vein of C. S. Forester's swashbuckling Horatio Hornblower series. He'd stockpiled more than thirty blank Big Chief tablets back home, their pages waiting to be filled.

But Harris, who'd spent his working life hustling from one news story to the next, wasn't going to be rushed. From now on, he'd set his *own* deadlines. "Do you remember in the picture *Easy Rider*, when the guy takes off his watch and throws it away?" he asked Kuehl. "Well, I've done that. It's whatever time I want it to be."

Harris would disappear for the rest of the decade. During that time, he continued to report on crime—this time as a novelist. He remained fascinated by real-life murderers. And when he returned to the public eye, he brought some of them along with him.

CHAPTER 4

"WE DON'T INVENT
OUR NATURES."

FBI special agent Robert Ressler would never be able to recall the exact year Tom Harris came into his life—and with good reason. For much of the 1970s and 1980s, Ressler was preoccupied with his day job: talking to serial killers.

Born and raised in Chicago, Ressler was an army veteran and criminology student who'd joined the FBI in 1970, right as the Bureau was about to undergo a series of drastic shifts. Longtime director J. Edgar Hoover, known for his combative personality and controlling leadership, would die in May 1972 after a long day at the office (the cause of death was a heart attack, apparently brought on by high blood pressure). A few days after his passing, the doors opened at the FBI's new training academy in Quantico, Virginia. Built for an estimated $24 million, the facilities included forensic science classrooms, a number of laboratories, and dormitories that could house more than two hundred students at a time.

By that point, the FBI was more than sixty years old. The high-tech facility was a sign that the Bureau was looking to evolve. "I will be more responsive to innovative ideas than Mr. Hoover might have been," noted L. Patrick Gray III, who had taken over as acting FBI director. "I'm a different sort of guy." Gray didn't last long in the job, thanks partly to his role in the Watergate cover-up (apparently, one of Gray's "innovative ideas" was to destroy incriminating documents). But that pledge of change came true in the decade ahead, as evidenced by the creation of what would become one of the FBI's most prominent divisions: the Behavioral Science Unit, or BSU.

Launched in the fall of 1972, the BSU incorporated a new process known as "profiling," in which experts studied crime scenes and police reports, looking for patterns that might illuminate a violent offender's tendencies and methodologies. Such details could be used to generate a "profile" of a likely offender, one that would list several possible characteristics—race, age, even employment status—and attempt to provide a psychological framework for that person's crimes. "Human behavior is much too complex to classify," noted a 1980 FBI internal report on profiling, "yet attempts are often made to do so with the hope that such a vastly complicated system can be brought into some control."

The goal of the BSU was to reduce the man-hours required to carry out investigations, as well as to provide insight into how *other* offenders might act in the future. Throughout the 1970s, the unit was short-staffed and hardly glamorous—a "back room" endeavor, according to a former member. Yet Ressler was eager to join the BSU. He'd spent his early years at the FBI working in cities such as Chicago and New Orleans, where he had handled everything from forgeries to fraud to organized crime. After joining the BSU in the mid-1970s, he quickly began educating himself on profiling.

As part of his BSU duties, Ressler gave lectures about the mindsets of well-known murderers, such as Charles Whitman, who'd killed more than a dozen people in a 1966 mass shooting in Austin, Texas. He also traveled around the United States and abroad, taking part in criminal science training sessions. It was while attending a symposium in England, Ressler claimed, that he came up with a new term to describe those who commit multiple murders: "serial killers."

The phrase was partly inspired, Ressler said, by the serial flicks he'd watched as a kid, in which heroes such as the Phantom would find themselves stuck in one cliff-hanger after the other. "In dramatic terms, this wasn't a satisfactory ending, because it increased, not lessened the tension," Ressler said. "The same dissatisfaction occurs in the minds of serial killers. The very act of killing leaves the murderer hanging, because it isn't as perfect as his fantasy."

Ressler would soon become restless and dissatisfied at Quantico. He was especially frustrated by his lectures on criminal behavior. He worried that he was simply regurgitating out-of-date information—that neither he nor his students were learning anything *new* about why people kill.

His concerns were shared by FBI special agent John Douglas, who'd joined the BSU in the late 1970s. Douglas had spent the early part of his FBI career investigating bank robberies and murders. Over time, he had learned to spot an offender's "signature," his term for "what the perpetrator has to do to fulfill himself." After arriving at Quantico, he sometimes sat in classes in which visiting police officers had more expertise than the agents teaching them. "There'd be a lecture on, say, Charles Manson," Douglas recalls. "And all of a sudden, a hand would go up in class and someone would say, 'I worked the case, and you're totally wrong.'"

In the late 1970s, Ressler and Douglas were paired up for what were known as "road schools," in which they traveled to police departments around the country to talk shop with cops. Ressler, who was nearly a decade older than Douglas, had been doing such trips for a while, using them as opportunities to collect case files on local crimes in the hope of learning more about violent offenders.

But there was only so much information the two men could glean from scouring regional police cases—and as a result, only so much they could teach others. If Ressler and Douglas wanted to learn more about why some people commit horrific acts, they'd have to go straight to the source: the killers themselves. The two men began making trips to correctional facilities around the country—sometimes together, sometimes with other agents. By flashing their credentials, they could get valuable face time with men who'd committed violent crimes, in order to "find out what it was like through *their* eyes," as Douglas put it.

One early subject was Edmund Kemper, a towering, brawny California man who'd murdered two family members when he was still a teenager ("[I] just wondered how it would feel to shoot grandma," he said). A few years later, having been released from a state hospital, he went on an early-1970s killing spree around Santa Cruz (which was then "the serial-murder capital of the world," according to Douglas). Kemper's victims were mostly female college students, though he also killed his own mother and one of her friends. In many instances, he mutilated the victim's body and had intercourse with her remains.

Ressler and Douglas would each meet with Kemper several times at a prison in Vacaville, California. The two men were struck by the killer's size, as well as his smarts: "[Ressler] and I worried he was a lot brighter than we were," noted Douglas. In his conversations with the agents, Kemper recounted his life and his many murders in a mild-mannered, analytical fashion. He explained that his impulse to kill had been driven by violent fantasies he'd harbored since his youth. "I'm sorry to sound so cold about this," he said during one chat. "But what I needed to have was a particular experience with a person, and to possess them in the way I wanted to. I had to evict them from their human bodies."

Despite Kemper's pragmatism, Douglas found him surprisingly engaging, even funny at times. For decades, the popular perception of mass murderers was that they were unhinged lunatics, an idea put forth in movies and on TV. Yet the BSU agents would find that some interviewees were capable of carrying on conversations for hours. "Many of these guys are quite charming, highly articulate and glib," Douglas noted.

At first, such meetings were conducted without the knowledge or permission of the agents' higher-ups at the FBI, who were enraged when they learned about the off-the-books interviews. "We had to tell them, 'Look, we're trying to figure out the *why*s of their behavior: their motivation, their victim selection, their pre- and postoffense behavior,'" Douglas says. "Because *why* plus *how* equals *who*."

The FBI's top brass relented, and Ressler and Douglas were able to keep the interview project going, spending hours with some of the most feared criminals in the country, including Charles Manson, the California cult leader whose acolytes had murdered nine people in the summer of 1969. Ressler was struck by Manson's emotional intelligence, as well as his "manipulative genius"—the way he controlled others not through intimidation but through *ingratiation*. Manson would break down their mental defenses and become the dominant voice in their heads, ultimately persuading his faithful that they *wanted* to kill (the LSD he made available to many of his followers likely helped). As he explained to Ressler, "I'm not a real big guy—I have to get things using my brain."

In most of the interviews, the BSU agents would ask those violent men—and they were *all* men—about their personal histories. They learned that during adolescence, many of the killers had begun exhibiting the same antisocial behaviors, such as torturing animals. The agents also quizzed their subjects about the nauseating nitty-gritty of their offenses: What did they do after murdering a victim? Did they collect souvenirs? Take photographs? And how did they process what they'd done—if they even processed it at all?

That curiosity was shared by many Americans. Throughout the late 1970s, it seemed as though a new headline-making killer was emerging every few months. On the West Coast, Los Angeles residents lived in fear of the "Hillside Strangler," who'd committed a series of brutal murders around the city. In the Midwest, there was John Wayne Gacy, a part-time clown whose home in Des Plaines, Illinois, was littered with the remains of more than two dozen victims, most of them teenage boys. And on the East Coast, there was New York City's "Son of Sam," who gunned down young men and women, often attacking couples as they sat in parked cars. Over the course of two tense years, Son of Sam killed six people and sent letters to police and the press featuring potential clues about his identity. When compared to the complicated brutality of the decade's other publicized killers, Son of Sam's murders seemed almost like an "old-style crime," Andy Warhol wrote in a 1977 diary entry. "Notes to the police, an M.O., killer on the loose, all that. People seem sort of happy to see a pattern. Son of Sam is nostalgia, almost."

Though Ressler's "serial killer" term wasn't yet being widely used, such crimes were being covered in newspaper articles and TV broadcasts and books, turning murderers into household names. The exploits of the "Zodiac Killer," who'd haunted northern California in the late 1960s, were fictionalized in the hit 1971 film *Dirty Harry*. Manson and Son of Sam, meanwhile, inspired bestselling books. By decade's end, one serial killer had even been transformed, grimly, into a sort of perverse pinup: Ted Bundy, a thirtysomething former law student who was in the late 1970s suspected of committing countless sexual assaults and murders. Bundy's youth, good looks, and relative charm earned him near-constant press—he was, after all, "the all-American boy," as one reporter noted. He even inspired the occasional tongue-in-cheek tribute. One novelty T-shirt featured the phrase "Ted Bundy is a one-night stand," while a fast-food vendor offered up "Bundy Burgers." And when Ann Rule, a crime writer who'd worked with Bundy at a Seattle crisis center, published her 1980 book *The Stranger Beside Me*, it quickly became a bestseller.

The rising profiles of killers such as Bundy, whose 1979 murder trial aired on national television, was a sign to many Americans that the country was in the grip of a mass-murder epidemic. And it prompted some journalists to ask what the FBI was doing to prevent it. "The Behavioral Science Unit was getting a lot of media attention," notes FBI special agent Roger Depue, who'd joined the unit in 1974. "We had people who were interested in coming down to the unit and talking with the agents."

In early 1980, the *Chicago Tribune* ran a front-page story about the "little-known FBI unit" that was using criminal profiles to examine violent offenses—and often getting results. The story chronicled the BSU's role in solving a particularly unpleasant case in Sacramento, California in 1978: Five people had been murdered in close proximity to one another, with some of the bodies exhibiting signs of cannibalism. Ressler and an FBI colleague helped draw up a profile of a possible suspect, based in part on BSU's research. They theorized that he was a twenty-seven-year-old undernourished white man with a history of mental illness—most likely schizophrenia—and a penchant for torturing animals. An investigation finally led the Sacramento police to Richard Chase, who fit the FBI's exact description, down to his age. Chase, who'd later earn the nickname "Vampire Killer," died by suicide in prison a few years after his arrest.

At the time the BSU assisted with the Chase case, the unit was still small, with close to a dozen agents. Their work sometimes confounded their colleagues. In the unit's early days, Douglas said, many within the FBI—and in the greater law-enforcement world—saw the BSU's approach to solving murders as "worthless bullshit." Yet over time, the BSU found admirers around the country. In 1979, it received about fifty requests for profiles from law agencies; the next year, the number doubled. More field agents were going to Quantico so they could study criminal behavior, and share what they learned with others across the country. The BSU was becoming known, in Ressler's words, as "a clearing house for bizarre, seemingly motiveless murders."

It was during that period of high notoriety that Ressler got a message from the FBI's public affairs desk, asking if he'd meet with a writer curious about the BSU's work. The guy was a novelist, one who had some admirers within the FBI. And he needed help in learning how to catch a serial killer.

Before dropping out of sight in 1975, Tom Harris seemed excited to get to work on his follow-up to *Black Sunday*. In his interview with *Book-of-the-Month Club News*, he described the joy he'd sometimes felt while writing his debut novel. "Do you remember when you first learned how to ride a bicycle?" he asked the journalist Linda Kuehl. "Remember that funny feeling when you finally got going and you realized, 'By god, I can ride that damn thing?'"

That enthusiasm proved to be short-lived. Just a few months after the release of *Black Sunday*, while signing a copy of the novel for a friend, Harris added an inscription about his struggles: "I thought that doing the next book would be easier, but I'm finding out different."

It was a cryptic sigh, one that offered little insight into how or why he'd gotten derailed. In fact, the years immediately following the publication of *Black Sunday* are among the least documented of Harris's life, though the writer was clearly experiencing a bit of wanderlust. He began spending more of his time in Sag Harbor, a village within Long Island's Hamptons enclave that had served as a refuge for generations of novelists, including James Fenimore Cooper and John Steinbeck. Harris also became enamored with Italy, zipping through the streets of Rome in his Alfa Romeo. Around that time, he met Pace Barnes, a book and magazine editor who'd become Harris's partner for the rest of his life (and who shared his no-interview policy).

Though Harris had initially planned to write an adventure novel, at some point in the 1970s—whether out of frustration, boredom, or some combination of both—he abandoned that idea in favor of something far more sinister. He had witnessed all sorts of crimes during his journalism days, and now violence was everywhere he looked. As he later told a colleague, he'd gone out for a walk on a beach one afternoon and observed "a great agitation" in the otherwise crystal-clear water. "[It was] in the distance, but close enough that I could actually see that something was eating something else," he said. "Everything is fine on the surface, and underneath, it's all this carnage."

Harris wanted to capture that feeling in his next novel, which he'd eventually title *Red Dragon*. It would follow a vile murderer, a damaged criminal profiler, and the madman who manipulates them both from a cell. As with *Black Sunday*, Harris's new book would find him leaning heavily on his journalism background, applying arcane facts to distressingly believable fiction. And because *Red Dragon* had dealt with multiple serial killers, Harris eventually reached out to the FBI, asking to meet with agents who specialized in murder investigations.

By then Ressler had become accustomed to journalists asking questions about the Behavioral Science Unit—though he wasn't always thrilled by the way the media portrayed the BSU's work. "They make profiling seem like a magic wand that, when available to police, instantly solves the crime," he said. Harris, though, didn't want to glamorize the unit's work. He wanted to grill the BSU agents about the science of catching killers— and then incorporate his findings into a work of fiction.

It was an audacious request. Luckily for Harris, *Black Sunday*, which by then had sold more than 2 million copies, had found a wide readership within the FBI. "After the Olympics where the Israeli team was murdered, we had a keen interest in all terrorist stories, whether they were fictional or actual," says former BSU agent Depue. "We read *Black Sunday* and thought it was a really excellent book. So Harris's name was known to us."

That made it easier for the writer to get access to the Bureau's Washington, DC, headquarters, where he was escorted by Bill Trible, a special agent in the FBI's public affairs office. Trible would be one of Harris's key contacts at the Bureau throughout the 1980s, as well as a friend and semifrequent dining companion. "He was interested in just about every-thing," says Trible. "Firearms, motorcycles, literature, forensics, arts, and architecture, European and American history. Every time we'd have a dis-cussion, I'd always feel afterward that I'd just read a very good book."

With Trible's assistance, Harris would meet with a handful of BSU agents, including Ressler, whom Harris inundated with questions: What would the FBI's role be in a serial killer case? How did it work with local police? And perhaps most crucially: How is a profile created?

During their time together, Ressler showed Harris slides relating to some of his most notorious interviewees, most notably Edmund Kemper and Richard "Vampire Killer" Chase. The agent also told Harris about the BSU's in-prison interviews and its practice of bringing in psychiatrists for consultations. "He just let me drone on and I'd think he wasn't paying attention," Ressler said. Later, he realized that "Harris was like a sponge—saying nothing but absorbing everything."

In addition to Harris's in-person meetings with Bureau agents, he would have had access to the FBI's monthly in-house publication, the *FBI Law Enforcement Bulletin*. A sort of academic journal/PR newsletter, the *Bulletin* documented the FBI's post-Hoover techniques and technologies, with stories that were sometimes contributed by agents themselves, often written in a dry, just-the-facts style (sample sentence: "Seldom will the lust murderer use a firearm to kill, for he experiences too little psycho-sexual gratification with such an impersonal weapon"). One article in 1978 examined how human bite marks, even those left on a piece of gum, were increasingly being used to solve homicides and sexual assaults. The next year, a *Bulletin* report looked at advancements in using latent prints—that is, prints left on human skin—to identify murderers.

In March 1980, the *Bulletin* ran a lengthy primer on profiling—an ac-knowledgment that a practice once treated with skepticism within the Bureau was now inching toward acceptance. The *Bulletin* piece made the case that in the decade ahead, profiling would become a more necessary skill. As its authors noted, profiling offered a new way to answer the first question invariably raised at the scene of a violent crime: "Who would do a thing like this?"

Harris had wondered the same thing. But his curiosity about human behavior wasn't limited to the likes of Kemper and Chase. He also paid close attention to the FBI profilers themselves. They were people who'd voluntarily stood face-to-face with murderers, and who'd sometimes faced grave consequences, including drastic weight loss, pseudo–heart attacks, and ceaseless stress. Harris was fascinated by the idea of turning over one's life and one's mind to some of the most terrifying humans imaginable—so much so that he decided to make a profiler the main character of his next work, a novel that would be written under dark skies and in tragic circumstances.

CHAPTER 5

"MY GOD, WHERE DID THAT COME FROM?"

On an afternoon in September 1979, Linton Weeks was working at Volume One bookstore in Clarksdale, Mississippi, not far from Harris's hometown of Rich, when a familiar-looking customer came through the door. The man wore glasses and a beard, and his head was covered in curls. It didn't take long for Weeks to figure out his guest's identity. For a while now, rumors had been circulating around the Delta that Tom Harris had come home.

Weeks played it cool. "*Black Sunday* was pretty good," he said by way of greeting. "The fact that you are a good writer shone through it all."

Harris nodded politely and expressed his gratitude. Then, in a quiet voice—which Weeks described as "Southern, worldly and charged with irony"—he asked for help in tracking down a particularly hard-to-find book: Alexandre Dumas's 1873 cooking guide, *Grand dictionnaire de cuisine*.

It was an unusual request, one that Weeks initially took as "pure pretension." He'd come to understand the significance of the Dumas book in the months and years ahead, during which Weeks and his wife, Jan, would become friendly with Harris. The couple lived in a cabin on nearby Moon Lake, and on some afternoons, the author would drop by with a pickle jar containing martinis, which the friends would drink as they sat and stared at the water. "The Mississippi Delta," Harris proclaimed, "has the most beautiful sunsets of anywhere on earth."

That wasn't why he had returned home to Mississippi. Harris told Weeks he'd found it difficult to write in Sag Harbor—which very well could have been the case. But he had never strayed too far from the Delta. In 1978, Harris had enrolled in a Monday-night art class at Delta State University, where an impressed instructor had told him, "Your drawing is so good, you can illustrate your next book." And by September 1979, he had relocated full-time to the family home in Rich to see his father, W.T., through an unspecified illness. The writer spent his days tending to the ailing W.T., and his nights in a neighbor's shotgun shack in the middle of a large cotton field. That was where Harris worked on what would become *Red Dragon*.

While typing away in his shack, he could hear wild dogs panting as they roamed outside in the dark, their voices howling in unison during a full moon. On some nights, he would walk the fields himself, wandering far from the house. "When I looked back from a distance," Harris wrote, "the house looked like a boat at sea, and all around me the vast Delta night."

As he stood in the dim light of the fields, surrounded by little more than the sounds of snuffling dogs, his thoughts turned to *Red Dragon*'s troubled antagonist, Will Graham, a skilled former FBI profiler who left the Bureau due to a pair of traumatic events. Early in his career, Graham had shot Garrett Jacob Hobbs, a serial killer known as the "Minnesota Shrike"—an incident that had led Graham to seek help in a mental hospital. After returning to the FBI, he suffered a near-fatal stabbing, prompting a haunted Graham to quit the Bureau for good.

As Harris worked on his novel in that vast cotton field, alone after hours of tending to his dying parent, he found himself empathizing with his put-upon hero. "At the time, I myself was accruing painful memories every day," he noted, "and in my evening's work I felt for Graham." That didn't mean that Harris would take it easy on him. *Red Dragon* begins with Graham's former FBI boss, Jack Crawford, pulling the ex-agent out of retirement. The Bureau needs Graham's help in finding a murderer police have dubbed the "Tooth Fairy." He's a nocturnal killer who's butchered two families in the suburbs of the South, timing his crimes to occur during a full moon, and leaving telltale bite marks on his victims.

Graham doesn't want to be pulled into the hunt for another serial killer. But he can't help himself. He has what Harris described as an "uncomfortable gift," the rare ability to empathize with a killer's motivations and methods—so much so, it's as if Graham *becomes* the murderer, albeit temporarily. As *Red Dragon* noted, "There were no effective partitions in [Graham's] mind. What he saw and learned touched everything else he knew. Some of the combinations were hard to live with. But he could not anticipate them, could not block and repress. . . . His associations came at the speed of light."

For Graham, tracking down the Tooth Fairy will be a devastating task, one that will require the help of the very person who, years earlier, had gutted him with a linoleum knife: Dr. Hannibal Lecter, aka "Hannibal the Cannibal." The two men have a complicated past. But Graham believes Lecter's the only one who can provide insight into the Tooth Fairy's means and methods—and who can help the profiler understand how this new serial killer thinks.

Graham and Lecter's first encounter in *Red Dragon* proved to be a struggle for Harris, for whom writing meant waiting. He described the novelist's role as akin to being a companion or caretaker: His characters were the ones on a journey, and he was merely tagging along. "When you are writing a novel, you are not making anything up," he explained. "It's all there and you just have to find it."

So it was with "some trepidation," he noted, that he accompanied Graham on his trip to visit Lecter. As he worked in his cabin, writing *Red Dragon*, he followed his damaged hero as Graham descended into the bowels of the Chesapeake State Hospital for the Criminally Insane, where Lecter is kept in a maximum-security wing.[*] The first time readers meet Lecter, the doctor's asleep on a cot in his cell, a copy of Dumas's *Grand dictionnaire de cuisine* sitting open on his chest. He and Graham are

---

[*] In the initial printings of *Red Dragon*, Lecter's home was referred to as the Chesapeake State Hospital for the Criminally Insane. It would be retitled the Baltimore State Hospital for the Criminally Insane in the novel *The Silence of the Lambs*.

separated by the steel bars of Lecter's cell, as well as by a protective wall made up of floor-to-ceiling nylon netting.

Once Lecter awakes, it becomes clear that such restraints haven't dimmed his powers. Blunt and bitchy—and eager to have a project—Lecter quickly makes Graham the topic of conversation. He quizzes the former agent about his emotional state, his dreams, even his aftershave (which Lecter, with his refined sense of smell, recognized as soon as the agent entered his lair). "Graham felt that Lecter was looking through to the back of his skull," Harris wrote in *Red Dragon*. "His attention felt like a fly walking around in there."

Their first meeting concludes with Lecter cruelly reminding Graham of the trait the two men have in common: Lecter may have murdered as many as nine victims (at least that the police know of), but Graham had fatally shot Garrett Jacob Hobbs. They may have been on opposite sides of the bars, but Lecter sees a murderous kinship in Graham.

"Do you know how you caught me, Will?"

"Good-bye, Dr. Lecter. You can leave messages for me at the number on the file." Graham walked away.

"Do you know how you caught me?"

Graham was out of Lecter's sight now, and he walked faster toward the far steel door.

"The reason you caught me is that we're just alike" was the last thing Graham heard as the steel door closed behind him.

Harris wrote that first-ever appearance of Hannibal Lecter in a rush, his notes "spilling into the margin and over whatever surface was uppermost on my table," he recalled. "I was worn out when it was over." After Harris finished, there was a full moon over the cotton fields, and thirteen dogs were howling on the cabin's front porch. By his estimate, he would go on to revise that initial moment between Graham and Lecter a hundred times. With each new visit to Lecter's cell, he said, he whittled down the "superfluous static, the jail noises, the screaming of the damned that had made some of the words hard to hear."

For Harris, the process of bringing Lecter to life had been exhausting—and unnerving. "I was not comfortable in the presence of Dr. Lecter, not sure at all that the doctor could not see me," he wrote decades later. "Like Graham, I found, and find, the scrutiny of Dr. Lecter uncomfortable, intrusive, like the humming in your thoughts when they X-ray your head."

If that humming felt familiar to Harris, it's because Lecter reminded him of an old, ominous acquaintance: Alfredo Ballí Treviño, aka Dr. Salazar, the elegantly composed, hyperinsightful murderer who'd dismembered his lover in the late 1950s, and whom Harris had encountered while visiting Mexico for *Argosy* magazine. In a 2013 introduction to *The Silence of the Lambs*, Harris described writing the scene in which Graham approached Lecter's lair. "Who do you suppose was waiting in the cell?" Harris asked. "It was not Dr. Salazar. But because of Dr. Salazar, I could recognize his colleague and fellow practitioner, Hannibal Lecter."

That line was immediately seized upon as evidence that Ballí was the "real-life Lecter"—a perception Harris later tried to discourage. "I won't say he was the model for Hannibal Lecter," the author noted in 2019. Certainly, the two killers had plenty in common. Both possess an icy verbosity and imposing manner—as well as what Harris described as "a peculiar understanding of the criminal mind." The doctors even match up physically: In *Red Dragon*, Harris notes that Lecter is a "small, lithe man," the exact term he'd use decades later to describe Dr. Salazar. And both prisoners stared back at their inquisitors through maroon-colored eyes (though only Lecter's, *Red Dragon* notes, "reflect the light redly in tiny points").

But to conclude that Dr. Lecter *was* "Dr. Salazar," or vice versa, was the kind of reductive statement that would make Hannibal the Cannibal click his tongue in condescending disagreement. For starters, the two killers' offenses and methodologies differed greatly. Ballí had confessed to just one murder, in which he had drugged, dismembered, and cut up a young lover before burying him in the ground. Lecter, by contrast, approaches his murders as though they were works of art. According to *Red Dragon*, one of his early victims was a hunter whom Lecter had stabbed, laced to a pegboard, and then adorned with arrows. As a finishing touch, he had rearranged the corpse so that the man resembled a vintage medical illustration known as "Wound Man." Lecter wasn't the kind of madman who'd stuff someone's remains into a box and dump them into the ground—a déclassé demise, if ever there was one.

There's another key difference between the doctors: Ballí's murder was a crime of passion. Lecter, however, spent his early years killing for fun. "He did it because he liked it," Graham tells a police detective. "Still does. Dr. Lecter is not crazy, in any common way we think of being crazy. He did some hideous things because he enjoyed them." Those hideous things, according to *Red Dragon*, include an attack on a nurse who got too close to Lecter during an exam: "She managed to save one of her eyes," Graham is told. "His pulse never got over eighty-five. Even when he tore out her tongue."

By the time Harris wrote *Red Dragon* in his Delta cabin, he'd spent nearly half his life studying crime up close—from Waco to Mexico to New York City and various points in between. When it came to murder, he was an unaccredited scholar. And with *Red Dragon*, he was drawing on years of dark knowledge.

So while he no doubt saw glimpses of Ballí when he stumbled upon Lecter, there were other killers lingering in that cell at the Chesapeake State Hospital for the Criminally Insane. Lecter had the smarts (and apparent appetites) of the accused cannibal James H. Coyner. He had some of Charles Manson's knack for intimidation and ingratiation. There were also similarities between Lecter and Edmund Kemper, both pragmatic conversationalists who'd tortured animals in their youth (an act that was "the first and worst sign" of violent tendencies, Graham noted in *Red Dragon*). And it was likely no coincidence that Lecter was conceived around the time newspapers were covering Richard Chase, the "Vampire Killer" who'd boasted of drinking some of his victims' blood.

Ballí, Manson, Coyner, Kemper, Chase—by the end of the violent 1970s, they were all part of a larger swirl of sadism. And they weren't alone; Lecter was an unnatural by-product of years' worth of bloodshed—his small, lithe body containing a multitude of murderers.

You are not making anything up, Harris had said. *It's all there and you just have to find it.* And in Lecter, Harris had found a plausible monster—one who would forever seem real not just to readers but to the author himself. "When in the winter of 1979 I entered the Baltimore State Hospital for the Criminally Insane and the great metal door crashed closed behind me, little did I know what waited at the end of the corridor," Harris wrote. "How seldom we recognize the sound when the bolt of our fate slides home."

Throughout the writing of *Red Dragon*, Harris fretted, fussed, and agonized. According to his Delta neighbor Linton Weeks, the author saw "each sentence [as] a jewel, each paragraph a bracelet." Over time, his Mississippi home began to morph into a small library, dotted with overflowing ashtrays and stocked with research materials: gun magazines, a Bible, star charts, an Italian cookbook. *Red Dragon* had engulfed him. "After this one," he said while working on the novel, "I'm going to take off a month and give way to liquor and licentiousness." He planned to be in Italy when the final pages of *Red Dragon* came together. That was a pricey work trip, especially considering that he had told Weeks—perhaps jokingly—that he had just "two hundred bucks" in his bank account.

Harris was still at work on *Red Dragon* when, in May 1980, his father passed away at the age of sixty-six. If that slowed Harris's writing, it wasn't for long. On November 4 of that year, Linton and Jan Weeks visited the author at his home, where they watched TV as Jimmy Carter acknowledged his loss to Ronald Reagan, a violation of Harris's no-news policy. The nearly completed manuscript of *Red Dragon* was laid out on a floor, piled up chapter by chapter. Soon afterward, Harris FedExed his pages to his agent, Gloria Safier. Then he drove to Memphis and celebrated the completion of *Red Dragon* by watching the sunset over the Mississippi River with a bottle of champagne. It wasn't exactly a night of full-on licentiousness, but it would do.

By that point, it had been five years since *Black Sunday* had landed on the bestseller lists. So Harris's editors at G. P. Putnam's Sons were no doubt feeling equally jubilant when the *Red Dragon* manuscript arrived—and proved to be worth the wait. It was speedy, succinct, and packed with unpleasant intel Harris had discovered in his research. But unlike Harris's globe-trotting debut, with its many terrorists and crime stoppers, it focused on a smaller cast of characters, all of them troubled.

There's Lecter himself, of course—though he appears in only a few chapters, and is kept obscured even while in plain sight. In fact, given how much he looms over the action in the book, it's remarkable how little information Harris divulges about him in *Red Dragon*, which treats the character as a sort of shadows-dwelling second banana. There are small teases of Lecter's past dusted throughout Harris's book: We learn that he worked as an emergency room doctor before setting up his psychiatry practice. And it's revealed that he was once injected with truth serum to try to force a confession, and responded by giving up a recipe for dip.

Red Dragon also displays Lecter's taunting, erudite cruelty: While Graham is on the hunt for the Tooth Fairy, Lecter sends him a letter, written on heavy mauve-colored stationery, in which Hannibal the Cannibal once again argues that he and the former agent aren't really that different. "We don't invent our natures, Will," Lecter writes, "they're issued to us along with our lungs and pancreas and everything else. Why fight it?" (Or, as the reputed cannibal James H. Coyner once said, *What is to be, will be.*)

Lecter then brings up the "Minnesota Shrike," the serial killer Graham had shot and killed a few years earlier, resulting in his stint in a mental institution:

> I want to help you, Will, and I'd like to start by asking you this: When you were so depressed after you shot Mr. Garrett Jacob Hobbs to death, it wasn't the act that got you down, was it? Really, didn't you feel so bad because killing him felt so good?
>
> Think about it, but don't worry about it. Why shouldn't it feel good? It must feel good to God—He does it all the time, and are we not made in His image?

Aside from such flashes of nastiness, the Lecter of *Red Dragon* is an elusive subject. "I don't think we're any closer to understanding him now than the day he came in," laments Dr. Frederick Chilton, Lecter's rigid caretaker. "I think he's afraid that if we 'solve' him, nobody will be interested in him anymore, and he'll be stuck in a back ward somewhere for the rest of his life."

In *Red Dragon*, Lecter is portrayed as an object of fascination among fellow psychiatrists, who ask him to contribute articles to their academic journals and show off letters from Hannibal the Cannibal on their walls. He's also found a fan in the Tooth Fairy, who keeps a collection of Lecter's press clippings. Though Lecter doesn't take up many pages in *Red Dragon*, Harris makes it clear that he is the killer *other* killers look to for inspiration and approval. Which makes sense: If you *had* to be a madman, wouldn't you aspire to be like Lecter, the most intelligent, most refined, most *accomplished* figure in a bloody field?

Harris lays out the Tooth Fairy's m.o. with terrifying specificity and efficiency throughout *Red Dragon*: After choosing his victims and scoping out their homes, the Tooth Fairy attacks in the middle of the night, killing the family members before arranging some of their corpses around a bed. He then places mirror shards over the mother's eyes, and looks at his own reflection in them while having sex with her. His crimes are so sensational that at one point in *Red Dragon*, a character sports a T-shirt emblazoned with the phrase "The Tooth Fairy Is a One-Night Stand"—an echo of the real-world design dedicated to Ted Bundy.

Unlike Lecter, who's largely obscured in Harris's novel, the Tooth Fairy has his entire sad, sticky life laid out in *Red Dragon*. Harris reveals early on that he's actually a loner named Francis Dolarhyde, a technician at St. Louis's Gateway Film Laboratory, where he examines home movies from around the country, hoping to find desirable families to victimize. Dolarhyde plots his crimes from an isolated, rambling home in rural Missouri—an existence that allows him to travel and commit murders without anyone noticing he's gone.

Harris doesn't merely detail Dolarhyde's digressions; he explains how that monster got his start: He was abandoned at a young age by his parents and raised by a cruel grandmother, who threatened to castrate him for wetting the bed. Decades later, after a troubled adolescence and early life, Dolarhyde has an epiphany when he spots William Blake's early-1800s painting *The Great Red Dragon and the Woman Clothed with the Sun*. It's a nightmarish watercolor, based on a passage from the Book of Revelation, depicting a winged, muscular beast descending upon a woman as she reclines near a crescent moon. Seeing the painting convinces Dolarhyde to believe he's in the process of "becoming" the Red Dragon itself—a feeling confirmed when he begins hearing the creature's voice in his head, commanding him to kill.

Graham's task in *Red Dragon* is to act as sort of moving-target middleman between the Tooth Fairy and Lecter, absorbing as much information as he can from one killer while desperately tracking down another. His search for Dolarhyde, much like the pursuit of the terrorists in *Black Sunday*, is chronicled with a level of procedural detail that's both bewildering and enthralling. Harris drops readers directly into the crime scene and spatters them with information—as in a passage in which Graham roams one of the family's homes, looking for "blood-drop trajectories":

> He went over the upstairs room minutely, trying to match injuries to stains, trying to work backward. He plotted each splash on a measured field sketch of the master bedroom, using the standard comparison plates to estimate the direction and velocity of the bloodfall. In this way he hoped to learn the positions the bodies were in at different times.

"Comparison plates"? "Bloodfall"? It was nerdy, giddy stuff. So were the bite patterns Graham finds on a partly nibbled chunk of cheese and the latent prints that are pulled from a corpse's eyeball. Harris may have been a quiet presence while visiting the FBI, but he'd clearly vacuumed up every detail he could find. Reading *Red Dragon* was like getting a behind-the-scenes tour of the Bureau's labs and conference rooms—the kinds of places where high-end lasers were used to find clues; hair samples were scrutinized in brightly lit, draft-free examination rooms; and a pair of human hands might be found sitting around in a box, preserved in dry ice.

Harris's meticulous approach to *Red Dragon* applied not just to his research but to his prose: When his publisher sent Harris a copyedited final manuscript for review, the author deleted every comma that a young editor had inserted, exerting a level of creative control he'd enjoy for his entire career.

Finally, in the spring of 1981, *Red Dragon* was ready to go to press. And though the novel wouldn't arrive in stores until fall, there were clear signs that the public, and the publishing industry, were eager for Harris's return. That April, Harris had received a cable from his agent, Gloria Safier, informing him that the book club rights for *Red Dragon* had just been sold for more than $250,000, a jackpot sum. A subsequent paperback rights deal would earn Harris an additional $1.6 million. By then, Harris had left Mississippi and relocated to Italy. Writing from Rome, he responded to Safier's cable with a note that winkingly celebrated his ever-increasing good fortune: "These mink socks tickle!"

The first major review of *Red Dragon* appeared in the pages of *The Washington Post* on Halloween 1981. The writer didn't waste any time getting to the point: Harris's new book was "probably the best popular novel to be published in America since *The Godfather*." The *Post* critic went on to praise *Red Dragon*'s "raw, grisly power," noting that Harris's sentences had "the ferocious focus of a clean white light." Reading the book, he declared, was like "[slipping] into the driver's seat of a Rolls Royce, where everything is muted and everything works."

Clearly, Stephen King was impressed.

He wasn't alone. Most of the responses to *Red Dragon* were laudatory. A few critics were irked by Harris's techno-obsessed detailing: "There's too much fingerprinting," complained the *Los Angeles Times Book Review*. And there was some tut-tutting about *Red Dragon*'s violence, with a critic at *The Philadelphia Inquirer* comparing the novel to *The Texas Chain Saw Massacre*, the bloody 1974 cult hit that had been partly inspired by Ed Gein's murders. *Red Dragon*, the *Inquirer* reviewer noted, was "the most repulsive book I have ever read."

But most readers could handle the novel's darker turns. *Red Dragon* quickly found its way onto several bestseller lists, where it sat alongside such terrifying titles as King's killer dog thriller *Cujo* and *A Few Minutes with Andy Rooney.* As grim as its contents might have been, *Red Dragon* became a mainstream must-read—the kind of book that would be in constant demand at libraries and spur numerous book club conversations. At the Carnegie Public Library in Clarksdale, Mississippi, where Harris had spent so much of his childhood, officials held a "Lunch at the Library" discussion of Harris's novel, just a few miles from the isolated shack where the author had first encountered Lecter. ("Coffee and cold drinks will be available," the library promised.)

There were numerous reasons for *Red Dragon*'s instant takeoff—its galvanic plotting, its rich characterizations, its menacingly cool-sounding title—but a crucial factor in its success might have been that by the fall of 1981, Americans had become freaked out by crime. Though the decade was still young, homicide rates were rising in some cities, and the world had just witnessed a wave of assassination attempts: In the months leading up to *Red Dragon*'s release, the former Beatle John Lennon and Egyptian President Anwar Sadat had been shot dead, while US President Ronald Reagan had been injured during an attempt on his life.

The country was also still dealing with two headline-making serial killer cases. In Atlanta, Georgia, a music promoter named Wayne B. Williams had recently been arrested on suspicion of killing more than twenty children and young teens in the area. And in Wichita, Kansas, the search was on for the "BTK Strangler"—short for "bind, torture, and kill"—who was believed to have been responsible for more than a half-dozen local murders. (In his letters to police, BTK claimed that he'd been compelled by a monster in his brain named "Factor X"—not too dissimilar from the "Dragon" that Dolarhyde converses with in his mind.).

To many critics, Harris was holding up a broken mirror shard to the country. And the reflection wasn't pretty. "These frightening days, when it seems you can be murdered just for the look on your face, it's simple enough to understand the appeal of Thomas Harris's 'Red Dragon,'" declared *The New York Times*. A critic for Virginia's *Richmond Times-Dispatch* noted the book's "cold, hard look at a kind of horror that is a threat to everyone." And in his *Washington Post* write-up, King made the case that *Red Dragon* was more than just mere late-night entertainment;

it was an essential document of its era. "The best popular fiction can combine art with nearly devastating insights into The Way We Live Now," he wrote. ". . . The prose in this novel is in perfect sync with the pulse of the times, and in the end we may sense that the Red Dragon in these pages is real enough . . . too real."

Red Dragon also had several fans within the FBI's Behavioral Science Unit—for obvious reasons: Though the BSU is just a background player in Harris's novel, *Red Dragon* introduced the concept of profiling to millions of readers. There was a sense of pride among some BSU agents that their work had helped yield such a satisfying read. "I thought *Red Dragon* was a fine piece of literature—the best in the series," notes Depue, who later helped found a forensics company, The Academy Group Inc., featuring a red dragon as part of its logo.

If Harris was pleased by the response to *Red Dragon*, he kept it to himself. Aside from his new author photo, in which he hid behind dark-colored sunglasses, he once again remained obscure. He emerged only once, to respond to a small *Red Dragon* controversy. In the book, it's revealed that Francis Dolarhyde was born with a cleft palate—a condition he shared with Dykes Askew Simmons Jr., the convicted murderer that Harris had interviewed in Mexico. A few years after the book's release, in 1983, a Pittsburgh group had organized a letter-writing campaign to the author, complaining that Dolarhyde's cleft palate unfairly stigmatized children who shared his condition. Harris's novel, one parent claimed, made the kids seem like "potential monster[s]."

Remarkably, Harris wrote back, agreeing that people needed more education about cleft palates—and defending his work. "Nowhere in *Red Dragon* do I indicate that his physical defect was the cause of his behavior," he replied, his words underlined and italicized for emphasis. "That would be an absurdity, as offensive to me as it is to you."

The flare-up was further evidence that *Red Dragon*'s breakout character was Dolarhyde—not Hannibal the Cannibal. The mindset of the Tooth Fairy "scared the shit out of me," remembered *L.A. Confidential* and *The Black Dahlia* author James Ellroy, who was just starting his crime fiction career when he encountered *Red Dragon*. To most reviewers, Dolarhyde was the book's main menace, with Hannibal merely an also-ran villain. In the synopsis printed on the novel's dust jacket, Lecter didn't even warrant a mention.

Yet it's Hannibal the Cannibal who gets the last laugh—if not the last word—in *Red Dragon*. The book concludes with a violent showdown at Graham's home in Marathon, Florida, where Graham's wife, Molly, shoots Dolarhyde repeatedly at close range—blowing "a rat hole through his thigh" that finally kills him. Before he dies, Dolarhyde manages to shove a knife into Graham's face, disfiguring him both physically and emotionally.

While in the hospital, Graham receives another note from Lecter, again on his telltale mauve stationery. It was the doctor who'd provided Graham's Florida address to Dolarhyde, and as punishment, Lecter's cell has been cleared of reading materials, leaving him with nothing to occupy his time. He's clearly bored—to Lecter, a situation that's even worse than being stabbed and left for dead. By the end of *Red Dragon*, even Hannibal Lecter thinks the world has gone a little mad. "We live in a primitive time—don't we, Will?—neither savage nor wise," he sighs in his note. "Half measures are the curse of it. Any rational society would either kill me or give me my books."

Lecter then bids Graham a cruel adieu:

I wish you a speedy convalescence and hope you won't be very ugly.
I think of you often.

Hannibal Lecter.

It was a haunting send-off, one that allowed Lecter to roam freely in Graham's mind, as well as in the imaginations of millions of *Red Dragon* readers. It was a novel whose evils felt feasible—so much so, even Harris was taken aback by its dark powers. Before the book's release, he took a hardcover copy to the beach. As he read his own novel, he couldn't help but wonder "My God, where did that come from?"

Many people in Hollywood were wondering the same thing.

CHAPTER 6

"HE'S LETHAL."

For all of Harris's early career ambitions—his story pitches to magazine editors, his relocation to New York City, his fleeing the AP and writing *Black Sunday*—he kept as far away from the entertainment industry as possible. "Hemingway said that what you should do is take your book to the California state line, wait till they throw you the money, then you throw them the book," he told an interviewer. "And you turn around and drive home just as fast as you can go. That's not bad advice."

Harris's aversion to Hollywood became clear when the film adaptation of *Black Sunday* arrived in 1977. Unlike some of his best-selling contemporaries, including Peter Benchley (*Jaws*) and Mario Puzo (*The Godfather*), Harris had played no role in bringing his breakthrough book to theaters. He hadn't worked on the *Black Sunday* script, nor had he plugged the movie in the press. And there's no record of his attending the *Black Sunday* premiere in Los Angeles, which featured such superstar guests as Warren Beatty, Jack Nicholson, and Ringo Starr.

The movie they saw that night—directed by John Frankenheimer, a veteran of energetic global thrillers such as *The Manchurian Candidate* and *Seven Days in May*—turned out to be a bit of a slog. Starring Bruce Dern as Michael Lander, the sporadically zippy *Black Sunday* was hamstrung by overcrowded plotting, not to mention some dubious on-screen accents: The Swiss actor Marthe Keller played the Palestinian militant Dahlia Iyad, while the English-born Robert Shaw, hot off the success of *Jaws*, played a Mossad agent (thankfully, the Goodyear blimp played itself). Despite a high-profile marketing campaign that included a giant billboard on Sunset Strip, not to mention the built-in awareness of Harris's hit novel, the movie drifted away from theaters not long after opening.

Harris's antipathy toward showbiz, whatever the reasons, seemed to echo those of *Red Dragon* character Freddy Lounds, a tabloid reporter who fantasizes about selling out: "He had heard that Hollywood was a fine place for obnoxious fellows with money," Harris wrote. But even if the author shared Lounds's cynicism about the film industry, he wasn't going to turn away the producers eager to translate his work to the big screen. A few months before *Red Dragon*'s arrival, the gossip columnist Liz Smith noted that the book's film rights had sold for "six large figures," and that the movie version would be overseen by an uncompromising young director, David Lynch.

At the time, Lynch was known as the oddball behind a pair of unorthodox yet affecting black-and-white dramas: 1977's *Eraserhead*, about a wild-haired outsider taking care of a grotesque infant, and 1980's Oscar-nominated *The Elephant Man*, which tells the true story of John Merrick, whose disfigurement had caused a stir in Victorian England. Lynch had a knack for telling stories about serious, solitary men. So did *Red Dragon*'s initial screenwriter, Walon Green, whose credits included the rugged—and sometimes jarringly violent—new-Hollywood masterworks *The Wild Bunch* (1969) and *Sorcerer* (1977).

By the fall of 1983, Green had completed a draft of his *Red Dragon* script. Clocking in at 122 pages, it portrays Lecter—spelled "Lector"—less as a brilliant, world-renowned madman and more as a humorless shit. Lecter snarls at Graham from the get-go ("Will, is a pig's ass pork?" Lecter asks in response to one query). And he's prone to grandstanding taunts: "Remember when I cut you Will? The way it glistened . . ."

In the second half of Green's script, Lecter disappears altogether, replaced by the Tooth Fairy, whose skeevyness is presented in all its gory semiglory. At one point in Green's screenplay, Dolarhyde stands in the nude, "his hand [gripping] his erection" as he watches footage of himself nearly decapitating one of his victims.

Green's screenplay was a rough read—too rough, it turned out, for Lynch. Apparently even the guy behind *Eraserhead*, a movie in which a cooked chicken suddenly starts spewing out gobs of blood, had his limits. "I got sick of it," he said of *Red Dragon* in 1990. "I was going into a world that was going to be, for me, real, real violent. And completely degenerate." After deciding that the project had "No Redeeming Qualities," he backed out.

A new filmmaker soon took his place. Like Lynch, that writer-director possessed an assured yet hard-to-define visual style, as well as an understanding of seemingly unknowable men. And he wasn't thrown by a little bit of violence.

Growing up in Chicago, Michael Mann learned early on that crime wasn't some distant phenomenon that took place only in movies, books, and newspapers; it was part of the local history. "I don't know how many times we passed the Biograph [Theater] and my folks said, 'That's where they killed John Dillinger,'" Mann recalled.

He left the city when he was eighteen, embarking on an academic career that would include a two-year stint at the London Film School. After he returned to the United States, Mann worked on experimental films and documentaries before breaking into television. By the late 1970s, he had written for such prime-time essentials as *Starsky & Hutch* and *Police Story* and created the hit series *Vegas*. Like Harris, he was a mix of storyteller and reporter, often becoming obsessed with details. And as he worked on those shows, he became friendly with cops and ex-cons alike. Mann channeled their experiences into his on-screen characters, whether they were overdriven detectives or resourceful criminals. As a result, he said, "I just became the flavor of the month for a couple of years."

Mann was eager to move into directing, and after his success on TV, he was hired to rewrite a script titled *The Jericho Mile*, about a convict who discovers he's a skilled runner. ABC would eventually green-light *The Jericho Mile* as a TV movie—and give Mann his first chance behind the camera on a major production. He soon found himself on location in California's Folsom State Prison, working alongside convicts with handles such as "Mike the Iceman" while trying to steer clear of the prison's ever-present gang violence. "We had 13 stabbings and one killing during the 19 days in which we were shooting," Mann remembered. "So it was obviously a dangerous place."

The resulting film, with its mix of grit and grace, would win Mann a cowriting Emmy after its 1979 release. He followed that with the 1981 caper thriller *Thief*, starring James Caan as a nervy safecracker who pushes back against his boss. *Thief* was a story of existential alienation masquerading as a suspenseful heist flick—or maybe it was the other way around. And the film established some of the creative flourishes that would become Mann's trademarks in the years ahead: bold, nocturnal neon colors; an atmospheric synth rock soundtrack; and tough guys whose swagger comes with serious emotional baggage. Mann was fascinated by the ways of intelligent, headstrong, overly dedicated men—perhaps because he could relate to them. "I work to very, very fine tolerances," he said upon *Thief*'s release. "I make a lot of people who don't understand nuts."

In the wake of *Thief*'s release, Mann received a copy of *Red Dragon* from producer Richard Roth. The director loved Harris's writing—"It was the best detective story I'd ever read," he said—and shared the author's fascination with those who kill. Earlier in his career, the filmmaker had been in touch with a California man named Dennis Wayne Wallace, who'd been convicted of an appalling murder: In the summer of 1970, he had come to believe that his girlfriend, an Orange County go-go dancer, had become hooked on drugs. Wallace used a crowbar to kill a man he thought was her dealer, and dissolved the victim's body in a bathtub filled with sulfuric acid. According to one report, all that was left behind for police to find was a garbage bag containing "a single bone about seven inches long, nine teeth, and a small amount of flesh."

As it turned out, Wallace was schizophrenic, and his crime had been driven by delusions: The woman who was ostensibly his "girlfriend" barely knew him at all, yet he was convinced that the two were a couple. He even believed that they shared a special song: Iron Butterfly's 1968 proto-metal psych epic "In-A-Gadda-Da-Vida."

Wallace was found guilty of first-degree murder and sent to California Medical Facility in Vacaville, the same prison that housed serial killer Edmund Kemper. That's where Wallace struck up a correspondence with Mann, sending the director ramblings that Mann describes as "psych-type poetry." Eventually, Mann met with Wallace for at the prison. "I was kind of a cultural anthropologist," the filmmaker says, "trying to understand what his value system was, what he thought he was doing, what he wanted."

Mann was struck by Wallace's cleverness—in particular, the way he took advantage of the penal system psychologists who were caring for him. "He had the ability to answer questions in a way that could manipulate their diagnosis of him," remembers Mann, who saw in Wallace "a strong ego and incredibly low self-esteem." Wallace also apparently had a morbid sense of humor: According to Mann, he sometimes wore a hard hat featuring a decal from *Mad* magazine that read "Support Mental Illness, or I'll Kill You."

Mann collected years' worth of research on Wallace, hoping to write a screenplay about the killer's life. It never quite came together. "I couldn't find any traction with the correct story structure," he says. "So it became a very expressionistic piece."

Years later, while reading Harris's book, Mann was struck by the similarities between Wallace and *Red Dragon*'s primary killer, Francis Dolarhyde. Both had suffered abuse as children. And both were in the grip of dangerous fantasies. "What Dolarhyde wants is a reenactment—a form of street theater in which his desired circumstances have been made to come true," Mann says. "That invention of Harris's was stunning and brilliant."

And of course, Mann was compelled by Lecter. "He commits heinous crimes and talks about them with a stunning dispassion," he says. "The counterpoint of those two presentations makes him very, very dangerous." The director also realized a key part of Lecter's appeal: "Regardless of how much he's restrained or imprisoned, or shackled, Lecter is able to work his will. And in that sense, he's a wish-fulfillment character."

Like Harris, Mann had begun his career in the world of nonfiction—one of his first films had been a documentary about the 1968 student revolts in Paris—and he was constantly seeking out fresh intel: "For me, the most exciting drama always has a real heavy reality base." After accepting the *Red Dragon* gig, he visited the FBI, where he was able to meet with members of the Behavioral Science Unit, much as Harris had a few years earlier. Mann was given a tour of the Bureau's forensic labs and briefed on the latest tech and terminology, such as "leakage." The phrase had been coined by former BSU agent Roger Depue in the mid-1980s to describe the way serial killers sometimes betrayed their secret desires in their day-to-day lives. "If you have a very intense fantasy, it will leak out of you involuntarily," Depue says. "It will manifest itself in the books you read, the movies you watch—even your music."

Mann incorporated much of what he learned, including Depue's leakage theory, into his *Red Dragon* script, which he worked on while his career fortunes fluctuated wildly. His supernatural historical horror thriller *The Keep* was released in late 1983 only to be condemned with what the filmmaker described as "universal opprobrium—the worst reviews known to man." Less than a year later, NBC debuted *Miami Vice*, a pastel-colored, pop tune–powered cop drama for which Mann served as executive producer. The show would become a sensation, earning its star Don Johnson countless magazine covers and making Mann one of the first ever celebrity showrunners (one actor later described him as "the man who gave the world designer stubble"). *The Keep* may have crashed, but thanks to *Miami Vice*, many people in Hollywood were curious to see what the guy who'd reinvented the police procedural could do with Harris's hit novel.

Mann wouldn't be the only hard-charging showbiz figure shepherding *Red Dragon* to the screen. Warner Bros. had initially purchased Harris's book, but after development stalled, the movie rights to *Red Dragon*— and to Hannibal Lecter—had been sold to the Italian impresario Dino De Laurentiis. An ambitious dynamo who always seemed to have a cigar or two on standby, De Laurentiis had produced art house essentials such as Federico Fellini's Oscar-winning *La Strada* (1954), as well as American schlockbusters such as *King Kong* (1976). By the time he greenlit *Red Dragon*, De Laurentiis had been working in the film industry for nearly fifty years. He once told a reporter his stamina was the byproduct of what

De Laurentiis called "the three C's": *cuore, cervello*, and *coglioni*—Italian for heart, brains, and balls.

"Dino was entertaining to everyone who met him," notes Jude Schneider, who worked as a production executive for the producer in the late 1980s and early 1990s. "He was charming, and also a little bit of a gangster." De Laurentiis was known for his tenacity and his shrewdness—especially when it came to budgets. Anthony Hopkins, who'd worked with De Laurentiis several times, once affectionately paid him Hollywood's highest compliment: "He's lethal."

De Laurentiis had recently built a sprawling series of soundstages across thirty-two acres of land in Wilmington, North Carolina—a miniature Hollywood that featured a fake New York City backlot, a special effects shop, and an on-site chef whom De Laurentiis had imported from Rome (he was one of several Italian workers brought to the studio, some of whom spoke little English).

North Carolina didn't require De Laurentiis to hire union workers, allowing him to make movies for much less than they'd cost in Los Angeles or New York. The official budget for Mann's *Red Dragon* adaptation was $14 million, which was relatively cheap (Mann would later say that the film had cost closer to $11 million). At that price, it was nearly impossible for De Laurentiis to afford any of the big-bucks stars he wanted to play the troubled former FBI profiler Will Graham. The producer's wish list apparently included Paul Newman, Richard Gere, and Mel Gibson—all A-list actors who likely had no interest in starring in an independently made thriller. Those weren't the only names being floated around for Graham. Gossip columnist Liz Smith, a ravenous *Red Dragon* fan, at one point lobbied for Kevin Costner to get the role, though it was unclear if that was based on reporting or wishful thinking.

Mann's choice for Graham turned out to be a name that few people recognized. William Petersen was a stage actor in his early thirties who hailed from the director's hometown of Chicago, and whose nascent film career had gotten its start with a brief appearance in *Thief*. Petersen was rangy and handsome, with an intensity that prompted one *Newsweek* critic to excitedly declare him "the next Robert De Niro!" But *Red Dragon*'s main benefactor, De Laurentiis, had no idea who Petersen was. In fact, the actor said, "*nobody* knew who I was—I didn't have an agent."

When Petersen took his first meeting with Mann, the actor was filming the movie that would give him his breakout role: William Friedkin's gnarly neo-noir *To Live and Die in L.A.*, in which Petersen starred as a corrupt Secret Service agent. He and Mann initially got together to discuss a sprawling cops-and-robbers saga that Mann had recently written, and that would be released years later as *Heat*. After a while, the two men's conversation shifted toward *Red Dragon*. Petersen realized Mann was aiming to make a new kind of thriller, one that relied less on blood and gunplay and more on psychology and mood. "He wanted to create a real visual aura for the film," Petersen recalled. "Instead of the movie coming down into the audience and scaring people, people would actually go up onto the screen. [They'd] be drawn into the actual beauty of the film, and the story would work underneath in a more emotional, interior way."

After landing the *Red Dragon* role in 1985, Petersen began hanging out with members of the Chicago Police Department's Violent Crimes Unit. The actor was also sent to the FBI, where he spent time with BSU agents, including Depue. "He was a good student," Depue recalls. "We talked about some of the more unusual and violent kinds of cases." There were plenty to choose from. At the time, a series of seemingly connected murders was taking place across southern California, all attributed to a figure dubbed the "Walk-In Killer"—so named for his habit of sneaking into homes at night, much like the Tooth Fairy. During his sessions with the FBI, Petersen met with some of the profilers who were helping to investigate the Walk-In Killer case. "I was asking them, 'How do you survive? You've got kids at home,'" the actor remembered. "They just said, 'We're men and fortunately we can compartmentalise.' Of course, you don't really turn it off."

Petersen spent nearly a month and a half researching his role as Will Graham—at which point Mann stepped in. "Michael said, 'You know what, you need to stop doing this,'" the actor recalled. "'Because at a certain point, you become a little inured to it.' And he wanted to make sure that that didn't happen, because my character has to deal with an emotional fine line."

Mann was less hands on when it came to the actor playing the film's vicious Francis Dolarhyde. The director had considered more than fifty performers for the part before finally meeting with Tom Noonan, a towering former high school basketball player who'd started acting in his late twenties. Because Noonan was so physically imposing, his early film roles had found him playing "a bunch of weirdo parts," the actor said. "I am sort of weird, but not *that* bad."

Noonan had been put off by the grisliness of the *Red Dragon* script. *Jeez, I don't want to do this*, he thought. *This is really upsetting.* But he needed the work, so he showed up for an audition, where he was forced to wait for hours to see Mann. By the time his name was called, "I was really fucking pissed off," he remembered. "I was going to get in there and read the fucking scene, and just leave."

Once inside Mann's office, he skipped the small talk and began running through the script with a woman from the film's casting department. The mood in the room soon became tense. "I didn't do anything, but she started to get really frightened of me, which made me feel really excited and full of myself," he said. Noonan was overwhelmed, he recalled, by "this feeling of power." True to his word, he finished the scene and stormed out of Mann's office without a word. The next time they talked, Mann offered Noonan the role of Dolarhyde. Before shooting began, Mann asked the actor if there was anything he could do to help him prepare for the part. "[I said], 'It'd be great if I never had to see anybody in the movie who's trying to kill me, or who I'm trying to kill,'" he remembered. "Which is basically everybody."

That meant that Noonan would have minimal contact with his castmates, all of whom were largely unknown, like Joan Allen, a Chicago actor who'd recently broken through on the New York stage. She was cast as Dolarhyde's unlikely love interest, Reba, a young coworker at Gateway Film Laboratory who is blind, and who inadvertently brings Dolarhyde's sadness to the surface. The role of FBI bigwig Jack Crawford, meanwhile, went to Dennis Farina, a fortysomething stage actor and ex–Chicago cop who, like Petersen, had made his big-screen debut in *Thief*.

With just a few months to go before filming on *Red Dragon* began,

Mann didn't yet have his Hannibal Lecter—though he did have a promising candidate: Brian Dennehy, the broad-shouldered character actor recognizable to audiences from such hits as *Semi-Tough* (1977) and *First Blood* (1982), as well as numerous TV credits. Dennehy bore little resemblance to the "small, lithe" Lecter of Harris's book—the actor described himself as more of "a pro football type"—but he'd impressed Mann in a supporting role in *Jericho Mile*. Even better: He had no hang-ups about playing a cannibalistic killer. "He campaigned for it, and it was pretty much decided he was going to do it," Mann remembered.

So the director was surprised when Dennehy called him in the summer of 1985—and essentially gave the Hannibal role away. "I'm going to prove to you what a good friend I am," he told Mann. "You know how much I want to do Lecter? There's somebody *better* you gotta go see."

CHAPTER 7

"ANYBODY THAT'S TOO CLEVER HAS TO BE A LITTLE BIT NASTY."

Brian Cox was more than two decades into his acting career when he suddenly became the next big thing. He'd grown up in the 1940s and 1950s in Dundee, Scotland, where his parents had sent him off to the local movie theater as often as four days a week. "That was where I got my yearning to be an actor—watching Marlon Brando and Spencer Tracy," he said.

At the age of fifteen, he dropped out of school and embarked on a yearslong pursuit of stage work, one that would find him joining numerous repertories and companies. But American theatergoers didn't take note of Cox until his appearance in a tough drama titled *Rat in the Skull*, which opened off-Broadway in 1985. *Rat in the Skull* starred Cox as a Protestant detective from Northern Ireland who's tasked with interrogating a suspected IRA bomber. *The New York Times* declared Cox's performance a "tour de force" in its review, and later declared the actor to be "something of an overnight sensation." By then, Cox was thirty-nine years old.

Another Cox fan was *Red Dragon* casting director Bonnie Timmermann, who asked the actor to audition for the film after seeing him onstage. Timmermann, who'd found numerous new stars while working on *Miami Vice*, had an unusual request: During Cox's camera test, she asked the actor to turn his head away, so she couldn't see his face. Eager to please, Cox agreed. "It was kind of a different vibe, you know?" he recalls.

Once the read-through was finished, Cox asked why Timmermann had wanted him obscured. She explained that she'd arrived late to see *Rat in the Skull* and had had to sit in an area where she could only hear him. "But I was so entranced by your voice," she told Cox. "It was your voice that did it for me."

Mann eventually caught *Rat in the Skull* for himself and was equally impressed. "The character became so internalized within him," the director says of Cox's stage performance. "His performance had intensity, and muscularity, and a certain three-dimensional quality"—all traits that would make for a powerful Lecter. Mann had found his cannibal.

Cox would be appearing in just a few scenes in *Red Dragon*. But landing the part was a midcareer milestone. After years of stage and British TV work, he'd finally nabbed a substantial Hollywood role. "It was my bid to do movies, which is what I wanted," he says. Mann's decision to hire him would set an inadvertent precedent, making the actor the first of four consecutive non-American performers to portray Lecter. "I've got a theory about that," Cox said, "which is the fact that anybody that's too clever has to be a little bit nasty—and therefore has to be played by a European."

Besides, it wasn't as if the United States had a monopoly on monsters. While preparing for *Red Dragon*, Cox would reconnect with a figure who'd long fascinated and terrified him: Peter Manuel, an infamous Scottish serial killer who had been hanged in 1958 following his convictions for a series of sexual assaults and murders. "I was obsessed with him as a kid," Cox recalls.

Manuel, who was born in the United States but raised in Scotland, was described by one newspaper as "more horrible than anything that ever came out of the depths of Loch Ness." From a young age, it was clear that Manuel "[lived] in a world of bizarre dreams, conjured up to swell his ego," as one journalist noted. Growing up, he stole money from a local chapel, spread strange lies about his father being killed in the electric chair, and idolized the likes of John Dillinger and Al Capone. In his early thirties, he embarked on a series of assaults and murders that stumped police for more than a year, and his eventual trial captivated Cox.

"He conducted his own defense, and he was very relaxed," the actor remembers. What especially struck Cox, he said, was that Manuel "had no sense of right or wrong—a kind of absence."

Cox kept Manuel in mind as he prepared for *Red Dragon* in 1985. He also followed the ongoing legal case of Ted Bundy, the serial killer whose death sentence had recently been upheld by the Florida Supreme Court. Bundy's infamy had increased in the years since his arrest, and by the mid-1980s, there were several books about his murders in stores, including *The Only Living Witness, Bundy: The Deliberate Stranger,* and *Ted Bundy: The Killer Next Door.* As one critic noted, in terms of publicity, Bundy "threatens to outstrip Jack the Ripper."

For Cox, understanding Bundy was a key to understanding Lecter. "Bundy could have had a great career as a politician—he was very smart, very articulate," he observes. "But he'd made a sort of pact with himself to just be that malevolent force, because he couldn't resist it. It's who he is. It was Bundy's weakness. It was Peter Manuel's weakness. And it's kind of Lecter's weakness, you know—clearly a brilliant man, but he has this flaw: He likes to kill and partly eat people."

Cox would have a few months to mull over his *Red Dragon* character before his *Rat in the Skull* run ended. Mann's film was set to begin shooting in September 1985—a time when the phrase "serial killer" was becoming a fixture of daily newspapers across the country. That month, there were tales of mass murders in Detroit, Seattle, and Los Angeles. At one press conference, a veteran investigator guessed that between 250 and 500 serial killers were currently at large—though he stated that was a lowball estimate.

As if readers needed more reason to be jumpy, there'd recently been a break in the case of California's Walk-In Killer—or, as he was now known, the "Night Stalker." By the fall of 1985, the murderer's body count was believed to be as high as fifteen. But with the help of souped-up technology, including a $35,000 laser detection machine, police had finally zeroed in on a suspect named Richard Ramirez, a twenty-five-year-old drifter. The news sent the public into a frenzy ("Manhunt Under Way for 'Night Stalker'" read one headline). And in September 1985, Ramirez was finally apprehended when a crowd chased him down in East Los Angeles, where one pursuer beat him on the head with a fence post. "Thank the Lord," Ramirez said, "I've been caught."

That wild confrontation took place a little more than a week before cameras were scheduled to roll on Mann's film. And more on-the-loose killers would emerge in the months ahead. When Harris's novel had been released, Dolarhyde and Lecter had seemed like the kind of made-up monsters found only in the darkest dwellings of fiction. Now they had real-world competition.

Even before shooting on *Red Dragon* got under way, it was clear that it was going to be a tight, tough production. The movie would be shot in several locations, including North Carolina, Florida, and Washington, DC. The filmmaker would be working with not only a cast of relative newcomers, but also several non-English-speaking crew members De Laurentiis had brought in from Italy. Throw in *Red Dragon*'s draining subject matter, and there were all the elements you need for a grinding gig. "The film was not a fun time," Petersen said.

The difficulties started early on. Mann was just a few weeks into production when a tractor-trailer containing $300,000 worth of equipment was stolen from a Radisson Inn parking lot in Atlanta. Then there were flare-ups with the crew: According to Noonan, on the actor's first day of work—for a scene in which Dolarhyde is sitting in a van outside Reba's home—Mann became frustrated by "a little tiny imperfection" in the vehicle, Noonan recalled. "You'd never have seen this in a million years. He complained to the producers. He was really upset." As a result, Noonan said, members of the film's art department were immediately dismissed.

"I learned over time that you really don't talk back to him or give him shit, ever," said Noonan. "He's like Napoleon." To Petersen, the filmmaker brought to mind a different fearless leader: "I often compare him to Bill Belichick. There is no part of the thing that he is not completely involved in, from the buttons on my jacket to the lenses he uses for his camera."

That included the film's budget. Mann, who'd spent the last year dealing with the granular aspects of making *Miami Vice*, kept a close eye on the film's financial reports—a pursuit that led to tension with De Laurentiis. "I got into some huge battles with him," recalls Mann, who at one point confronted De Laurentiis about overtime charges at his North Carolina facility. "I would question him, and the response would be 'Michael, why do you have to be that way?'"

The two also argued over the film's title, as De Laurentiis insisted that *Red Dragon* be rechristened. Numerous reasons for the switch have been given over the years: According to one account, he felt burned by the recent commercial failure of his crime drama *Year of the Dragon* and believed that the D-word was cursed. The producer's wife and creative partner, Martha De Laurentiis, would later suggest that there had been concerns that moviegoers would think that *Red Dragon* was about communism. And according to Mann, there were concerns that some would even mistake the film for "a chop-socky movie from Hong Kong."

A prolonged debate followed between the filmmaker and the producer, with De Laurentiis ultimately winning. To find a new name, Mann offered crew members cash prizes of up to $200 for the best suggestion. He'd wind up receiving more than a thousand submissions. "One of my favorites," he said, "was 'Don't Go For a Ride with Francis Dolarhyde.'" (The *Manhunter* title was likely derived from the *Red Dragon* novel, which features a fleeting mention of "federal manhunters.")

The back-and-forths with De Laurentiis had become a source of frustration for Mann. But he didn't have much time to deal with them. The *Manhunter* script was more than 140 pages long, which was a demanding tally for any film and an usually high one for a thriller. In order to get what he needed, he and his crew would have to work punishingly long hours in less than two months. In Harris's book, Graham's wife, Molly, observes that "time is luck." Mann would use that line in his script and live by it on his set. "If he could shoot twenty-four hours around the clock," Joan Allen said of the director, "he'd say, 'Let's go for it.'"

Occasionally, Mann got what we needed using guerrilla tactics. For a *Manhunter* scene in which Graham examines evidence while on an evening plane ride, Mann and his team bought tickets for a United Airlines flight from Chicago to Orlando, timing the four-hour trip so that they'd be airborne during sunset. As the sky began to darken, he and his team got out of their seats, grabbed their equipment from their carry-on luggage, and began shooting. "We just reconstituted ourselves into a film company," he said. "A couple of the stewardesses got upset."

Most of the time, though, Mann didn't have to sneak around to get what he needed. During his preproduction meetings with the FBI, he'd arranged for access to the Bureau's J. Edgar Hoover Building in Washington, DC. He was later given permission to shoot a few key scenes of Graham, Crawford, and the film's on-screen agents examining evidence in actual FBI forensic labs. "They never let anybody in," Mann said at the time. "[But] they're very concerned about this kind of crime. It's on a big upswing." *Manhunter* would serve as a showcase for some of the FBI's latest tools: pinpoint-precise lasers for detecting fingerprints; bulky microscopes for analyzing hair. The criminal sciences had never been depicted as thoroughly or as beautifully. In one striking moment, an investigator examines a note written by Dolarhyde while working in a darkroom immersed in bloodred light.

It was one of many enthralling scenes Mann would create with *Manhunter* cinematographer Dante Spinotti. Born in Italy, Spinotti had been working largely on TV films in his home country when he met De Laurentiis. "My aim was to do movies in the USA," he says. "A race car driver dreams of Formula One. A filmmaker dreams of Hollywood."

De Laurentiis invited him to North Carolina to meet with Mann, who looked at some of his work and showed him *Thief*. In their earliest conversations about *Manhunter*, Mann told Spinotti about the film's use of color. "He told me green represented danger and tension," Spinotti remembers, "and we spoke about blue representing a sort of intensity." Mann handed him an image from the Belgian surrealist painter René Magritte's "Empire of Light" series. It featured a placid blue sky hovering over a darkened house with green-hued doors. The Magritte painting was alluring yet ominous, and Mann wasn't the first filmmaker to turn to it for inspiration: Years earlier, the image had been the basis for a scene in Friedkin's horror hit *The Exorcist*. "Michael said, 'This is the movie,'" Spinotti recalls. "I said, 'Okay, great.'"

As the *Manhunter* crew zipped from one location to the next, Mann and Spinotti began collecting a succession of evocative images: There's Graham's wife, Molly, covered in the midnight blue haze of their ocean-side bedroom. There's the doomed tabloid reporter Freddy Lounds, glowing a sickly orange after being set afire by Dolarhyde and strapped to a runaway wheelchair. And there's Graham himself, standing in the middle of a rainbowlike supermarket aisle, trying to explain his deadly work to his young son.

Yet the most striking color in *Manhunter* is the Colgate white look of Lecter's cell. When Cox first appears on-screen, he's wearing an ivory-hued jumpsuit and lounging in a windowless, monochromatic room: white walls, white bars, and white furniture. The only pops of color come courtesy of Cox's black, slicked-back widow's peak, as well as a few academic journals and markers Lecter keeps on his shelf. "Lecter's personality was so strong that I wanted to neutralize everything about his environment," Mann notes. "It would be like a blank sheet of paper, so that whatever was in there—and whatever he was wearing—stood out."

Two locations would be used to create Lecter's home at the Chesapeake State Hospital for the Criminally Insane. For the building's hallways and exteriors, Mann headed to the High Museum of Art in Atlanta, an imposingly all-white modernist mecca. Lecter's cell, meanwhile, was located on a soundstage at De Laurentiis's North Carolina studios. That was where Cox and Petersen shot their characters' first scene together. As Graham tries to recruit Hannibal to help in the hunt for the Tooth Fairy, the two men stare at each other through the bars with a mix of animosity and curiosity:

GRAHAM: Thought you might be curious to see if you're smarter than the person I'm looking for.
LECTER: Then, by implication, you think you're smarter than me, since you caught me.
GRAHAM: I know that I'm not smarter than you.
LECTER: Then how did you catch me, Will?
GRAHAM: You had disadvantages.

LECTER: What disadvantages?

GRAHAM: You're insane.

Though the meeting between Lecter and Graham lasts on-screen for barely five minutes, Mann spent days filming the sequence, giving Cox time to try out the character in a variety of ways. "I played it broader, I played it louder, I played it more forceful, I played it more violent," he said. "My bias was always to be a little bit more hidden, a little bit more unrevealed." That was the version of Hannibal the Cannibal that wound up in *Manhunter*. Lecter comes off as impudent, blunt, and seemingly a bit *bored*—but it all feels like a ruse. The moral and emotional vacuum Cox had observed in the Scottish killer Peter Manuel would also be found within the Lecter of *Manhunter*.

The character's final moment in the film consists of a brief but crucial phone call with Graham. The profiler has become stuck in his search for the Tooth Fairy, and he's still trying, in Lecter's words, "to get the old scent back again"—to understand a killer's *why*s and *how*s. Lecter doesn't think that Graham needs to search too hard for the smell, reminding the ex-profiler that Graham had shot and killed the murderous Garrett Jacob Hobbs—and that it had felt good.

LECTER: And why shouldn't it feel good? It must feel good to God. He does it all the time. God's terrific! He dropped a church roof on 34 of his worshippers last Wednesday night in Texas, just as they were groveling through a hymn to his majesty. Don't you think that felt good?

GRAHAM: Why does it feel good, Dr. Lecter?

LECTER: It feels good, Will, because God has power. And if one does what God does enough times, one will become as God is. God's a champ. He always stays ahead. He got 140 Filipinos in one plane crash last month.

Cox played the phone call scene splayed out on Lecter's bed with a hand casually draped over his head, and his sock-covered feet propped up against the cinder-block wall. It's an oddly comic image—one that was inspired, Mann said, by the 1959 Rock Hudson–Doris Day romantic comedy *Pillow Talk*. And the moment could have been even broader: At one point during filming, Cox had Lecter serenade Graham with Stevie Wonder's recent Oscar-winning hit "I Just Called to Say I Love You," though that moment didn't make the final cut.

Cox's time on the *Manhunter* set in North Carolina was brief and relatively painless—something that couldn't be said for the actor playing Francis Dolarhyde, Lecter's pen pal and fan. By the time Noonan showed up for work, he'd gained thirty pounds of muscle, and his blond, thinning hair had grown out to mid–mullet length. The transformation would give Dolarhyde an alienlike appearance—one that Noonan's castmates would rarely see up close, thanks to the actor's decision to isolate himself during filming. "I traveled on different airlines, I stayed at different hotels, and [crew members] all had to talk to me as 'Francis,'" Noonan recalled. "It created this atmosphere on the set where people were frightened of me."

Even Mann abided by those rules—for the most part. One day while Cox was in a makeup room, the director attempted to introduce *Red Dragon*'s murderous mutual admirers. "Noonan just ran away screaming, 'I don't want to meet him,'" remembered Cox. "Mann had to chase him down the corridor, shouting, 'But he's your friend!'"

It was Dolarhyde's skeevy, isolated headquarters that would serve as the setting of *Manhunter*'s violent finale, one that's sparked by a pair of potentially deadly epiphanies: In a dreamlike sequence full of bright light and loud new-wave guitars, Dolarhyde visualizes Reba, his sorta girlfriend, kissing one of their film lab coworkers; the moment exists only in his mind, but it's enough to prompt him to fully embrace his Red Dragon rage. As for Graham, he takes inspiration from one of Lecter's teachings—"If one does what God does enough times, one will become as God is"—to push himself deeper into the Tooth Fairy's thinking, finally connecting the murders to Dolarhyde.

That's all followed by a climactic shoot-out at Dolarhyde's home, which had been saved for *Manhunter*'s final two days of work. The filmmaking team would be working on a set built for the production in a swamp alongside the Cape Fear River. "It was at a very spooky place," Mann said. "Ocean fog would come in and you couldn't see ten feet in front of you."

The killer's dreary home also affected the mood of the *Manhunter* crew. "Everybody was way inside the content of the movie," Mann says. "The movie had become their environment." And some were eager to escape. Right before the production's final days in North Carolina, members of the special effects team quit en masse, apparently frustrated by the long hours. Their departure posed a problem for Mann, who had to scramble to pull together *Manhunter*'s effects-heavy climax, in which Graham crashes through a kitchen window and shoots Dolarhyde dead. It was a fast and unforgiving sequence, one that would provide a sudden surge of ferocity in an otherwise slow-burning film. And Mann knew exactly what song he wanted to use as its backdrop: "In-A-Gadda-Da-Vida," the pulsing, gurgling Iron Butterfly number that Dennis Wayne Wallace had mistakenly believed to be his personal love song.

For much of Mann's script, the filmmaker remained loyal to Harris's novel: Though he had omitted several chapters' worth of backstory, Mann had treated the author's dialogue and characters with care, expertly distilling long back-and-forths into just a few exchanges. And he had taken pains to recreate some of *Red Dragon*'s smallest details. In *Manhunter*, Graham carries a Bulldog .44 Special revolver loaded with Glaser Safety Slugs, the same hardware name-checked in the book.

But the third act of Mann's film would represent a notable departure from Harris's novel. Whereas *Red Dragon* had concluded with Dolarhyde emerging from hiding to attack Graham, *Manhunter* would turn the profiler into the aggressor. He breaks into the killer's lair with focused fury as "In-A-Gadda-Da-Vida" becomes increasingly louder and more torturous. The hypnotic mano a mano would end with Dolarhyde dead on the floor, his blood spreading around his corpse like dragon wings.

Without an effects team to handle the bullet-blasted gore, Mann and his team had to scramble, sometimes relying on DIY supplies picked up at a local 7-Eleven, including pork brains and condiments. "All of a sudden it was Filmmaking 101," Petersen said. "[They were] shooting ketchup through a tube onto the wall." Finally, just after 6:00 a.m., filming on Petersen and Noonan's final showdown was completed. The two actors had stayed away from each other for months—"I never met Billy until he came through the window," Noonan said—and they decided to get breakfast together. The *Manhunter* shoot had exhausted them both. "The whole thing was hard," Petersen later said. Coming from the theater, Petersen was used to going onstage, playing his part, and then hitting the bar. "This was much more of a war of attrition; you had to somehow survive to the end."

And for Petersen, the end came much later than expected. Not long after filming wrapped, the actor was back in Chicago, rehearsing for a play. But he found that he was still talking like Graham. He eventually dyed his hair blond, "just so that I would look in the mirror and see a different person," he said. The experience of making *Manhunter*—of being plugged into the mind of a serial killer—"had just creeped in."

Even after Mann stopped production on *Manhunter* in the fall of 1985, there'd be no chance for him to decompress. Time is luck, after all, and the filmmaker needed whatever spare second he could get not only to edit his film but to oversee a new season of *Miami Vice*, as well as an NBC drama he was developing titled *Crime Story*. "I was going a little crazy," he said, looking back. "I was doing too much."

It didn't help that he and De Laurentiis were still feuding. According to Mann, at some point during the editing process, the producer wanted to recut *Manhunter*, spurring the director to take legal action. "Basically, I sued him to say, 'You can't touch the movie,'" remembers Mann, who'd negotiated to have the final cut of the film's US version. "We got into this big beef that went all the way into postproduction."

The battle ended, Mann says, when De Laurentiis finally saw *Manhunter* in full: "He responded to the movie in a very positive way." Not everyone shared De Laurentiis's enthusiasm for *Manhunter*—at least not at first. Petersen watched the film in Mann's editing room, and afterward, the director asked for his thoughts. Petersen's one-word response: "Interesting." "To this day, I can't believe it came out of my mouth," the actor recalled. "You say that to an artist, and you may as well just shoot 'em in the heart. But I was so completely kind of boggled by watching the film."

Petersen's disorientation was due in part to the fact that he was still getting used to seeing himself on-screen. But being "kind of boggled" by *Manhunter* was an understandable response. Mann had preserved the procedural details and criminal mind insights of Harris's novel, while adding his own narrative flourishes: the guitars and keyboards that creep up on the speakers; the ethereal visuals that seem as though they might bleed off the screen. The result is a methodical thriller in which horrendous deeds are granted an almost majestic beauty. There are moments in *Manhunter* in which the film breaks from reality entirely, as when Graham, standing in an all-white bedroom, watches as the mirrored eyes of one of the Tooth Fairy's victims begin to glow. Or when Dolarhyde imagines Reba being with another man—a delusion Mann illustrates with almost heavenly lighting and an anthemic, guitar-heavy score.

Such fantastical moments are countered by *Manhunter*'s gleaming display of real-world tech: lab-born lasers, high-end computers, Teflon-coated bullets. The crime-solving aspect of *Manhunter* feels so grounded, so clearly of our world, that it makes the film's unthinkable crimes seem all the more plausible.

Watching *Manhunter*, it was hard to tell if it was supposed to be a gritty thriller, a transportive art house drama—or both. Anybody expecting Mann to deliver a bunch of cheap shocks was sure to be disappointed. "He didn't want to make it one of these movies where the audience is on the edge of their seat and you get all these fake scares," Noonan said. "It just sort of builds up and up and up in a very quiet way."

That posed a big challenge for Mann as his film headed to theaters in the summer of 1986. "*Manhunter* is a real hard movie to sell," the director said shortly before its release. The film's theatrical trailer did its best to capture *Manhunter*'s vibe, playing up its moody tone and slick visuals while adding a few lines of tough-talking narration. But without a major star in the cast, the film had a difficult time attracting press, and interviewers weren't always sure how to approach *Manhunter*'s unseemly subject matter. At one point during the movie's PR campaign, Noonan made a disastrous appearance on *The Morning Show*, a daily chat fest hosted by Regis Philbin and Kathie Lee Gifford (its title would later be changed to the better-known *Live with Regis and Kathie Lee*). The problems began when the actor was jokingly introduced as a serial killer. "Kathie Lee was sort of being a drag, sort of making fun of me," Noonan recalled. "Finally I turned to read to Regis and said, 'What is her problem? You know, I'm being very normal here, and I don't know why she has to do this.'" The producers cut to a commercial break, during which Noonan was asked to leave.

Ultimately, *Manhunter* was a film that would need support from critics—many of whom turned out to be politely unimpressed. While it was hailed by critics in *Newsweek* and *Time*—in which Richard Corliss described it as "a police procedural with some smart new fangles"—its supporters were in the minority. "The main trouble is Mr. Mann's taste for overkill," noted *The New York Times*' Walter Goodman. "Attention keeps being diverted away from the story to the odd camera angles, the fancy lighting, the crashing music, and you realize you're being had. It's like catching a glimpse of the gimmicks in the magician's bag."

Sheila Benson's review in the equally influential *Los Angeles Times* derided Graham as a "klunker of a hero" while dismissing *Manhunter* as "all flat, brilliant, reflective surfaces." And though critic Rex Reed had loved Harris's novel—calling it "the most galvanizing history of a heinous crime since Truman Capote's *In Cold Blood*"—he felt that Mann had gone soft on the story's violence. "We don't even see the murders in the picture," Reed complained on his TV show *At the Movies*, "Instead of the nerve-frying action you should get, you get clinical discussions about how the latest FBI technology works." (Reed also admitted that he'd dozed off during his screening.)

Manhunter did find some admirers, including *Chicago Tribune* critic Gene Siskel, who praised Mann's color scheme, Petersen's performance, and the film's sustained tension: "You want to look away from the screen, but you can't." At a time when some critics were suspicious of superslick music videos—not to mention visually vigorous blockbusters such as *Top Gun*—the brilliant, reflective surfaces of *Manhunter* seemed to some to be a little *too* polished. Which, of course, was the whole point. "It was designed to be handsome because of the subject matter," Mann said. "I could have made a very gritty, very realistic movie that would have had a tremendous amount of power, and I'd have everybody in the men's room and woman's room 20 minutes in."

Absent from most of the *Manhunter* reviews, good or bad, was any mention of Hannibal Lecter—or, more specifically, "Hannibal Lecktor," as his name had inexplicably been modified for the film. A few critics called out Cox's performance, including the *LA Times*' Benson, who called the actor "brainy, powerful, focused" and added that Lecter "could probably run for governor from behind bars and win if he simply put his mind to it." For the most part, though, Lecter was viewed in much the same way as he was in the reviews of Harris's novel: as either a nonentity or a backup madman.

Shrugging reviews, a tricky tone, a low-wattage cast: *Manhunter* had everything working against it when the film finally opened in theaters on August 15, a lousy time to debut an R-rated grown-up thriller. The box office was led that weekend by a surprise-hit remake of the horror classic *The Fly*, and James Cameron's recently released sequel *Aliens* was still pulling in viewers. That didn't leave much room for *Manhunter*, which earned barely $2 million in its first weekend, all but dooming it to a slow fade-out from theaters.

Before the movie could disappear from view altogether, though, it enjoyed a weeklong run at Showcase Cinema, a two-screen venue in downtown Clarksdale, Mississippi, less than a half-hour drive from where Harris had grown up. In a newspaper advertisement, the theater trumpeted the fact that *Manhunter* was "based on the novel *Red Dragon*, by the Delta's own Thomas Harris from Rich, MS." *The Clarksdale Press Register* even ran a news article about the film's arrival, describing Harris as a "local boy made good."

Harris likely would have quibbled a bit with that "made good" assessment—at least when it came to *Manhunter*. "He didn't like it much," a relative said. "He didn't think they did it any justice."

Unlike Stephen King, who had been vocal about his displeasure with

Stanley Kubrick's 1980 adaptation of *The Shining*, Harris kept his gripes about *Manhunter* private, having realized the wisdom of Hemingway's showbiz adage: "Throw them the book, grab the money, and drive home as fast as you can." Besides, by the time *Manhunter* came and went, he'd long since moved on to his next novel. It would take him most of the 1980s to complete it, his writing process once again deepened and delayed by years of research. During that time, few people knew what his third book would be about. And nobody knew what it would be called—even Harris. In fact, it wouldn't be until his last day of work on the novel, in the late 1980s, that he looked down at the last five words of his book and saw the perfect title staring back at him: *The Silence of the Lambs*.

PART 2
FIRST LOVE

*The Silence
of the Lambs*
(1988, 1991)

CHAPTER 8

"SOME PEOPLE ARE JUST BORN EVIL."

Athena Varounis made her first arrest for the FBI in 1981 at a diner in Jersey City, New Jersey. She'd been sent there as a new agent, tasked with finding a waitress working the lunch shift. "Her name was Joann, and she had floated bad checks or some shit," recalls Varounis. Once inside the restaurant, Varounis spotted her target, who was carrying a tray of food and wearing a name tag that read JOANN. The rookie moved in quickly. "I said, 'My name is Athena Varounis. I'm an FBI agent. You're under arrest.'"

Joann didn't try to run. Instead, she fainted. "The Coke went flying here, the sandwich went there, and she went on the floor," says Varounis, who was about to read the woman her rights when a training agent stepped in. "No, no, no," Varounis was told. "They have to be conscious when you arrest them."

It was an inauspicious start to Varounis's hard-won FBI career. She'd spent part of her childhood in Edison, New Jersey, and attended college to pursue painting. But after graduating, she had decided to get into law enforcement. "Why? I have no idea," she says. "I just felt responsible for people. And I wanted to do something significant."

When Varounis applied to be a police officer in Edison in 1976, she was turned down. "The mayor and police chief said, 'There's no way a girl's ever going to be a cop,'" recalls Varounis, who instead joined the force as a civilian, serving as both a crime analyst and a police photographer. One of her earliest assignments required her to take a picture of a corpse, so she grabbed her camera, climbed atop a table in a morgue, and clicked away while standing over the body. "The medical examiner had never seen a woman doing this stuff, and he almost joined the guy on the gurney," Varounis says. Afterward, the examiner gave her a tip on dealing with the dead: "He taught me that you put Vicks VapoRub under your nose, and that blocks the smell."

While working for the Edison police, Varounis applied to other law enforcement outfits, only to be rejected because she stood at five foot four, three inches shy of the official height requirement (the strict measurement, she says, was another barrier to keep women out). By the end of the 1970s, she'd realized that careerwise, she was stuck. "I was pretty depressed," she remembers. "I wasn't getting to be a cop. I wasn't sure what I was gonna do." She was about to apply for grad school when a pair of FBI agents who happened to be visiting her office in Edison asked if she'd consider applying to the Bureau.

Such a proposal would have been impossible only a few years earlier. During his long reign as the head of the FBI, J. Edgar Hoover had made it clear that, while women could fill clerical and secretarial jobs, they couldn't become agents. But by the 1970s, an equal rights revolution under way. In 1971, the Secret Service had admitted its first female agents, and a few years later, the United States Military Academy in West Point, New York, enrolled its female cadets—a move that angered many students. "I'm glad I'll be gone when they come," one senior grumbled.

The FBI had to keep up with the times, and in 1972, the Bureau finally swore in two female agents—one a former Marine Corps lieutenant, the other an ex-nun. But the number of women didn't increase much from then on. And in 1977, one of the FBI's few female recruits filed a class action complaint against the Bureau, alleging sexual discrimination when assignments were handed out. By the end of the 1970s, the FBI was in the middle of a PR crisis. And the Bureau remained overwhelmingly male. As a result, Varounis says, "they were under pressure to hire women."

Stuck in her New Jersey job, Varounis was eager to help with the

Bureau's enlistment efforts. After applying to the FBI, she found herself in Newark, New Jersey, where she and "a bunch of lumberjacks" underwent a series of academic and physical examinations. There were spelling quizzes—"I couldn't spell worth a flip, so I worked harder on that than I did on push-ups"—firearms drills, and physical fitness tests. At one point, Varounis was told to hold and aim a shotgun for one minute in order to demonstrate her upper-body strength. "I said [to the supervisor], 'Well, what do you want me to aim at?" she recalls. "He said, 'Anything you want.' Well, I aimed it at him. That did not go over well."

Despite her bluntness, or perhaps because of it, Varounis was called back for an interview. She endured a series of patronizing questions, such as: How would she find time to work in the Bureau *and* cook for her husband? ("I don't cook anyway, so he's on his own, whoever he is," she replied.) A few days later, a letter arrived, telling her to report for training. *Son of a bitch*, she thought, *I passed.*

Varounis endured months of training—"the sixteen longest weeks of my life," she says—before graduating from the FBI Academy in 1980. During the next few years, she would handle criminal cases on military bases around Washington, DC, an assignment that involved everything from shoplifting to murder. She also served on the FBI's Reactive Squad, dealing with bank robberies, kidnappings, extortions, and all sorts of unwanted nudity, sometimes rousing suspects from bed before they'd had time to get dressed: "They got a bazillion dollars, and they can't buy PJs. I saw so many naked men, I almost went to the convent."

In 1984, Varounis would find herself in the middle of a national crime story. That July, a wealthy bridge player named Edith Rosenkranz, whose husband, George, had helped develop the birth control pill, was abducted at gunpoint outside a tournament in Washington, DC. The kidnappers demanded a $1 million ransom, and the Reactive Squad was called in. After a pickup was arranged, Varounis found herself in a Chevrolet Cavalier following a van carrying Rosenkranz, the kidnappers, and a medical bag containing the cash. When the vehicle pulled over near the White House, Varounis was ordered to move in. "I ran up to Mrs. Rosenkranz, and grabbed her by the shoulders," she recalls. "She looked at me, and I said, 'FBI! You're safe!' She probably thought, 'Bullshit I'm safe! Where's the men? Who's this girl with a gun?'"

Two years after her work on the Rosenkranz case, in late 1986, Varounis got a call from a senior agent, telling her to wear something nice to work the next day. She'd been scheduled to have lunch at the J. Edgar Hoover Building with an author whose name she didn't recognize: Thomas Harris. She wasn't thrilled with the assignment. "I said, 'I'm not going to talk to any author.'" But she didn't have a choice. "The Bureau approves of this guy," she was told. "They like his work."

Varounis hadn't read any of Harris's books. But she *had* seen *Black Sunday*. So she was taken aback when the bearded, gently smiling Harris joined her table one afternoon at the J. Edgar Hoover Building cafeteria. "I'm thinking to myself, 'This is a sick puppy—and he looks like freaking Burl Ives!'" she says.

Harris began their conversation with a series of pleasant but banal inquiries about FBI procedures and paperwork. Things got more interesting when he asked Varounis about her experiences within the Bureau—her training, her responsibilities, her frustrations. He ran different hypotheticals by her: What would she do, for example, if she were alone in the home of a suspected murderer and the subject started walking away? "The appropriate thing to do is to back off and get backup—you can't shoot him," Varounis told him. "But what would *I* do? I'd go after the son of a bitch, 'cause he might have another victim in the house."

More queries followed. Varounis was struck by Harris's gentle interrogation style, one he'd developed during his years as a reporter. "He had a soft voice and soft approach," she says. "And he wasn't thinking about his next question—he was listening to my answer." She told Harris about frantically yelling "FBI! You're safe!" to the frazzled Mrs. Rosenkranz. And she talked about how whenever she felt down about her job, she'd unwind by doing laundry. ("There was something calming about it," she recalls.)

She also confided in Harris the many obstacles she'd faced as a woman in the Bureau, where she felt that many of her male colleagues didn't have her back—or simply didn't like her. "The men had never worked with women as equals before," she says. "There were no mentors, no role models. And you knew that, if you made a mistake, you were never going to be forgiven." Still, no matter how frustrating it could get at the Bureau, Varounis never let her emotions come to the surface. "I don't care what happens—you don't cry," she told Harris.

Their lunch lasted more than two hours. When it ended, Harris headed back into the noisy, dirty streets of Washington, DC. In the early 1980s, the city had come under attack by flocks of birds, which had taken up residence around the city's many museums and government facilities, dropping globs of shit upon pedestrians. "The FBI building looks like a concrete cage, and they were in every opening in the front of the building," Harris remembered. "So when you walked out, they flew. And when they flew, it rained." The birds had even migrated to the grounds of the White House, where staffers tried to scare them off by placing six-foot-long inflatable plastic snakes in the Rose Garden trees and blasting unpleasant sounds from what was described in one report as an "antilullaby tape."

But nothing worked. The birds wouldn't be deterred. They were smart, stubborn, and unimaginably tough. They were starlings.

For Harris's fans, the six-year gap between *Black Sunday* and *Red Dragon* had been frustrating but forgivable—after all, there were plenty of other globe-spanning thrillers to occupy their time as they awaited his next effort. But the final pages of *Red Dragon* begged for a more immediate follow-up. Harris still had to answer some crucial questions: Would Will Graham make a recovery and return to profiling? And whatever had become of Hannibal Lecter, last seen tormenting Graham from the confines of his cell?

At first, it seemed as though Harris's readers were in for a speedy resolution. In January 1983, Harris's longtime booster Liz Smith announced that the "good ole [boy] from Mississippi with a fevered imagination" had just signed a deal for his third novel, with St. Martin's Press. "It is still untitled," she noted, "and everybody involved is too refined to discuss the rather large amount of money being offered." A subsequent report pinned Harris's new deal at $750,000—a colossal advance, and one that would theoretically compel him to complete his new novel sooner rather than later.

But Harris couldn't be rushed. His next book would take much of the decade to complete, as he plunged himself deeper into his research than ever before. "This is not a guy who just jots and gives his book to an editor and says, 'Put it into shape,'" noted his editor Tom McCormack, who worked with Harris on his third novel. "He considers every single aspect of the story."

For Harris, the most essential aspect of his next book was the story's hero: a bright, forceful young FBI trainee named Clarice Starling. He had wanted to write a novel centering on a female character since the days of *Black Sunday*, in which the defiant terrorist Dahlia Iyad, an expert manipulator of damaged men, had propelled the book's narrative. "She was a distinct character," he recalled. "I liked working with her."

In *Black Sunday*, Iyad had been part of an ensemble. In Harris's new book, Starling would be the steely focal point. The novel found Harris unabashedly repurposing the plot of *Red Dragon*. Once again, the FBI's cruelly expedient Jack Crawford would cajole an underling to catch a serial killer—in this case, a murderer known as "Buffalo Bill." And once again, Hannibal the Cannibal would serve as the FBI's off-the-books consultant. But Will Graham would be gone this time around, having been scarred—literally and figuratively—when Lecter had sent Dolarhyde to kill him. ("Will's face looks like damn Picasso drew him, thanks to Lecter," Crawford notes.)

Instead, Crawford puts his trust in Starling, a blue-collar ambition machine carefully plotting her still young FBI career: "She knew what happens to a woman if she's ever pegged as a secretary," he wrote of Starling. "It sticks until the end of time."

Starling's concerns were well founded. In the mid-1980s, the Bureau's efforts to train and retain more female FBI agents were moving slowly. The workforce remained dominated by men—statistically as well as culturally: In one Los Angeles field office, female staffers were referred to as "cupcakes" by their male colleagues, some of whom displayed *Playboy* centerfolds over their desks. And though female agents were increasingly being deployed in everything from stakeouts to stings to drug busts, many old obstacles remained. "Women still have to prove themselves more than men do," one staffer told a reporter.

Harris wanted to talk to members of the next class of female agents to learn about their lives in the FBI. In doing so, he hoped to better understand Starling. She would be the most vital character in his new book, the only person capable of forging a connection, however fraught, with Hannibal Lecter. If Starling wasn't drawn properly—if she didn't contain the right mix of moxie and savvy—Lecter would simply wave her away. And so would readers.

Throughout the 1980s, Harris reached out to his various contacts at the Bureau, asking for introductions to female staffers. That was how he wound up having lunch with Varounis—the first of several conversations the two would have. He also wanted to meet with women in the Behavioral Science Unit, the group whose tech prowess and criminal mind savvy had lent *Red Dragon* its creepy credibility. He reached out to his old BSU source Robert Ressler, hoping that the agent would introduce him to a female profiler. There was only one problem: The BSU didn't have any female profilers. But Ressler *did* know someone Harris should speak with, a promising young agent in the Bureau's Baltimore Field Office.

Her name was Patricia Kirby, and though she was just getting her start at the FBI, she'd had plenty of experience dealing with violent criminals. Raised in what she calls a "very nice, very well-to-do" family in Baltimore, she had been encouraged by her family to seek out a low-key life. "My dad wanted me to work at the bank, get married, and start raising a family," Kirby remembers. Instead, she decided to earn an undergraduate degree in social psychology, and get into law enforcement. "When I came out of college," she says, "I was going to save the world."

She landed a job as a parole and probation agent before heading to Boston, where she studied criminology and worked in a program aimed at helping preteen offenders. "I thought, 'If we catch these kids early enough and we don't label them, we can turn them around,'" Kirby says. She soon came to a harsh realization: "These kids were given every opportunity under the sun. And some of them were just bad. At that point, I said, 'I think some people are just born evil.' That made me want to know 'Why did they do this?'"

Kirby returned to Baltimore, joining the city's police department in 1975. At the time, she was in her late twenties and one of just two female officers in her graduating class, making her presence on the force impossible to miss. When the *Baltimore Sun* published a profile of Kirby in 1976, the story's opening line asked, "What's a nice girl like her doing in a place like this?"

In her first year as an officer, Kirby made arrests in cases that ranged from narcotics to drunk driving to sexual assault. She'd eventually be named the city's first female homicide detective, patrolling the same neighborhoods that would later become famous on the HBO series *The Wire*. "You're right there with the blood and the guts and the pieces of brain laying on the sidewalk," she recalls. "I got a real good baptism by fire."

In the late 1970s, she attended a two-week training session at FBI headquarters in Washington, DC, where she sat in on a presentation by Ressler and John Douglas about the still-fledgling Behavioral Science Unit. "We all made fun of it," she says. "We thought, 'What are we going to learn about homicides from the FBI? *We're* the ones out here doing it!'" But she was intrigued by the profiling process and struck up a friendship with Ressler, who in 1979 convinced her to join the FBI.

Over the next few years, working from the Bureau's Baltimore Field Office, Kirby acted as a liaison with the BSU, assisting on cases involving serial killers, sexual assaults, and child murderers. She traveled to jails and prisons to interview violent offenders—including some that her male counterpoints wanted to avoid. "A lot of the men had trouble talking to child molesters, because they'd taunt them," she says. "They just didn't have the same issues talking to a nonjudgmental female as they did talking to a male."

Though Kirby didn't know it at the time, Ressler was occasionally feeding details about her progress to a third party with a keen interest in her work: Harris. "Ressler would tell him, 'I went on this interview with her at a prison, and this is how a guy reacted to her, and this is how she handled it,'" Kirby remembers.

At some point in the 1980s, Ressler set up a meeting between Kirby and Harris. The author didn't want Kirby to know why he wanted to talk to her—an unusual request, but one that didn't faze her. By that point, she'd fielded endless questions about being with the FBI. "I was five feet eight and 120 pounds," Kirby says, "and I was used to people asking 'What's it like for a young woman to go into an all-male maximum-security prison? How do you react?'"

The two met for lunch, and though Kirby would be hard pressed to recall much of their discussions decades later, she didn't withhold from Harris any details about the intensity of FBI life—including the difficulties women faced in law enforcement. "I was up front and honest," she says. "And he was very thorough." Harris, like other inquisitors, was particularly interested in her experiences talking to violent men. "He was trying to determine how a female main character would fly, and how realistic it would be," Kirby remembered, adding: "I think the impression oftentimes was that a woman is going to be cringing. So that's what I could tell Tom Harris: that a woman can do it, in many ways, better than a man. Because a woman will listen more and not judge. And that lack of judgment entices someone to be more forthcoming."

Harris and Kirby would wind up talking a few more times in the 1980s. During that time, he also kept in touch with Varounis, and met with an FBI agent named Carol Skiles, whom Harris later described as an "outstanding" agent who had helped him "[deal] with Clarice Starling" (Skiles died in 2009). Though it's not clear how many female agents the author consulted while working on his third novel, such conversations would play a major role in his understanding of Starling.

Harris's real-world research for his new book didn't stop there. He also needed to understand the novel's sadistic lead villain, Buffalo Bill. There was no way he could charm and disarm a mass murderer over lunch, of course. If the writer wanted to *really* learn about why men kill, he'd have to go to serial killer school.

CHAPTER 9

"SOMETIMES YOU REALLY HAVE TO SHOVE AND GRUNT AND SWEAT."

The bearded middle-aged guy sitting in the back of John Douglas's classroom at the FBI Academy in Quantico, Virginia, didn't say much. And while a few attendees were no doubt aware that the author of *Red Dragon* was in their midst, they were probably too distracted—or too freaked out—to care. Douglas's lessons, which covered topics such as criminal psychology and death investigation, were as intense as the man teaching them. "I'd show slides featuring these horrific pictures of victims and crime scenes," Douglas recalls. "Because of the subject matter, it was one of the most popular classes at Quantico."

If his students were hoping to become experts in the growing field of serial killer scholarship, they'd come to the right place. By the mid-1980s, Douglas had become an authority on mass murder—a distinction that had nearly killed him. In December 1983, just a few years into his career with the Behavioral Science Unit, he had awakened in a painful panic, convinced that he was being tortured by some of the violent criminals he'd apprehended. As he writhed in agony, Douglas realized that he was about to die. "I knew the way these guys operated," he later said. "They'd keep me alive as long as my body would hold out, reviving me when I passed out or was close to death, always inflicting as much pain and suffering as possible."

In reality, he had collapsed in a hotel room in Seattle, where he was investigating the case of the "Green River Killer," who at the time was believed to have murdered as many as twenty sex workers. It was one of the many investigations Douglas was working on at the time, and the strain of his job—the relentless workload, the endless travel, the pressure to bring closure to all those deaths—had sent the thirty-eight-year-old to the ground. "I was there for three or four days before they found me in a coma, paralyzed," he remembers.

It would take the agent months to recover, after which he returned to Quantico—and the BSU. That was around the time Harris showed up, asking to sit in on his classes, where the agent shared his knowledge of murderers from around the country, often revealing details that had been kept out of public view. After a class ended, Harris might head to an office shared by Douglas and Ressler. The agents kept eight-by-ten-inch color photographs of crime scenes spread out on their desks, and there were often maps on the wall marking the locations of victims' bodies. "We probably scared the hell out of him," Douglas says.

During their chats, Harris quizzed the famed profiler about past and current serial killers, including Ed Gein, the midwestern recluse who'd become an object of fascination/repulsion after his killing spree had been discovered in 1957. While at Quantico, Harris likely would have gotten a look at graphic images of Gein's handiwork, including his skin suit made from human remains. Such horrors apparently didn't upset the writer, who said little as he sat in Douglas's classroom and office, jotting down all sorts of gruesome data. The agent found Harris to be bright, quiet, and a bit awkward—"not exactly the kind of guy you go out and have a beer with."

A few years later, when Douglas got a chance to read Harris's third book, he realized just how closely Harris had been listening—and saw how the author had used some of his Quantico findings to create *The Silence of the Lambs*' murderous Buffalo Bill. As the novel begins, Bill is credited with the murders of at least five women, all of whom have been found flayed in a river. Harris then slowly revealed Bill's lethal process: He lures in a young woman by placing his arm in a cast and knocks her unconscious when she asks if he needs help. The woman wakes up afterward at the bottom of an eight-by-ten-foot cement pit, where she'll be slowly starved over the course of a week. The torture concludes with Bill shooting his victim dead and collecting parts of her skin, which he'll use to create a female bodysuit for his own use. Before abandoning the corpse, he might open the victim's throat and place inside it a pupa containing a death's-head moth, a rare insect whose body pattern resembles a human skull.

Douglas believed that Harris had based the fantastical Buffalo Bill on three real-world killers. First there was Gein, who had used some of his victims' remains to create items of clothing, including a vest and a belt made of human nipples. Then there was Ted Bundy, who'd sometimes elicit help from his victims by placing his arm in a sling and feigning helplessness. Bill was also modeled, Douglas believed, on a Philadelphia man named Gary Heidnik, who had been arrested for murder in 1987 after imprisoning six women in a plywood-covered hole in his basement.

Gein, Bundy, Heidnik—all three were discussed at Quantico at various points in the 1980s. But Harris's FBI education wasn't limited to mass-murder lectures and crime-scene photos. As a guest of the Bureau, he would have been invited to stay in one of the facility's guest rooms, giving him the chance to collect pages' worth of small yet vivid insights about life on the sprawling FBI campus. Harris saw the gray-colored case files in the BSU's offices. He noted the trainees returning from the shooting range with gunsmoke on their hands and grass stains on their windbreakers. And he glimpsed students dusting for fingerprints at "Anytown Bank," one of the many fake businesses located in the Bureau's Potemkin Village–like training area.

Such details would find their way into *The Silence of the Lambs*, which was written in various locations throughout the 1980s. Harris worked on parts of the book in Rich, where a neighbor let him use a small red frame house as a temporary office. He wrote in the morning and read all afternoon before having dinner with the now-widowed Polly. While back home, he took care not to discuss his work in progress. "He doesn't even tell his mother what he's doing," noted a relative.

As Harris forged ahead with his third novel, it became clear that his creative process hadn't gotten any easier in the years since *Red Dragon*. "Sometimes you really have to shove and grunt and sweat," he once said of writing. "Some days you go to your office and you're the only one who shows up, none of the characters show up, and you sit there by yourself, feeling like an idiot. And some days everybody shows up ready to work."

When Harris wasn't grunting and sweating in his Mississippi workplace, he might be found writing in his office in Sag Harbor, the beachside getaway that was now a frequent retreat for him and his partner, Pace Barnes. Over the years, the couple would become friendly with several Hamptons-dwelling writers and artists, some of whom would be treated to home-cooked meals at Harris's home. The author had become passionate about cooking, approaching his culinary work with his typical rigor: One night, over a dinner of squash blossoms, he explained to a guest the painstaking rituals that had gone into preparing the dish, down to the pipe cleaner he'd used to flush out bees hiding inside the flower.

To his Sag Harbor friends, Harris was an amenable oddity—a soft-spoken intellectual with an appetite for Jaguars, wild duck, and criminal ephemera. "I know Tommy Harris," said neighbor Betty Friedan, author of *The Feminine Mystique*. "He is this sweet southern person, and underneath is this sadistic imagination." Floyd Shaman, a Mississippi sculptor who visited Harris at Sag Harbor in the 1980s, said the author was "always thinking about strange things. I remember he told me he had just gotten some videotapes on how to pick locks and break into safes as part of his research." Harris also confided in Shaman, a fellow artist, about the hours and angst that went into each novel: "He really wants his books to go beyond thrillers."

Harris's Sag Harbor writing space, located a short walk away from his favorite grocery store, was a crooked room above a barbershop. That's where Harris awaited the arrival of the novel's many characters—including Lecter, who'd appear to him more fully formed, more visible, than he had in the past. Harris would bring Lecter further into the light, giving readers a better look at the doctor, with his striking red lips and the extra middle finger on his left hand, the result of a rare condition known as polydactyly. *The Silence of the Lambs* would also showcase Lecter's artistic skills: Using butcher paper and charcoal, he sketches extravagant illustrations of the skyline of Florence, Italy. And after meeting Starling, he draws designs for a wristwatch that features her head atop the crucified body of Christ.

The novel also fleshes out new details of Lecter's bloody past. In *Red Dragon*, his nine known murder victims were referred to only fleetingly. *The Silence of the Lambs* IDs some of his victims, such as the dull therapy patient Lecter had killed midsession, shoving a stiletto into the man's still beating heart while declaring "Looks like a straw down a doodlebug hole, doesn't it?" (Lecter later serves the man's pancreas and thymus at a high-society dinner.) And when Starling visits Hannibal the Cannibal in his cell, he recalls the census taker who'd annoyed him by trying to "quantify" him—never a good idea. "I ate his liver with some fava beans and a big Amarone," he tells the young trainee. "Go back to school, little Starling." (The wine choice would be changed to Chianti for the film adaptation.)

But the book's most insightful revelations about Lecter deal with the doctor's mood and mindset. The Lecter of *Red Dragon* had seemed comfortable in his cell, where he held snooty sway over his colleagues and could comfortably torment irritants such as Will Graham. When Starling visits Lecter in *The Silence of the Lambs*, half a decade has passed since the events of *Red Dragon*,[*] and a sense of melancholy has gripped Lecter. He's now well into middle age, and though he still enjoys a sick kind of celebrity—with one tabloid offering him $50,000 for one of his recipes—his savage exploits are slowly being overshadowed by a new wave of madmen. Even his fan mail has begun to slow down.

Hannibal the Cannibal now passes the time by drawing, reading, and tormenting his captors. "It takes an orderly at least ten minutes a day to remove the staples from the publications he receives," notes Dr. Frederick Chilton, Lecter's smug keeper. "We tried to eliminate or reduce his subscriptions, but he wrote a brief and the court overruled us."

But while Hannibal the Cannibal is far too smart to be bored—he can "entertain himself for years at a time," Harris wrote—his cell has begun to feel like a prison. "I've been in this room eight years, Clarice," he says. "I

---

[*] Harris never explicitly provides the years in which either novel takes place, though it's implied *Red Dragon* is set in the late1970s, and that *The Silence of the Lambs* takes place in the mid-1980s.

know that they will never, ever let me out while I'm alive. What I want is a view. I want a window where I can see a tree, or even water."

Such malaise hasn't weakened the doctor's manipulative powers. "If Lecter talks to you at all, he'll just be trying to find out about you," Crawford warns Starling "It's the kind of curiosity that makes a snake look in a bird's nest." And in Starling, Lecter has found the perfect target for manipulation. She's the first person to interest him in years: a woman raised in near poverty, trying to conceal her past as she attempts to rise in the ranks of an elite institution. For all the confidence Starling tries to project, she's still playacting in her role as an FBI trainee. She can help out at a grim autopsy, where she's taught to apply Vicks VapoRub under her nose. But when she's back at Quantico, overwhelmed by her work, she might be found seeking out the "comforting chug" of a washing machine.

Lecter senses in Starling a desire to be molded and mentored. She's not his equal, like Will Graham; she's a student. When she first visits him in *Silence*, her intent is to understand the thinking of a killer and see if Lecter can lead her to Buffalo Bill. But from the get-go, the doctor makes it clear that *he's* dictating the terms of their relationship—and that he has no time for questions from "little Starling":

> "Am I evil, Officer Starling?"
>
> "I think you've been destructive. For me, it's the same thing."
>
> "Evil's just destructive? Then storms are evil, if it's that simple. And we have fire, and then there's hail. Underwriters lump it all under 'Acts of God.'"
>
> "Deliberate—"
>
> "I collect church collapses, recreationally. Did you see the recent one in Sicily? Marvelous! The façade fell on sixty-five grandmothers at a special Mass. Was that evil? If so, who did it? If He's up there, He just loves it, Officer Starling. Typhoid and swans—it all comes from the same place."

• • •

Lecter insists that any attempts to analyze, categorize, or explain his actions are in vain. "Nothing happened to me, Officer Starling," he tells the trainee. "*I* happened. You can't reduce me to a set of influences."

It was another echo, perhaps unintentional, of James H. Coyner's comment to authorities shortly before he was tried and hanged for murder in Bolivar County, Mississippi, in 1935: "Everything we do or say is predestined, and we have no control over it." But Lecter's insistence that he arrived in the world fully formed—that he wasn't shaped by any outside force—is either an outright lie, an ego-fortifying boast, or a sign that he's in denial about his *own* backstory. He clearly sees one's past as a cheat code to their present, because in order to understand Starling, he begins asking about some of the most intimate details of her life. As they talk, the serial killer and the trainee agree to an ongoing quid pro quo: He'll provide insights into Buffalo Bill's behavior in exchange for Starling handing over her past traumas.

She agrees, letting the snake into the nest. Starling is by now desperate to find Buffalo Bill, especially after he abducts a young woman named Catherine Martin, the daughter of a powerful US senator from Tennessee. Though Lecter and Starling meet just a few times, their conversations grow more intimate. Lecter's questions to her are piercing and persistent—and sometimes shockingly inappropriate. But over time, he wears down her resistance. She tells him about the loss of her father, a night watchman killed on the job when she was a child. And she recounts running away while living on a relative's sheep and horse ranch in Montana, where Starling became terrified by the sound of the spring lambs being slaughtered. Lecter, after taking in Starling's case history, then reduces her to a set of influences:

"Do you think if you caught Buffalo Bill yourself and if you made Catherine all right, you could make the lambs stop screaming, do you think they'd be all right too and you wouldn't wake up again in the dark and hear the lambs screaming? Clarice?"

"Yes. I don't know. Maybe."

"Thank you, Clarice." Dr. Lecter seemed oddly at peace.

•••

Though she doesn't acknowledge it, Starling *also* finds peace during her talks with Lecter. Despite being warned by Crawford not to grow close to the doctor—"You know what he did to Will Graham," he says—she allows him access to her troubled childhood. In return, he performs a sort of psychological surgery, locating the connections between her tumultuous past and her urgent present. He's perhaps the first person in Starling's life to actually *see* her. Lecter may be a man-eater, but before he began dining on his patients, he was clearly a *very* good therapist.

Starling and Lecter would spend the rest of Harris's novel separated physically, if not emotionally. The book concludes with Starling rescuing the imprisoned Catherine Martin—"FBI, you're safe," she barks—and shooting Buffalo Bill while he is alone in his home. As for Lecter, he's now on the loose, having made a violent escape that left five casualties in its wake, including two officers (one of the victims, Harris wrote, "seemed to have exploded blood in the cell"). It's a daring feat, one that replenishes Hannibal's grody celebrity. "Lecter's gone platinum," Crawford tells Starling, "he's at the top of everybody's Most Wanted list."

But Hannibal is well hidden, having altered his appearance by injecting his nose with silicone gel. The final pages of *The Silence of the Lambs* finds him recuperating at a posh St. Louis hotel—and on his way to a vacation cottage where he'd hidden plentiful reserves of cash. He writes a letter to Starling, asking to stay in touch and promising not to harm her. "I have no plans to call on you, Clarice, the world being more interesting with you in it," he writes. "Be sure you extend me the same courtesy."

Lecter's kindness toward Starling may have been the novel's most unmooring revelation. In *Red Dragon*, Lecter is described by his captors as a sociopath, a monster, or some new strain of terror altogether. But in *The Silence of the Lambs*, his genial note to Starling proves that he *might* have a capacity for empathy—or at least an ability to fake it. In the same way that Lecter helps Starling see herself, Starling lets the reader see Hannibal the Cannibal for who he really is: a murderer, to be sure, but one who can exhibit signs of respect, even an odd kind of kindness—so long as the person standing across from his cell doesn't bore him. And so long as he gets something in exchange for his niceties.

By the book's last pages, which Harris completed in the late 1980s, Starling is resting soundly for presumably the first time in months, perhaps even years. "She sleeps deeply, sweetly," notes the book's final line, "in the silence of the lambs."

After typing those words in his Sag Harbor office, Harris felt "a stab of happiness" and let go of his desk. The room's floor was tilted, sending his chair backward until he slammed into a wall. The ending of *The Silence of the Lambs* had literally sent him reeling—a response that would soon be shared by millions of readers.

CHAPTER 10

"HE KNOWS ABOUT STRANGE THINGS."

When word got out in early 1988 that Harris had another book on the way—his first in seven years—the publishing world sprang into action. St. Martin's Press announced that the novel would enjoy an impressive initial print run of 200,000 copies. At a national booksellers' gathering that summer, the expectations for Harris's follow-up were so pitched that a reporter overheard the same refrain being repeated across booths and stalls: *"Hannibal Lecter is back!"*

A book like *The Silence of the Lambs* warranted a high-profile launch, one that Harris would have to endure without the help of his longtime literary agent and champion, Gloria Safier, who'd died in 1985. Safier was a book-industry lifer with countless connections to the Manhattan publishing scene (her client list included columnist Liz Smith, which explains how the gossip maven had landed all those items about the secretive Harris).

As Safier's successor, Harris chose another New York City titan, Mort Janklow, a lawyer/lit world superstar who'd worked with everyone from Jackie Collins to Henry Fonda to the ex–Watergate factotum John D. Ehrlichman. Janklow was an infamous figure in the book business, a press-savvy operator known for holding competitive bidding wars that could yield million-dollar deals. And because the agent had so many projects going at once, Harris wouldn't have to worry about being nagged for his next manuscript. "I never push him," Janklow once said.

In the months leading up to the release of *The Silence of the Lambs*, Janklow orchestrated a series of lucrative deals. The Book-of-the-Month Club picked the novel as its main selection for the group's nearly 3 million members. And the British rights to *The Silence of the Lambs* were sold for a whopping £250,000—yet another early sign of confidence in the novel's success, and a demonstration of the book industry's big-money muscle. The late 1980s had turned into a blockbuster era for authors and agents alike. Chain bookstores were becoming fixtures in malls and shopping centers across the country, making it possible for hit hardcovers such as Lee Iacocca's memoir *Iacocca: An Autobiography* and Donald Trump's *Trump: The Art of the Deal* to sell more than a million copies. As a result, some authors were getting seven-figure advances, and publishers were spending as much as half a million dollars on promotional efforts for expected bestsellers.

The arrival of *The Silence of the Lambs* would be announced with a modest yet assured marketing campaign—one that wouldn't involve Harris, who once again declined to hype the book. "He just won't do interviews," griped a St. Martin's employee. "It's a publicist's nightmare." Instead, Lecter would serve as the book's selling point, despite having been a mere supporting player in *Red Dragon*. In late August, St. Martin's Press ran a haunting newspaper ad in which Lecter—his wrist shackled, his skin gnarled—reaches for Starling's hand, accompanied by a forgivably gaudy tagline: "She has seen murder. She has met madness. Now she must use evil . . . to stop them both." By late summer, even the most casually informed book lover knew that Hannibal Lecter was once again heading to stores and library shelves.

And when the first wave of reviews of *The Silence of the Lambs* hit in the fall of 1988, they were across-the-board awestruck. "It isn't easy to explain why a civilized person would want to keep reading about such lunatic depravity," wrote *New York Times* critic Christopher Lehmann-Haupt. "But you do; you do." He praised the book's lucid horrors and marveled at the onslaught of technical arcana that Harris had assembled: "He knows about strange things, like the life cycle of lepidoptera, the legal spacing of fishhooks on a trotline, moths that live only on the tears of large land animals, and the amount of brain matter it takes to tan a hide."

But *The Silence of the Lambs* was more than a card catalog overview of Harris's busy mind. The years he'd spent sweating and fretting over his writing were evident across all 338 pages. The novel never lags or sags, instead maintaining a locomotive force that forces readers to run alongside, trying to keep up. And its most rattling passages are devoid of violence, yet inflated with terror. In a chapter Lehmann-Haupt described as "a tour de force of descriptive economy," Starling finds herself in a dark, decrepit, mice-ridden storage facility. Working off a tip from Lecter and operating under an impossible deadline, she decides to enter an abandoned Packard that appears to contain a long-abandoned dead body:

> The car springs groaned as she got inside and the figure shifted a little when she sat down beside it. The right hand in its white glove slid off the thigh and lay on the seat. She touched the glove with her finger. The hand inside was hard. Gingerly she pushed the glove down from the wrist. The wrist was some white synthetic material. There was a lump in the trousers that for a silly instant reminded her of certain events in high school.
>
> Small scrambling noises came from under the seat.

Released at a time when so many mass-market novels had become weighty in every sense of the word—several recent bestsellers, including Tom Wolfe's *The Bonfire of the Vanities* and James A. Michener's *Alaska*, had broken the six-hundred-page barrier—Harris's sharp, swift-moving storytelling was a welcome relief. *The Silence of the Lambs* wasn't always pleasant. But at least it went down easily. "It's marvelous, the best book I've read for a very long time," enthused *Charlie and the Chocolate Factory* author (and Willy Wonka creator) Roald Dahl, no stranger to stories of dark-minded madmen. "It is infinitely superior to any novel published this year."

And while reviews of *Red Dragon* often cast Hannibal the Cannibal to the side, *The Silence of the Lambs* clearly made him a star. "Lecter emerges as one of the great villains of thrillerdom," noted the publishing-business bible *Kirkus Reviews*. For many critics, Lecter stood out for his distressing relatability. "The closer Harris brings us to Lecter, the less chilling and loathsome he becomes," noted a critic in *The Asbury Park Press*. "We begin to empathize with him—at arm's length, of course—and, yes, even feel comfortable with him." (Maybe a little *too* comfortable: One female British cultural critic swooned over the killer, describing him as "my kind of man: intelligent, vicious, and totally untrustworthy.") Lecter loitered in readers' minds long after they'd put down *The Silence of the Lambs*, wondering about his fate. As one critic noted, "He remains at large. And he could be coming to get *you*."

But Lecter's potency, not to mention his humanity, would never have come to full power in *The Silence of the Lambs* if not for Clarice Starling. She was a rare character in the world of 1980s crime fiction—or really *any* genre of fiction: a young woman who doesn't overcome obstacles so much as she ignores them, trying to use her poise and smarts against the men who stand in her way. Starling was a breakout character for many readers, including one of the women who'd inspired her. Before the book's release, Harris sent Athena Varounis a copy of *Silence* with the inscription "Clarice Starling may be fiction, but her spirit is real. Now where do you suppose that came from? Thank you, Athena."

"I was so proud," says Varounis. "Tom took some of the stuff I told him and created this unique character who lived, breathed, felt, thought—and that felt super cool."

Patricia Kirby also read *The Silence of the Lambs* upon its release. By that point, she'd left the FBI, where she'd spent her last few years in the BSU, working as a profiler. She hadn't thought about her conversations with Harris since then. And she'd had no idea that she'd played a role in the book until she received a copy of the book from Ressler, the agent who'd brought Kirby to the FBI in the late 1970s. "It said, 'Dear Clarice—here you are,'" Kirby remembers. Reading the book, she admired Starling's toughness. And the relationship between Harris's young trainee and Crawford reminded Kirby of her own time working with Ressler.

By year's end, *The Silence of the Lambs* had become Harris's third consecutive bestseller and a fixture on holiday gift lists. A big-screen adaptation seemed inevitable. "If this one isn't immediately snapped up by a major studio," noted a critic in the *Cleveland Plain Dealer*, "somebody hasn't been paying attention."

The big studios *had* been paying attention. But when executives took a look at Harris's twisty, ensnaring, perfectly plotted thriller, many of them had a puzzling response: silence.

CHAPTER 11

"DADDY, YOU'RE NOT MAKING THIS MOVIE."

Bob Bookman needed a favor from one of the most powerful men in Hollywood. It was just a few months before the hardcover release of Harris's new novel, and Bookman had been sending copies of *The Silence of the Lambs* around town. A motion picture literary agent at the famed Creative Arts Agency, Bookman was looking to sell the film rights to *Silence*, a job that had proved to be surprisingly tough. "There was absolutely no interest in it," he remembers.

All of the major studios had turned down the book. Some executives noted the poor showing of the last big-screen Lecter adventure, *Manhunter*. Others were turned off by the novel's serial killer storyline. Though late-1980s audiences would happily show up on a Friday night to cheer supernaturally powered killers such as Freddy Krueger (*A Nightmare on Elm Street*) and Jason Vorhees (the Friday the 13th series), the crimes in Harris's novel weren't exaggerated slasher-flick kills; they were reality-rooted, scarily plausible stuff. There was worry that *The Silence of the Lambs* would be too much for sensitive filmgoers. "It was the typical Hollywood lemminglike mentality," says Bookman. "And at the time, the lemmings weren't making serial killer movies."

Even Dino De Laurentiis, the mogul who'd produced *Manhunter*— and who had contractual first dibs to bid on a *Silence of the Lambs* movie—wasn't interested in returning to Lecter's world. His film company had endured several recent box-office disappointments, including *Manhunter*, and De Laurentiis ultimately decided to pass on adapting *The Silence of the Lambs*. "Big mistake," he'd say years later.

With De Laurentiis no longer a possibility, Bookman continued to try to find a studio that would back the project. He knew that Ned Tanen, then the president of Paramount Pictures, had assigned an underling to read the book—and then rejected it. So the agent did something unprecedented: He called Tanen and asked if he'd give Harris's novel to someone else at the studio, just to get a second opinion. "I really believed in the book and thought it would make a really good movie—it was all about figuring out the material," Bookman recalls. Three days later, he got a verdict. The good news was that Tanen's second reader had loved the book. The bad news? Tanen *still* didn't want to buy it.

Not long afterward, Bookman heard from Fred Specktor, a longtime CAA agent who represented one of the more durable movie stars of the last few decades: Gene Hackman. The palooka-faced Oscar winner had never flinched at unsavory material, having starred in some of the 1970s bleakest masterworks, such as the hardboiled cop drama *The French Connection*, the nihilist neo-noir *Night Moves*, and the rank sex-ring thriller *Prime Cut*. By the late 1980s, Hackman had become a rarity—a middle-aged star who seemed to become more popular as he got older. At that point, he could pretty much do what he wanted. And now, after more than a quarter century in Hollywood, Hackman was eager to get behind the camera. "I've wanted to try directing," he said at the time. "And who else would hire me?"

While reading *The Silence of the Lambs*, Hackman realized that the book offered him a potentially showy supporting role—he thought he might want to play the diabolical Lecter—as well as a chance to kick-start his filmmaking career. He teamed up with Orion Pictures, the studio responsible for the recent Best Picture winners *Amadeus* and *Platoon*, and bought the book's film rights. According to Mike Medavoy, who was then Orion's executive vice president of production, the studio split the $1 million cost with Hackman's company.

The actor didn't just want to direct *The Silence of the Lambs*; he also wanted to try writing the script himself—an unusual request, given that he had no screenplay credits. He churned out a few dozen pages before realizing that he needed help. Which was how, in late 1988, Ted Tally found himself in a Chicago hotel room, listening as Hackman lay on the floor, discussing his vision for *The Silence of the Lambs*.

Tally was an acclaimed playwright and a justifiably frustrated screenwriter. He'd been in his twenties when his play *Terra Nova*, the story of the South Pole explorer Robert F. Scott, had opened to wide critical acclaim. But the show hadn't gotten too far in New York, and Tally had spent the next several years working on off-Broadway productions, while also scoring the occasional Hollywood gig. In the late 1980s, he had spent almost two years working on the erotic thriller *White Palace*, only to be replaced before production began. "I was furious," Tally recalls. "By that point, I felt very betrayed by Hollywood. I wasn't making it in theater, and I wasn't making it in film, either."

As it turned out, he knew another writer with a disregard for show business: Tom Harris. The two had been introduced by Tally's wife, who worked at a New York City art gallery where Harris was a client. "I had dinner with him a couple of times and told him I was a big fan of his work," Tally remembers. "And he said, 'Well, I have a new one you might be interested in.'" Tally read his advance copy of *The Silence of the Lambs* in two days. "I was beside myself," he says. "I thought, 'This is the kind of book that only comes around every ten years.' I thought it was like *The Godfather*—it had enough raw excitement to be a huge hit commercially."

Tally knew that there was little chance that he'd be hired to adapt *Silence*. His moviemaking experience was so minimal that he'd never even visited a film set. "I figured somebody had already taken the job—William Goldman or some other famous Hollywood screenwriter," he recalls. "I was moaning about that to my wife, and she said, 'Call your agent.'" When he did, he learned that *The Silence of the Lambs* had been picked up by Orion. Tally had worked on a script for the studio years earlier, and though that project had never gotten off the ground, Medavoy had liked Tally's work, and invited the writer to pitch Hackman in person.

After an introductory meeting with the actor near his home in Santa

Fe, New Mexico, Tally was called out to Chicago in the winter of 1988—right in time for a blizzard, and just days before Tally's wife was due to give birth to their first child. Hackman, who was in town to film a thriller titled *The Package*, had recently injured his back. He rested on the floor while Tally took notes on their spitballing session. "Luckily, I did most of the talking," Tally says. "I had a very hard time understanding what Gene was after. He would say odd things, like 'I see Clarice having flashbacks to her childhood, and her father is up in the sky when she looks up.'"

Tally took careful notes during those conversations with Hackman, collecting many of the actor's ideas into a story memo—one that included a description of a moment in which Starling reminisces about her late father:

> We see this memory visualized as a huge image in the sky, above the horizon line—a smiling man, in a dark suit, with a badge pinned to his lapel. He reaches down, swoops up a little girl into a hug, spins her around. It's Clarice as a child, age nine. The image rushes toward us, bigger and bigger, until it disappears.

During his talks with Hackman, Tally learned that the actor was already rethinking his decision to play Lecter: "He did say, 'Maybe Bobby will play Lecter,' but I didn't have the nerve to ask, 'Bobby who? Bobby Duvall? Bobby Redford? Bobby De Niro?' He just assumed that I would know who Bobby was." It was an early sign that the actor might not have a clear vision of what he wanted for *The Silence of the Lambs*.

Tally then returned home to New York City, where he began work on his first draft. A few months later, his progress would be interrupted by a phone call informing him that Hackman had dropped out. His decision to leave, Hackman later said, had been made during the March 1989 Academy Awards ceremony. Sitting in the audience, watching a particularly brutal clip from his film *Mississippi Burning*, he had begun feeling queasy and realized that he wanted a break from making violent films. According to Bookman, the actor's exit had also been influenced by his daughter, who'd read *The Silence of the Lambs* and urged her father not to get involved: "She called her father and said, 'Daddy, you're not making this movie.'" Both stories could be true—though it's equally likely that Hackman was simply overwhelmed by the prospect of being a filmmaker. "I didn't have the energy to do it," he later said. "It would have taken years."

In one blow, Orion Pictures had lost both its director *and* its big-name star. But the studio was still eager to proceed with *The Silence of the Lambs*. Medavoy bought out Hackman's share of the film rights and began looking for a new filmmaker. He needed someone who could maintain the chill of Harris's book without turning it into an exploitation flick—and who could find the humanity in a monster like Lecter.

CHAPTER 12

"I FELL MADLY IN LOVE WITH HER."

By the late 1980s, director Jonathan Demme had assembled a reliably unpredictable filmography. He had grown up in Miami, where his parents had taken him to regular Thursday-night screenings—everything from the sci-fi giant-insect flick *Them!* to the vibrant French tragedy *Black Orpheus*. By the time he was a teen, he was spending hours digging through piles of old newspapers, looking for vintage movie advertisements to add to his collection. Years later, while attending the University of Florida, Demme worked as a movie critic for a shopping newspaper in Coral Gables. He took in as many foreign releases as he could before heading to New York for a film publicity job.

The young film lover eventually connected with Roger Corman, the producer and diector known for feeding audiences a steady diet of low-budget, high-profit B movies, including *Little Shop of Horrors* and *X: The Man with the X-Ray Eyes*. Corman was always on the lookout for cheap, green talent, and he called Demme with an unexpected yet intriguing proposition: "How'd you like to write a screenplay for me—for a motorcycle movie?"

Demme agreed and wound up coscripting and producing the 1971 *Rashomon*-inspired biker drama *Angels Hard as They Come*, the first of several Corman releases he'd work on in the early part of the decade. "I kind of fell backwards into filmmaking," he said. "I didn't know what the hell I was doing." He learned along the way and made his directorial debut with the lively, lusty, oddly inspiring *Caged Heat*, a 1974 action drama about a band of female convicts who start an uprising at a corrupt women's institution. Promoted with a proudly sleazy tagline—"Women's Prison U.S.A.—Rape, Riot & Revenge"—*Caged Heat* earned solid reviews and wound up playing drive-in theaters and grindhouses for years.

Demme would eventually migrate out of Corman's stable and begin pursuing stories that veered wildly between genre and tone: His 1979 thriller *Last Embrace* channeled midcentury Hitchcock, while 1980's true-life tale *Melvin and Howard*—about a gas station worker whose name ends up in Howard Hughes's will—was a tartly bittersweet look at marriage and class. Such efforts seemingly had little in common. But Demme's films all displayed a fondness for outsiders, eccentrics, and uneasy heroes—as well as an aversion to good-versus-evil dynamics. "Characters who are just 'bad'—it's never that simple," he said.

In the 1980s, Demme's emotionally attuned, slightly skewed sensibilities would yield a 1940s-set romance (*Swing Shift*), a frisky concert doc (*Stop Making Sense*), and a yuppiefied screwball comedy (*Something Wild*). The director had accrued a following of critics and auteur-intrigued movie fans, none of whom had any idea what Demme might do next. "He was undefined," remembers Rick Nicita, Demme's agent for much of his career. "People couldn't quite figure him out." In 1988, Demme had his biggest commercial hit to date: *Married to the Mob*, starring Michelle Pfeiffer as an underestimated Mafia wife who falls for an FBI agent. On its surface, *Married to the Mob* was a colorful, tactfully zany confection. But once viewers got past Pfeiffer's overteased hair and *long-guy-land* accent, her character's desperation and loneliness became clear.

"There are dark parts to that movie," recalls Mike Medavoy, whose Orion Pictures had released *Married to the Mob*—and who sent a copy of *The Silence of the Lambs* to Demme soon after Hackman jumped ship. Even during his Corman years, when Demme had been making films aimed at the drive-in market, he'd never told a story as grim as the tale of Starling, Lecter, and Buffalo Bill. But many of the director's crowd pleasers had moments of sudden tension: In *Caged Heat*, a female inmate is forced to undergo a harrowing shock therapy treatment, and in *Something Wild*, a character is stabbed while looking directly into the camera, his face expressing a mix of pain, shock, and confusion.

Medavoy also knew that Demme was what he describes as "a visual guy," a director who could create a compelling look for a story that takes place across a series of stifling administrative offices, Bureau hallways, and prison cells. It also no doubt helped that Demme, who by then had directed four Academy Award–nominated performances, would be a draw for marquee actors who might otherwise recoil from *Silence*'s rough subject matter.

As it turned out, the director initially didn't want to *touch* Harris's book. "It wasn't the kind of thing that I find interesting," he said. "The idea of a film about a serial killer repels me." At the time, he and his producing partner, Ed Saxon, were looking for projects along the lines of *Married to the Mob*—crowd pleasers with a point. "We wanted to make movies that mattered," Saxon says. "Back then, if someone asked us what we were looking for, we'd say, 'Something that visualizes the humanity of disenfranchised people.' And a movie about a guy who skins people and a guy who eats people doesn't do that—unless you think cannibals are disenfranchised."

Despite his resistance, Demme eventually picked up Harris's book. After reading the first three pages of Harris's novel, all of which focus on Starling, he knew he wanted to make *The Silence of the Lambs* into a movie. "Ever since my days of working with Roger Corman, and perhaps before that, I've been a sucker for a woman's picture," he said. "A film with a woman protagonist at the forefront. A woman in jeopardy. A woman on a mission." He also noted, "I'm pulling for women. I've got enough estrogen in me to identify with women."

Demme's sudden enthusiasm for *The Silence of the Lambs* was also driven by his anxieties. "This country has a terrible mother lode of violence at its heart," he said. And though he had initially bristled at the idea of making a film about mass murder, he couldn't deny reality. "Serial killers exist," he said. "We actually have in our society men who go out and murder dozens of women—and is there anything being done about this problem?"

In January 1989, not long before Demme became involved with the film, Ted Bundy was executed in an electric chair. His death had been cheered by hundreds of celebrators outside the Florida State Prison—a reminder of Bundy's horrific crimes, and a sign of the public's bloodlust for revenge. *Red Dragon* and *The Silence of the Lambs* had bookended a decade that to many Americans felt besieged by violence. And by the time the 1980s were winding down, Demme felt a need to confront what he saw as a foul zeitgeist. "These aren't very funny times, are they?" he said. "Who's in the mood for laughing nowadays?"

When Tally learned that Demme was circling *The Silence of the Lambs*, he became "a little alarmed," he says. "I didn't know if he could pull off a scary movie." But during their first meeting, Demme told the screenwriter that he was committed to the story's more outré elements—and to Tally: "Jonathan said, 'Your life is going to change now. Nobody but you will ever work on this movie.'"

Tally may have been willing to join Demme for *The Silence of the Lambs*, but others weren't so sure. The director had hoped that the film would reunite him with Michelle Pfeiffer, but she was turned off by the fact that, by the script's conclusion, Hannibal Lecter has escaped to the outside world. "At the end of that film evil ruled out," she said. "I didn't want to put that out into the world." (Pfeiffer's agent also reportedly wanted $2 million for the role, which would have taken up a big chunk of the film's $19 million budget.) Demme then pursued the rising rom-com star Meg Ryan, who quickly declined, later saying that she had found the material to be "dangerous and a little ugly."

The director's next choice, *Blue Velvet*'s Laura Dern, hadn't yet headlined a film—but Demme wanted her nonetheless: "I said, 'This is the one.'" Executives at Orion disagreed, noting that Dern wasn't enough of a draw. So Demme kept looking. A new generation of young female stars had come of prominence in the late 1980s, and there were plenty of candidates. Some wound up on a list circulated by *Silence of the Lambs* casting director Howard Feuer. His suggestions for Clarice Starling included Madonna, Susan Sarandon, Joan Cusack, Frances McDormand, Julia Roberts, *Cheers* star Kirstie Alley, and *Manhunter*'s Joan Allen.

It's unclear if any of those performers were ever formally approached about the film. But one actor halfway down the list was *desperate* to be in *The Silence of the Lambs*. She was a recent Oscar winner, and a name even the most casual moviegoer would recognize. But whenever she was suggested to play Clarice Starling, Demme had the same response. "You know," he said, "I don't think Jodie Foster would be good in this part."

Though she was still in her twenties when she began pursuing *The Silence of the Lambs*, Foster was already a showbiz veteran. She'd been raised in Los Angeles, growing up with her single mom and three siblings in a house just a few blocks away from Hollywood Boulevard. Foster had landed her first role when she was three years old, appearing in a TV ad for Coppertone sun cream, and would spend the next several years starring in prime-time shows, Disney movies, and the occasional after-school special, such as 1974's *Rookie of the Year* (billed as "The story of a little girl with a lot of spunk—and talent for playing baseball"). She grew up on film and TV sets, which she treated like summer camp: a new adventure each time. "To me," she said, "eight months out of my life every year was spent getting up at the crack of dawn, eating shitty food and drinking shitty coffee and making things work."

In the mid-1970s, after playing a small role in Martin Scorsese's gentle widow's tale *Alice Doesn't Live Here Anymore*, Foster was approached for the director's follow-up: a violent urban nightmare called *Taxi Driver*, co-starring Robert De Niro. Scorsese wanted Foster to play Iris, a self-assured twelve-year-old prostitute working the streets of New York City, where she meets a disturbed Vietnam vet named Travis Bickle. Foster initially turned the part down: "I thought, 'What would my friends say?' I could just hear their little snickerings." But her mother, who was managing Foster's career, persuaded her to reconsider. Before filming began, Foster underwent a required psychiatric evaluation with the California Labor Board to ensure that she could handle *Taxi Driver*'s intensity. Foster passed; even though she wasn't yet a teen, she'd been around long enough to know that acting was all just pretend. "I was 12 years old," Foster said, "and had made more movies than anyone else on the film at that point."

Released in 1976, *Taxi Driver* was a violent shocker; it felt like a rageful response to the contagious despair brought on by the Vietnam War and Watergate. The movie earned Foster an Academy Award nomination, and in the years ahead, she graduated from kid-friendly films such as *Freaky Friday* to tougher, R-rated dramas, including the teen angst–ridden *Foxes* and the con artist tale *Carny*. She was drawn to characters who'd been ostracized—or perhaps had ostracized themselves. "Every acting part that I take is about redeeming somebody," she said. "Somebody that has been distrusted or disappointed, or somebody that's been shat upon, somebody that's been tortured. You sort of save them from being categorized easily or dismissed easily . . . it's like a mission or something."

Foster paused her acting career in 1980 to study literature at Yale University. One night toward the end of her freshman year, she returned to her dorm after a long study session and was greeted by a roommate yelling "Jodie, John Hinckley!" Foster knew the name; she'd received numerous admiring letters and even a few phone calls from Hinckley, a recluse who'd become obsessed with her. On March 30, 1981, in an apparent effort to impress the actor, Hinckley shot and wounded President Ronald Reagan, along with three others.

Foster met with the FBI and immediately became the subject of unwanted, and often terrifying, press attention. At one point, a photographer chased her down an icy street until she slipped and fell to the ground. As she sobbed in pain, her pursuer laughed and yelled "I got her! I got her!" as he kept taking photos.

Despite the scrutiny, Foster refused to leave school. When she returned to Hollywood, she starred in a series of well-intentioned but underwhelming dramas before discovering a screenplay titled *Witnesses*. Based on a true story, it follows a Massachusetts waitress who's sexually assaulted by three men in a bar—and who takes her assailants to court. It was tough material, and Foster's immediate response was understandably conflicted. As she told a reporter, she'd had two thoughts when she had read the script. The first was "Oh, yeah, this is what I've always wanted." The second was "Oh, no, this is what I've always wanted."

Despite her long-established skills and her Oscar nomination, Foster was asked to audition several times for the film—her first such tryouts in more than fifteen years—before landing the part. The production itself was rough: "I got very bruised in this movie," she said. But when the film was released in 1988 as *The Accused*, her tense performance, the best reviewed of her career thus far, became the movie's selling point. *The Accused* opened at number one at the box office, and a few months later, Foster won the Academy Award for Best Actress in a Leading Role. Within Hollywood, the Oscar for *The Accused* was seen as her comeback moment—despite her being only in her midtwenties.

In the months following her Oscar victory—"that year before you hand over your tiara," Foster said—she had the power to handpick her next projects. And the actor was determined to make *The Silence of the Lambs*. She had read the book, and after falling hard for Clarice—another in a long line of misunderstood characters—she tried to secure the book's film rights. Upon learning that they'd already been snapped up, she called Tally. "I'd never met her," the writer says. "She was campaigning for the part. She said, 'Maybe someday you'll write a great part for me.' I said, 'I think I already am.' And she said, 'I know you are.'"

Tally thought that Foster would be the ideal candidate to play Starling. So did Saxon. And so did Orion's Medavoy, who met with Foster in his Los Angeles office, where she gently pleaded her case. "There's nothing better than to have a really good actor want a part enough to push for it," the Orion executive says.

Demme, though, resisted all of those entreaties, for a simple reason: *I wouldn't believe Jodie Foster in that part*, he thought. For what it's worth, Foster wasn't too sold on him, either. "I was worried about Jonathan," she said. "I thought, '*Married to the Mob*—My God. He's going to grab onto the kitsch part. He's not going to respect Clarice.'"

The two had a meeting in which Foster explained to Demme what had drawn her to Harris's book in the first place. "There's are all these movies with men going in and saving a bunch of people and doing one thing or another," she told the director. "But this story is about one young woman trying desperately to save the life of another young woman. And in order to do that, she's faced with the overwhelming obstacle of all these men."

After Foster left, Demme thought, *I'm going to take that theme, and claim it—but I'm still not going to cast her*.

At Orion's urging, Demme had another sit-down with Foster. After they bade farewell, the director reflected on Foster's determination and realized that she was Demme's favorite kind of hero: a woman on a mission. "I thought about how much she loved that part," he said. "I fell madly in love with her." It had taken a while, but Demme had finally come to recognize the obvious: Jodie Foster *had* to be Clarice Starling. In August 1989, she was hired for the role, signing on for about $1.2 million—her first acting payday since winning the Oscar.

At the time Foster joined, Tally was still revising his script. Hackman's airborne flashbacks were gone, and Tally had also excised some of the novel's less cinematic moments, including a subplot involving Jack Crawford as he cares for his dying wife, as well as much of the backstory about Buffalo Bill. Along the way, he received pages of feedback from the film's creative team, often collected in lengthy script-note memos. In one missive, Saxon requested a change to what would become of Lecter's signature lines: "Let's say 'lima beans,'" he wrote. "No one knows what fava beans are!"

When reminded of his comment decades later, Saxon let out a long laugh. "Jonathan was a guy who was just fascinated by the margins," he says. "Occasionally, it could be distracting from the story, so it was often me trying to pull things toward the middle." His suggestion to remove the "fava beans" line—which remained in the film—was a "wonderfully idiotic example of why you always take what's good and leave the rest."

Tally worked on his screenplay in an office at the Writers Guild of America headquarters in midtown Manhattan, where he sat not far from Robert Benton, the two-time Oscar-winning screenwriter whose credits included *Bonnie and Clyde* and *Kramer vs. Kramer*. Like many others in the industry, Benton had read and loved *The Silence of the Lambs*. He didn't envy Tally's assignment. "I thought it would've been one of the hardest films to do in history," Benton says. The two met occasionally to talk shop, and at one point, Tally expressed his frustration that when all was said and done, the story he was telling came down to a woman in a basement with a madman—something moviegoers had seen countless times before. To which Benton replied, "That's the ending you've promised the audience—you *have* to do it."

While Tally worked on delivering his script in time for the film's fall start date, executives at Orion were scrambling to undo a knotty legal issue that dated back to the days of *Manhunter*. As part of the original film deal, Dino De Laurentiis had secured the rights to any *Red Dragon* characters that appeared in a sequel. That meant that Tally couldn't use the name "Dr. Hannibal Lecter." Instead, in early iterations of his *Silence* screenplay—and in some of the filmmakers' memos—Lecter was referred to as "Dr. Leopold Strang" or "Dr. Quinn." The studio eventually called Bookman, asking for help. "They said, 'We have a real problem here—nobody can come up with a better name than 'Hannibal Lecter,'" Bookman says.

Eventually, Bookman negotiated a modest deal between the studio and the impresario, allowing Orion the use of the *Red Dragon* characters for just one film. Afterward, De Laurentiis would once again control Harris's characters—a move that would lead to legal skirmishes down the road.

For now, though, the *Silence of the Lambs* team had the rights to Lecter. And by the end of 1989, the actor who would play Hannibal the Cannibal would be making a pilgrimage across America, heading toward the film's set. It was the latest destination in a long, often frustrating journey that had started many years and many thousands of miles before.

CHAPTER 13

"I USED TO FEEL LIKE A CLOSED FIST."

By the late 1980s, Anthony Hopkins figured that his Hollywood career was over. The Welsh-born actor had spent much of the decade living in the United States, where he split his time between the stage and the screen, building an utterly respectable career. He had played a compassionate doctor in David Lynch's *The Elephant Man*; a murderous ventriloquist in the cult thriller *Magic*; and the real-life convicted child murderer Bruno Hauptmann in the TV movie *The Lindbergh Kidnapping Case*, for which he had won his first Emmy (he'd get his second a few years later, for playing Adolf Hitler in *The Bunker*). Hopkins often inhabited madmen or sickos, yet he could locate flashes of pathos or longing in even the most despicable character. "You have to play an evil monster as a human being," he said.

Hopkins had seen plenty of banal maliciousness while growing up in post–World War II Europe, where he had felt stupid and useless, a self-described oddball whose teachers constantly reminded him of his failings. "Our education was hideous—a lot of corporal punishment," he said. "I was terrible in everything." As a teenager, he took inspiration from his local movie star, Richard Burton, the stage actor and then-ascendent Hollywood dynamo who lived near Hopkins in a working-class Welsh seaside town. At the age of fifteen, Hopkins knocked on Burton's front door to request an autograph, catching his hero in midshave ("I remember that stare, with his green eyes," Hopkins later said). Afterward, as the young boy was walking home, Burton and his wife cruised by in their Jaguar. "I wanted to become somebody like that," Hopkins said. "I just didn't want to be what I was."

He began performing a few years later, using the stage to work out his antisocial tendencies, which he could suppress for only so long. "I used to feel like a closed fist," Hopkins said. "I'd be angry at the audience and angry at other actors." He accumulated several screen and theater credits throughout the 1960s and 1970s; during that time, he also earned a reputation as a gifted but combative collaborator, prone to on-set outbursts and private drinking. One day in late 1975, he woke up in an Arizona hotel with no idea how he'd arrived there. He immediately swore off alcohol and found his rage subsiding as a result.

Newly focused, Hopkins steered himself toward movie stardom, saying yes to paycheck dreck such as the 1980 drama *A Change of Seasons*, which found him in the hot-tubbed embrace of Bo Derek—exactly the kind of film that soon soured him on Hollywood. By 1989, he'd returned to the United Kingdom to focus on TV and stage work. One day, while taking a break from a play, he caught a London screening of *Mississippi Burning*, the film that had driven Gene Hackman away from Hannibal Lecter. As the credits rolled, Hopkins felt a tinge of regret. All those years of working in Hollywood, yet he'd never gotten a chance to be part of a big, important, everyone's-gotta-see-it studio production. "That part of my life's over," he told himself. "I suppose I'll just have to settle for being a respectable actor poncing around the West End, and doing respectable BBC work for the rest of my life."

Not long afterward, he got a call from his agent, asking if he'd be interested in a project titled *The Silence of the Lambs*. His initial response was muted enthusiasm; he thought that it sounded like the title of a children's story. And besides, there was no firm offer on the table. Worried that he'd get too excited for a job that might never materialize, Hopkins initially skimmed Tally's script, which had so frightened the actor's wife that she couldn't even get through it. But after reconsidering and reading a few pages, he realized that *Silence* tapped into the sense of alluring fear that he'd felt as a child while watching *Snow White and the Seven Dwarfs*. "My favorite character was the witch," he said. "*She* was the interesting character to me. And I used to love watching Bela Lugosi in those *Dracula* movies."

Lecter was part of that long line of canny villains, and as Hopkins familiarized himself with Tally's script, the doctor began to take shape in his mind. "I somehow knew everything about this man," he said. "I'd see him in this halflight, in his oakwood office in Baltimore, dark hair slicked back, white shirt, black suit, beautifully manicured hands, black shiny shoes. A man with luminous eyes. Like a machine." His perception of Lecter was based in part on a stern acting instructor he'd once studied under—a man who "would just take you apart intellectually," Hopkins said. Even the word "Lecter," he realized, had a sense of rigid malice. "It sounds like a black, shiny ebony box," he said, "full of shiny silver instruments."

Hopkins's own name wasn't known to most American moviegoers, meaning that he'd have some high-profile competition for the role. "Every male in the business wanted to play that part," said Demme, who needed an actor who could differentiate the Hannibal of *The Silence of the Lambs* from the arch Hannibal that Brian Cox had played in *Manhunter*. Demme had admired Mann's film back in 1986 and decided to rewatch it before making *The Silence of the Lambs*. "I didn't get very far," he said. "I saw one Lecter scene, and I thought, 'Oh, my God. That's not *my* Dr. Lecter.'"

To help in the hunt for Demme's Lecter, Saxon had put together a casting memo in May 1989, naming seventy-five potential candidates for the character who, at that point, was still named "Dr. Quinn." The list was a wide-ranging, spitballing assortment of late-1980s male performers, including David Bowie, Harrison Ford, Robin Williams, Charles Grodin, Steve Martin, Tom Hanks, Jeremy Irons, Al Pacino, Bill Murray, and Warren Beatty. Demme was also apparently interested in an English stage actor named Edward Petherbridge, who'd starred in the original London production of *Rosencrantz and Guildenstern Are Dead*, and who was scheduled to discuss the part with the director in person in the summer of 1989.

It's unclear if that meeting ever happened. But according to Saxon, only two A-list stars were ever seriously considered for the Lecter role.

One was Sean Connery, the ex–James Bond whose good-guy persona Demme felt would make for a perversely compelling villain. The other was Jack Nicholson, who was *everybody's* go-to choice in the late 1980s, and who'd just starred in the summer blockbuster *Batman*. Either name would have greatly increased the film's box-office prospects—while also running up its relatively slim budget. But after Connery and Nicholson passed, Demme set his sights on Hopkins, whose intelligence and humanity had been well deployed in *The Elephant Man*.

"There's just something about him that makes you feel, 'Here's a man who's a lot smarter than you,'" the director said of Hopkins. "And that's fundamental to Lecter. This is someone who indeed is brighter than almost anybody else he ever encounters." Demme made the pitch directly to Hopkins when the two met in London, telling the actor that Lecter, despite his evil acts, was a smart and semidecent guy who just happened to be "trapped in an insane brain." As Hopkins later recalled, "I think he was right, because what Lecter is really—it's an old-fashioned word to use—but he's a gentleman. He has finesse. He's not Buffalo Bill. When he kills, it's fast and deadly."

Demme returned to America more convinced than ever that he'd found his Hannibal. "I'd like to think Tony got just the joke about Doctor Lecter that nobody, save Tom Harris, may have gotten," he said. Medavoy had pushed for Robert Duvall to get the part: "I said, 'I don't understand why you're doing it with a British guy,'" the executive recalls. But he and Demme reached a compromise, and by December of that year, Hopkins had officially signed on for the film, for which he'd receive $600,000.

The actor's original agreement included a "Conduct of Artist" clause, which stated that Hopkins would behave "in such a manner as to avoid offending any large and definable segment of the population." To the filmmakers, the idea that Hopkins's off-screen activity would somehow denigrate a film about a murderous cannibal was hilarious: "Love THIS—for Lecter??" Saxon scribbled next to the clause, which was later struck.

At ten a.m. on October 16, 1989, the cast and filmmakers assembled in Orion's offices in Manhattan, where they held the first run-through of Tally's script. "Table reads are weird, because you'll have one person who's mumbling and another person who's onstage at Carnegie Hall," recalls Saxon. "Tony was somewhere in between."

That was by design. Hopkins saw Lecter as calm, focused, *secure*. His many inspirations for Hannibal included a nightmare the actor had experienced for years. It found Hopkins answering a doorbell at his home— only to be greeted by the sight of a man standing under a streetlamp, gazing directly at him. Hopkins decided to adopt the man's blank expression. "If you stare at someone for more than 10 seconds, it scares them," he said. "I knew instinctively that I should be absolutely still." He also knew that there'd be expectations that he play Lecter as some sort of raving monster. So he took the opposite approach: *Play him nice.*

At the table read, Hopkins debuted Lecter's icy but melodious voice, for which he blended those of three chatty troublemakers: Truman Capote, the high-pitched author of *In Cold Blood*; HAL 9000, the menacingly even-tempered robot of Stanley Kubrick's *2001: A Space Odyssey*; and the Bryn Mawr–bred motormouth Katharine Hepburn. When combined, the trio's inflections amounted to what Hopkins described as "a cockamammy American accent." After trying out his voice in front of the *Silence of the Lambs* team, "I knew I had got them all," he said, "because there was this amazing silence at the end of my first speech, and Demme then let out a, 'My God, yehhh.'"

Not long after the New York meeting, Hopkins headed to Utah, where he was set to star in the thriller *Desperate Hours* alongside the on- and off-screen tough guy Mickey Rourke. The shoot was miserable, and after filming wrapped in December, Hopkins decided to decompress by hopping into a rented Pontiac and making the nearly two-thousand-mile drive from Salt Lake City to Pittsburgh, where *The Silence of the Lambs* would soon start filming. He wanted to see as much as he could of America, a country that had tempted and intrigued him for decades.

Over the next several days, he canvassed the country, listening to cassettes of Handel and Mozart. As he traveled, he tried to stay out of the sun; the *Silence of the Lambs* makeup team had asked him to arrive as pale as possible to help with his transformation into Lecter. And he did his best to achieve a Lecter-like litheness, sticking to a diet of fish and salad.

As Hopkins zipped from one state to the next, he was unknowingly tracing a map of recent American violence. He made a stop in Durango, Colorado, where a serial killer was suspected of being responsible for the recent deaths of two young men. From there, he headed toward Oklahoma City, the stomping ground of a still unknown murderer who'd targeted at least three women starting in the 1970s. And Hopkins would soon pass through Dallas, where three victims had recently been strangled to death by the same man. It seemed that each city Hopkins visited had its own gory history, its own homegrown monsters. They were further proof that the imaginary killer he was about to play had not been invented so much as been summoned up from the country's bloodstained terrain.

CHAPTER 14

"I JUST WANTED TO DROP HIM ON THE SPOT."

After agreeing to star in *Silence*, Hopkins had attempted to read a biography of Ted Bundy—only to quickly toss it aside out of disgust. *I don't need to know all that stuff*, he thought. *Don't want to.*

Some of his costars and colleagues, however, wanted to learn as much as possible about serial killers—and the men and women who pursued them. In the summer of 1989, Saxon wrote to the FBI's Office of Public Affairs, requesting permission to visit Quantico and meet with agents and teachers. He included a copy of Tally's *Silence* script and listed Demme's big-screen achievements. (Saxon also noted that *Silence* coproducer Kenneth Utt had worked years earlier on *The French Connection*, a film that surely had some fans within the Bureau.)

For Demme, the prospect of cozying up to the FBI, even in the name of research, was an uneasy one. "As soon as I started paying attention to how this country works," the director said, "I became very concerned about the FBI." Those concerns didn't diminish during the 1980s, as the Bureau endured heated criticism of its surveillance of private citizens, and as new revelations came to light about the Bureau's decades-old targeting of Dr. Martin Luther King Jr. "They are helpful to society in some ways, and are a menace to society in other ways," he said of the FBI. "They are the White House police force—what do you expect?"*

Foster understood Demme's reservations about the Bureau. "Some of the institutions they are there to protect, I don't much agree with," she said. And she had her own private (and no doubt complicated) relationship with the agency after its handling of the Hinckley case. But she didn't want *The Silence of the Lambs* to play as an anti-FBI screed. Before shooting began, she sat down with Demme to share a burger and discuss the film. Using a combination of persuasion and soft power, skills she'd mastered over her decades in Hollywood, she reminded the director that the movie couldn't afford to get mired in politics. "In all responsibility to women being victimized all over the world, you can't portray these FBI people as, 'Oh, those goofy Republicans,'" she told Demme. "If you want me to be your hero—want some member of the FBI to be your hero—and you want to believe in us, you've got to portray us in the correct way."

Members of the Bureau were equally nervous about how the FBI would be depicted in *The Silence of the Lambs*. Not long after Saxon sent a copy of the script to the Bureau for review, he received a multipoint memo from the Bureau's Office of Public Affairs. "We most definitely share your goal to produce a movie that is at the same time entertaining and authentic," wrote Milt Ahlerich, the office's assistant director.

That said, the FBI did have some notes. It contended that, as a student, Starling would *never* be sent to meet with the likes of Hannibal Lecter: "We may be over sensitive on this one point," Ahlerich noted, "but we believe that the FBI will look foolish assigning a trainee to a major case." In a follow-up letter, he expressed hope that *The Silence of the Lambs*—with its kidnapping and cannibalism—could be "a PG rather than an R rated film."

Many of the changes the Bureau requested could be easily navigated

---

* Demme's FBI comments were made during a January 1991 press conference for *The Silence of the Lambs*. His criticisms of the bureau were later marked for removal from the event's official transcript, and got little coverage at the time.

or outright ignored. The FBI needed the filmmakers as much as the filmmakers needed the FBI. Harris's novels had raised the public's awareness of the once obscure Behavioral Science Unit—and, in doing so, helped burnish the BSU's reputation. A film version of *The Silence of the Lambs*, especially one featuring an Oscar-winning star such as Foster, could be a monumental public relations win for the Bureau, in much the same way that the 1986 hit *Top Gun* had boosted the visibility of the US Navy. As the memo from the FBI's Office of Public Affairs noted, *The Silence of the Lambs* had the potential to "show the American public that violent crimes such as serial murders are seriously being addressed."

The FBI ultimately pledged to collaborate, even granting Demme permission to shoot on location at Quantico. In October 1989, several members of the film's creative team arrived at the FBI Academy, including production designer Kristi Zea. Though she'd collaborated happily with Demme on *Married to the Mob*, Zea at first wanted nothing to do with *The Silence of the Lambs*. "I was appalled by the script," she recalls. "In a way, Hannibal was glorified. His whole demeanor was so intoxicating—he was like a spider to a fly. I told Jonathan, 'I don't want copycat crazies imitating these murderers. I don't want to be responsible for that kind of inspiration.'"

But she trusted Demme, which was how she found herself wandering the sterile offices and classrooms of the FBI Academy, marveling at their blandness: "I said to Jonathan, 'We can't use this—it's the most boring place I've ever seen.' And he said, 'That's the point.'" The antiseptic environment of Quantico, where violence existed only in the abstract, as a training tool, would be a striking contrast to the grisly, real-world crime scenes depicted in *The Silence of the Lambs*.

At one point, Zea and Demme visited Douglas in his Behavioral Science Center office, located in a windowless former bomb shelter sixty feet below ground. "It was very tight quarters, and it was all cinder block, with no windows," Zea says. "I was already beginning to feel claustrophobic when I walked into his office, which was ridiculously small. On the walls was a case that he was working on, so there were pinned-up pictures of dead bodies. And I realized that I had to get out of the room."

Demme, though, would wind up spending several days in Douglas's office. The agent had been tapped as a sort of serial killer *consigliere* for the filmmakers—an assignment that initially didn't thrill him. "When I heard they were coming down, my attitude was 'Okay, they want to learn about this stuff—they're going to have to see it,'" he says. "I wasn't going to let them Hollywood-ize this, like it was some joke."

But he quickly realized that Demme and Saxon's interest in his work was genuine. As a result, he says, "I opened everything up." He told his guests about his time interviewing murderers such as Richard Speck, a Chicago-area drifter who'd killed eight student nurses in one night in 1966. Douglas also handed over shocking photos of some of Ed Gein's gory creations, most likely the same images Harris had seen when he'd visited Quantico a few years earlier. The agent even offered his own succinct analysis of how Lecter approaches the world. "He's incarcerated," he told the filmmakers, "but his mind is free."

Saxon and Demme would make more than a half-dozen trips to Quantico during the course of making *The Silence of the Lambs*. The director may have been wary of the FBI, but his time with Douglas, as well as with several other agents, altered his perception of the Bureau. "I don't have mixed feelings about the Behavioral Science Unit," he said. "They're fantastic."

Not everyone walked away from the BSU offices feeling quite as optimistic. Prior to filming, Douglas also spent a few days with the man who'd be playing his on-screen doppelganger: Scott Glenn, the intense character actor who'd recently been cast as Starling's paternal (and sometimes patronizing) FBI boss, Jack Crawford. Glenn had known Demme since the early 1970s, when the actor had starred as a heroic biker in the Demme-produced *Angels Hard as They Come*. In the years since, he had portrayed a series of bad dudes—some good-bad, some just *bad*-bad— in films such as *Urban Cowboy* and *The Right Stuff*. Off-screen, he was a tough figure in his own right, having survived a series of physical and emotional endurance tests: He'd served in the Marine Corps, worked on the set of the chaotic *Apocalypse Now*, and been friends with Miles Davis. He wasn't the type who'd get rattled easily.

Glenn was introduced to Douglas at Quantico where he talked to the agent in his office, surrounded by crime-scene photos. "After I'd been there for a few days, I said, 'Thank you for letting me become part of your world,'" the actor recalled. "And he said, 'You're not really a part of my world. You want to *really* become a part of my world?'"

Glenn accepted the challenge, and Douglas gave him some audiotapes the agent had used for his classes at Quantico. They had been made by the convicted murderers Lawrence Bittaker and Roy Norris, who'd kidnapped, tortured, and killed five young women in southern California in 1979. While their victims were still alive, Bittaker and Norris had recorded the sounds of their suffering. After listening to those terrible noises for a few minutes, Glenn turned off the tape player and marched toward Douglas, who was waiting for him in a hallway. The actor was enraged. "I just wanted to drop him on the spot, you know," he recalled. "He said, 'Now you're part of my world.'"

Douglas claimed that he hadn't been trying to provoke the actor. Instead, the longtime BSU agent, just a few years removed from the stress-induced coma that had nearly killed him, wanted Glenn to understand what it was like not only to encounter violent crime but to actually *live* with it nonstop. "It is not the kind of work you can shut down at the end of the day," Douglas said. The combination of stress and excitement felt by many Bureau employees was encapsulated by a series of signs nailed to a tree at the Quantico training grounds. They'd later appear in the opening moments of *The Silence of the Lambs*, as if to warn viewers what lay ahead: HURT, AGONY, PAIN, LOVE IT, PRIDE.

Though several members of *The Silence of the Lambs'* cast and crew would end up passing through Quantico, it was Foster who received the most attention when she showed up for a multiday training session in November 1989. The actor did her best to avoid being noticed—"dressing way down, keeping completely low key," she said—but it was hard for the star of such hits as *Freaky Friday* to blend in easily. Students couldn't help but notice her when she joined their classes—and sometimes couldn't resist approaching her. At one point, while she was dining in the Quantico cafeteria, she was asked to sign another diner's tray.

Foster didn't have much time to give autographs. Her Quantico itinerary, which had been planned out carefully by the Bureau, was intense. On her first day, she was scheduled to attend a new-trainee class called "Kidnapping Practice," observe a lesson about court procedure, and meet with Douglas. Day two would be far more taxing. According to the actor's all-caps itinerary, she endured a fast-moving gauntlet of tasks:

*FIREARMS AND DEFENSIVE TACTICS

*TRAINING ON THE OBSTACLE COURSE

GYM SESSION: "BULL IN THE RING"

*PRACTICE FUNWORK—DRAWING WEAPON, SPEED-LOADING, DROP-AND-ROLL OVER

*WORK WITH OTHER INSTRUCTORS ON PHYSICAL MOVES

When she wasn't working on her FBI-approved "physical moves," Foster spent some of time at Quantico—both before and during the filming of *The Silence of the Lambs*—meeting with female agents and trainees. That included Varounis, who ran into Foster on the FBI gun range, and who served as an unofficial consultant for the filmmakers while they were at Quantico: During a dinner with Demme and the producers, Varounis opened the conversation by asking: "So, guys—what propaganda has the FBI fed you all day? What kind of crap have you been looking at?"

Foster also had a series of conversations with Mary Ann Krauss, a special agent who had a long history with the FBI. Krauss's mother had worked for the Bureau during World War II ("She would never tell me what

---

* A defensive exercise used by the bureau for many years, "Bull in the Ring" requires a trainee to don boxing gloves and stand in place as a series of opponents approach to trade blows. As one FBI instructor told trainees before a session in 2006: "We're classmates, pals and friends. But for the next hour, we're not . . . it's going to hurt."

she did," Krauss says). And while growing up in Meridian, Mississippi, a state where the Bureau had had many agents stationed during the civil rights era, she had known several FBI employees. "Everything about the Bureau appealed to me," she says. "I enjoyed Nancy Drew mysteries when I was a kid. And I was never one to play with dolls—I was a tomboy."

Krauss got her start with the Bureau in 1980, working as a Spanish-speaking tour guide at FBI headquarters. She became a special agent in 1986, and by the end of the decade, she had handled surveillance investigations, undercover work, kidnappings, robberies, murders, and more. She'd also been involved in a couple of serial killer cases. Along the way, Krauss had learned to keep her emotions in check. "I always tried to impart to women 'Hey, don't be crying in front of people—they don't want to see it,'" she says. "At the Bureau, there was not much room for tears. You had to suck it up so you could work the case and deal with it later on."

In 1989, as the *Silence of the Lambs* movie was coming together, Krauss's higher-ups tapped her to work on the film, telling her it would be "a positive recruitment tool" for the Bureau. Krauss was selected in part because she was near Foster's age. But the agent also had a few things in common with Clarice Starling. Both women spoke with a discernible twang, both had rural backgrounds, and both had lived around lambs as children. "We spent months grooming and caring for these animals," Krauss says, "and couldn't help but become close to them."

She was given a copy of the script and asked to contribute feedback. Later, she found herself dining with Demme and Foster. "They wanted me to draw a picture for her of my work life and what made me interested in the Bureau," she says. The two women met several times at Quantico, often talking shop: Krauss told Foster about the effects of water on a corpse and let the actor handle her revolver, which the star "treated like a prize," Krauss says. And while Krauss was a bit guarded around Foster—"Headquarters had told me to be careful," she remembers—their conversations occasionally got personal: "Jodie asked, 'Are these guys chauvinist? Or do you feel like you're included as a female?' And I told her, 'I feel like one of the guys. If they talk trash, I just enjoy it and go on—I don't take objection.'"

During their talks, Krauss was impressed by Foster's smarts and seriousness. "She wasn't one to be overexuberant—and that's what they always train us to be: 'Don't get excited to the point you look silly,'" she recalls. "I told her, 'You could be a great agent.' And she said, 'Yeah, but then I'd be here every day—and I like to take time off.'"

Though the FBI had given its blessing—and opened its doors—to Demme and his cast, the filmmakers weren't going to get much assistance from Harris. The author's resistance toward Hollywood apparently hadn't lessened since the days of *Manhunter*. Demme did his best to get Harris involved: Before production began, he called the writer and told him that when shooting was finished, he was welcome to give notes on the first cut—"because he'd be likely to be the toughest critic," the director said.

But Harris wasn't interested. "Don't take this the wrong way," the author said, "I'm glad you're making the movie, but I'll probably never see it." He told Demme about an interview he'd read with the author John le Carré, the creator of a famously unassuming spy named George Smiley. After Alec Guinness had begun playing Smiley in the late 1970s, le Carré could no longer write about Smiley without thinking of the on-screen version. In effect, the character had been stolen from him. And Harris didn't want the same thing to happen with Lecter. He knew he might lose control of the cannibal—especially, Demme noted, "in the hands of someone like Anthony Hopkins."

There was another reason Harris didn't want to get involved with a film version of *The Silence of the Lambs*: The experience with *Manhunter*, he would later admit, had left him "sort of down on the movies." Still, he liked Demme and didn't want to shut the door on their relationship altogether. In the summer of 1989, he sent the director a fax from Sag Harbor: "Good luck with *The Silence of the Lambs*."

At that point, the book's recently published paperback edition was on the *New York Times* bestseller list, further stoking excitement for a big-screen version. But to no one's surprise, Harris didn't publicly celebrate the success of the book. One of the few purported sightings of the author in the late 1980s took place at a party in a Beverly Hills bookstore. The shop's owner, spotting Harris in the wild, quickly ducked into a storeroom and grabbed some novels for the author to sign. It couldn't have been more than a minute or two before the excited owner returned to the floor, books in hand.

By then Harris had already disappeared.

CHAPTER 15

"DR. LECTER IS IN ACTION."

In late 1989, the *Silence of the Lambs* team arrived in Pittsburgh, where they tried to stay as far from sight as possible. The film had already attracted plenty of press attention—it was, after all, a pedigreed adaptation of a best-selling book—and Demme demanded a closed set. With few exceptions, no reporters or photographers would be allowed at Keystone Commons, the industrial park that would double as the film's bustling HQ.

Built on the site of a recently closed Westinghouse Electric Corporation plant, where workers had spent years building train-sized electrical generators, Keystone Commons was spacious, versatile, and relatively isolated. It would serve as the home of *The Silence of the Lambs*' most elaborate sets, including Lecter's quarters at the Baltimore State Hospital for the Criminally Insane. Unlike *Manhunter*, which had found Lecter dwelling in a spotless cell in a pristine modernist building, *The Silence of the Lambs* would send the doctor to a dingy, subterranean room far from view. "I figured they'd put Lecter in the basement of some place as dismal and weird as possible," recalls production designer Kristi Zea, whose research for *The Silence of the Lambs* found her examining photos of old jails, including the facilities used to house defendants during the Nuremberg trials of the 1940s.

But designing Lecter's cell would require some modern innovations. The protective measures described in Harris's novels, which have the doctor behind a wall of bars and a layer of nylon netting, wouldn't work on-screen, as they'd obstruct Lecter from view. Zea tested a variety of designs for Lecter's cell, but none worked; no matter how far apart the bars were spaced, they always got into the way.

After some trial and error, Zea took inspiration from the transparent walls she'd spotted at New York City liquor stores. "They put plexiglass everywhere," she says, "so you could see all the liquor bottles, but you couldn't get to it. You had to put your money through the slot." Zea decided to use a series of see-through panels, made of one-inch plexiglass, for the outward-facing wall of Lecter's cell. She then added holes along the top and bottom so the doctor could carry on conversations—an idea suggested, she says, by the safety partitions employed by taxicab drivers.

Placing Lecter behind glass wouldn't just make him easier to see; it would give moviegoers an almost subliminal sense of his unique status, and reinforce the idea that Lecter was a very different kind of killer. "Everyone else in the institution would have bars," says Zea. "But this guy would be like a bug—a *specimen*." And unlike in *Manhunter*, where the doctor had been presented under bright lights, he'd dwell in a shadowy cell lit by cinematographer Tak Fujimoto, a veteran of several Demme productions. "I don't think we've ever been Gee-Whiz kind of boys," Fujimoto said of his and Demme's visual approach. "We've always tried to put the goods before the audience and just show it to them without being overly dramatic." In *The Silence of the Lambs*, Lecter would appear to viewers the same way he might have appeared to hospital staffers: as a murky figure who seems to blend into the darkness.

Lecter's lair was ready and waiting for Hopkins when he arrived on the *Silence of the Lambs* set in Pittsburgh in early 1990. The actor would shoot the majority of his scenes in a little more than a month, including the moment Lecter first meets Starling.[*] That was the film's make-or-break

---

[*] Though Lecter's cell was created on a set at Keystone Commons, two other Pittsburgh-area locations were used for the sequences set at the Baltimore State Hospital for the Criminally Insane: The hospital's exteriors were shot

sequence, one that would take place about twelve minutes into the movie. By that point, viewers would have already heard a series of on-screen warnings and legends about the dreaded "Hannibal the Cannibal." If Hopkins could connect with audiences from the get-go, he knew, they'd stay with him for the rest of the film. "It's like Bogart in *Casablanca*," he said. "Everybody talks about Rick for so long that when he finally appears, you believe everything they've told you about him." But if Lecter didn't live up to the audience's anxious expectations—if he didn't ooze the perfect cocktail of charisma and cunning—the rest of the movie could be a slog (or worse, a joke).

As Demme staged Lecter's first scene, he asked Hopkins how the actor wanted the character to be introduced—not just to Starling but to millions of moviegoers. "Jonathan said, 'Would you like to be lying on the bed or sitting in a chair, writing or drawing or reading?'" the actor recalled. "I said, 'I'd like to be seen standing upright at attention in the middle of the cell.'"

Demme agreed to run a quick camera test to see if Hopkins's idea worked. The results thrilled the director, who wound up using the setup for Hannibal the Cannibal's first appearance in the movie. As Starling approaches Lecter's cell, she finds him gazing directly at her with a semi-pleasant grin and an unwavering stare. "I know what scares people," the actor said, "and I believe that stillness is the key."

For viewers, the effect of seeing Lecter for the first time was one of serene eeriness. It was as though Hopkins had conjured up his recurring nightmare about the strange man under the streetlight—and then delivered it straight to the audience's collective unconscious. "I want them to see a very nice, charming, erudite, smiling man saying 'Good morning'—which would be terrifying," the actor said. (The character's introductory scene could have been even more eerie: During preproduction, Hopkins

at Western Center, a facility for mentally ill and disabled patients. And the facility's hallways were filmed at the Allegheny County Jail.

tested a pair of lenses that would have given him Lecter's maroon-colored eyes, but the effect was abandoned before filming began.)

Throughout *The Silence of the Lambs*, Lecter presents a sort of chilling blankness—one that's accentuated by his wardrobe. For the initial scenes of Hannibal the Cannibal in captivity, he wears a blue jumpsuit that stands out, just barely, against his earth-toned, rock-fortified cell. The look was courtesy of the film's costume designer, Colleen Atwood, who just a few years earlier had created Lecter's getup in *Manhunter*—a fact she hadn't volunteered to Demme when she was brought on for *The Silence of the Lambs*. "Jonathan didn't know me that well," Atwood later said, "but I found out he really did not want to hire the crew from *Manhunter* to do *Silence of the Lambs*. He hired me, then the producer looked at my credentials rolling his eyes saying, 'Oh my god, she did *Manhunter*.' The whole movie I was saying to myself, 'I haven't told Jonathan.'"

Atwood created Lecter's distinct looks in *The Silence of the Lambs*, including a grubby straitjacket, as well as an all-white ensemble that inevitably gets splattered with blood (not Lecter's own, of course). In each of his on-screen appearances, Lecter had to look "super precise," Atwood noted. "There was nothing that was wrinkled, it was totally under his control."

But Lecter's most memorable accoutrement in *The Silence of the Lambs* is the protective mask he dons for trips outside the asylum. In Harris's novel, Hannibal's face guard is described as a simple hockey mask. ("It was as effective as a mouthpiece," the author wrote, "and not so wet for the orderlies to handle.") Hopkins tried out a variety of athletic head coverings, including a fencing mask, before a member of Atwood's team reached out to Ed Cubberly, a New Jersey–based intensive care nurse who designed NHL goalie masks in his spare time. Cubberly had no connection to the film business, and had never heard of *The Silence of the Lambs*. But a member of the film's prop department team had tracked him down, to see if he'd be interested in taking a stab at creating Lecter's mask. When told that Lecter liked to eat people, Cubberly replied, "So, you want me to make you a muzzle?"

Cubberly began looking at photos of retro fiberglass goalie masks he'd built and quickly sketched a design for a covering that would obscure the lower half of Lecter's face, leaving his eyes exposed. He added bars over the mouth—"to make it look mean," he said—and constructed a raw-looking, greenish brown plexiglass prototype. The mask took about two days to design and produce, and when Cubberly handed it over to the filmmakers, he suggested that they not paint it. Lecter's mask may have been ugly, but it looked exactly like something you'd find in a subterranean cell.

Cubberly's mean-looking creation would appear briefly but unforgettably in the film. During the search for Buffalo Bill, Lecter has a grotesque face-off with Ruth Martin, the posh and powerful southern senator whose daughter has been kidnapped by Buffalo Bill. To play Martin, Demme had turned to the veteran actor Diane Baker, whose big-screen career included such films as Alfred Hitchcock's out-there 1964 thriller *Marnie*, and the lively 1965 noir mystery *Mirage*.

Baker had known Hopkins for years, their paths having crossed at various times in London and Los Angeles. The two would be reunited for a tense scene set in an airplane hangar in Memphis. Lecter has agreed to give the senator information that might lead to the rescue of his daughter. But he can't resist toying with her.

> **LECTER:** Tell me, Senator: Did you nurse Catherine yourself?
> **SENATOR MARTIN:** What?
> **LECTER:** Did you breastfeed her?
> **SENATOR MARTIN:** Yes, I did.
> **LECTER:** Toughened your nipples, didn't it? Amputate a man's leg, and he can still feel it tickling. Tell me, Mom: When your little girl is on the slab, where will it tickle *you*?
> **SENATOR MARTIN:** Take this . . . *thing* back to Baltimore!

When Baker arrived on set and witnessed Hopkins in his full Lecter getup, which included not just his mask but also his dirty straitjacket and orange jumpsuit, she was taken aback. "It was appalling to see him and hear the words come out of his mouth, because you couldn't see his lips," she recalls. "It was terrifying." Perhaps as a result, their initial attempt at playing the scene found both actors operating at a high pitch: "He made it more disgusting, and I reacted with more disgust, and we got it out of our system. Jonathan walks right over to me and whispers, 'Okay, that take is history—now do it again.' And Anthony and I realized that he wanted [our performances] to be more internal and not crazy."

The final version of the scene would be more restrained but no less intense, with the senator trying to keep her rage at bay while Lecter, who hasn't had fun like this in *years*, tortures her with a series of lies and taunts. Their exchange ends with Lecter's cruel kiss-off: "Oh, and Senator, just one more thing," he coos. "*Love* your suit."

When Hopkins wasn't creeping out his costars on the set of *The Silence of the Lambs*, the actor spent his downtime consulting his script, which he'd annotated with illustrations of Lecter (one drawing featured Hannibal in a prison suit, alongside a scribbled description from Hopkins: "As fit and fierce as a caged panther"). Hopkins also enjoyed what would turn out to be his last blast of anonymity. He could sometimes be found dining alone at a Pittsburgh restaurant, lost in an Edith Wharton novel. Few passersby recognized him, and those who did occasionally confused him with *another* on-screen psycho: "Aren't you—or weren't you—Tony Perkins?" one admirer asked him.

Even when Hopkins was back at Keystone Commons, the actor was very much in his own world. Though he did joke around with the crew— at one point doing an impersonation of Rocky Balboa while dressed in full blood-spattered Lecter gear—he rarely socialized with his colleagues. "You finish your job at the end of the day, and go your way," he explained. He likely wouldn't have had much time to hang out anyway: Because Lecter was such a solitary character, often stuck behind a cell or a mask, Hopkins interacted on-screen with just a handful of other actors. One of them was Anthony Heald, who played *The Silence of the Lambs*' slippery Dr. Frederick Chilton, the mental hospital administrator who makes a fumbled pass at Starling—and who sees Lecter not as a patient to be observed but as an asset to be exploited. Chilton is a delightfully despicable bad guy, the kind of hiss-worthy snoot whose preening ambition only makes Lecter seem all the more likable.

At the time he was approached for *The Silence of the Lambs*, in the summer of 1989, Heald was a fortysomething stage star who'd just earned a Tony nomination for his role in the musical *Anything Goes*. "I was kind of a hot property in New York theater," he recalls. "But in terms of film and television, I'd never had major billing." Demme was a fan of the actor and asked him to meet to discuss *The Silence of the Lambs*. Heald hadn't read the book, so he picked up a copy in a drugstore and tore through it in one night. During his talk with Demme, he pitched himself as Chilton: "I said, 'I always play these lovable nerds, and I think it'd be interesting to have a tension between the nerd quality and the sleaze element.'"

Demme demurred, telling Heald that he was considering an older actor to play Chilton. It's also possible that he wanted the doctor to be played by a more recognizable face; early casting wish lists for the film included such potential Chiltons as Rick Moranis, *Saturday Night Live*'s Phil Hartman, director David Cronenberg, and disgraced Watergate player G. Gordon Liddy. But after an early script meeting—one held before Hopkins was cast—Heald had impressed Demme by reading Lecter's part with Foster. Not long afterward, he was cast as the detestable Dr. Chilton.

Heald would spend his time in Pittsburgh working with both Foster and Hopkins. Chilton treats both of their characters with a sort of impatient prickliness, and early on during filming, Demme had given the actor some guidance about Chilton's state of mind: "He leaned in and said, 'You're desperate to go to the bathroom,'" Heald recalls. As much as he enjoyed his time on the set, Heald was convinced that playing Dr. Chilton—at that point his biggest on-screen role—wasn't going to do much for his film career. "I was so convinced this was going to be a flop," he says. "Just *convinced*. Every time I watched the dailies, I thought, 'What are you doing?'"

Heald was thrown by the number of close-ups Demme was employing for the film—shots that were so head-on that the actors appeared to be speaking directly to viewers. It was a technique Demme had noticed in several Alfred Hitchcock films, including *Psycho*, which ends with the killer Norman Bates grinning madly at the audience. Demme and cinematographer Fujimoto had experimented with this intimate (but potentially off-putting) style on *Something Wild* and *Married to the Mob*. They'd embrace it fully while shooting *The Silence of the Lambs*. As Demme noticed, the close-ups conveyed the intimacy between "two people, fighting their way into each others heads."

Hopkins and Foster shot many of their scenes together from a distance—physically and emotionally. "He would do a whole day inside the prison cell, and they wouldn't let him out," Foster recalled. "We'd just do his side. And then the next day, we'd do my side." She added, "When you literally almost never see your partner except behind glass, it just creates this very strange atmosphere on set."

Demme's unusual approach to the asylum scenes was initially a cause of concern for producer Ed Saxon. Throughout filming, members of the film's creative team would often meet at night at Pittsburgh's Westin William Penn Hotel, which served as *The Silence of the Lambs'* headquarters. A projector was set up in a makeshift screening room so the filmmakers could review the previous day's footage. After spending one session watching countless close-up takes of Lecter talking in his cell, Saxon walked away feeling "totally depressed," he says. "I thought, 'This is just Little Red Riding Hood: *I'm going to eat you, little girl.*' It was a reasonable insight into what was going on. But it was also totally wrong when it came to the quality of the work. When you're in the middle of it, you just don't know."

In addition to their moments together at Lecter's cell, Hopkins and Foster would be brought closer—briefly but memorably—for a sequence filmed inside a cavernous space at Pittsburgh's Soldiers & Sailors Memorial Hall. It was a stately, decades-old building that, for *The Silence of the Lambs*, would be converted into the Memphis courthouse serving as Lecter's temporary home. As he awaits transportation back to his asylum, Lecter sits inside what Demme described as "a giant birdcage"—a steel cell plopped in the middle of the room, giving him a 360-degree view of his surroundings. That's where he's waiting when Starling comes to visit him one last time. By that point in the film, she's closer than ever in her search for Buffalo Bill. But she still needs Lecter's advice.

At first, the doctor taunts his guest's persistence. "People will say we're in love," Lecter purrs. He quickly returns to their quid pro quo arrangement, extracting more painful personal memories from the FBI trainee. Before they part, Lecter pays Starling a respectful farewell—"Brave Clarice. You will let me know when those lambs stop screaming, won't you?"—and hands the agent some of her FBI case files. As the papers pass between them, Lecter touches Clarice's forefinger with his own—the first moment of physical connection between the two isolated, yet deeply intertwined, characters. "It's almost a shock to the audience when they actually touch," Tally noted. "But I think you approach these scenes exactly as if you were writing a sort of courtship between two lovers."

That exchange would prove to be a rare moment of vulnerability in the film. Once Starling is safely away from the Memphis courthouse, Lecter finally makes a daring escape from his cell. After ordering a dinner of extra-rare lamb chops, he uses a homemade key fashioned from a stolen pen to break free of his handcuffs before attacking the two officers left to guard him. One victim is bitten on the cheek, slammed against the cell walls, and maced in the eyes; the other is beaten repeatedly with a police baton, his blood spurting elegantly over Lecter's white prisoner uniform. "After all that passivity," Demme noted of the scene, "Dr. Lecter is in action."

Following that initial burst of violence, Lecter calmly cues up a recording of Bach's *Goldberg Variations*. Then he *really* gets to work. Using one victim's pocket knife, he carves off the face of one officer, which he'll use to disguise himself. And he disembowels the other, draping the man's corpse on the outside walls of his cell and arranging the body so it looks like an angel (complete with a red, white, and blue banner as "wings"). The resulting tableau, which Tally had described in his script as a "brief snapshot from hell," was inspired by the macabre paintings of the English artist Francis Bacon, as well as by some nauseating photos that production designer Kristi Zea had found, including shots of splayed beef carcasses. When Zea's research material for *The Silence of the Lambs* was later sent to the American Museum of the Moving Image, a museum employee cataloging the images became physically ill.

But as vivid as Lecter's on-screen destruction might have seemed, Demme actually doesn't linger on it for long. Instead, he allows viewers' imaginations to do most of the work. "We wanted to show [the bloodshed] at a great distance," he explained, "so that you could get the totality of it without having to have your nose right in the gory specifics."

Lecter's escape from the "birdcage" was one of the last sequences Hopkins would film in Pittsburgh in early 1990. Much of the remaining action would focus on Foster. Though their characters forge a perverse bond in *The Silence of the Lambs*, the actors themselves had spent barely any time together. That was the result of the production logistics, as well as a mutual sense of intimidation. Foster had been nervous around Hopkins ever since he had transformed into Lecter during their initial script read-through. "He brought that voice out, and I kind of got scared of him," she said. Hopkins, meanwhile, had been daunted by Foster's pedigree. "I was scared to speak to [her],' the actor recalled. "I thought, 'She just won an Oscar.'"

That shared unease continued until Hopkins's final day on the Pittsburgh set. "I was eating a tuna fish sandwich," Foster said. "And he sidled up to me, and I had a sort of tear in my eye. I was like 'I was really scared of you!' And he said, 'I was scared of you!'"

Afterward, the two hugged. But while Hopkins would soon have some time away from the world of *The Silence of the Lambs*, Foster would spend much of her remaining weeks chasing down the film's lead villain—a bad guy so sadistic that he makes Lecter look mild by comparison.

CHAPTER 16

"THAT WILL MAKE YOU FUCKING CRAZY."

In Harris's *Silence of the Lambs* novel, the author noted that Jame Gumb—the skin-carving murderer whom the police have dubbed "Buffalo Bill"—is a "white male, thirty-four, six feet one inch, 205 pounds, brown and blue eyes, no distinguishing marks." Judging by some of the actors who appeared on an early casting memo, the filmmakers felt they could adjust that description a bit. Among the names lobbed about to play Gumb were Charles Grodin—who'd also been ID'd as a possible Lecter—as well as Art Garfunkel, Nicolas Cage, Daniel Day-Lewis, Alec Baldwin, and the fitness expert Richard Simmons. It was a wild list of possibilities, and proof that the casting of Buffalo Bill could go in just about any imaginable direction.

One of the lesser known performers on the list was Ted Levine, a stage and TV actor then in his early thirties. Levine was a self-described "rocking hillbilly Jew" who'd spent several years working in Chicago theater, where he'd gotten to know William Petersen. In 1985, while hanging around Miami, he had used Petersen's name to talk his way into the wrap party for *Manhunter*—another odd connection between the two films. Levine's act of cocky ingenuity apparently impressed Michael Mann. The two got to know each other, with Mann eventually casting Levine as an eccentric Mob henchman in the prime-time series *Crime Story*, which debuted in 1986 and lasted for just two seasons.

In the years after that show went off the air, Levine appeared in such dramas as 1988's *Betrayed*, in which he played a hot-headed white supremacist, before being offered the role of Gumb. The actor became fixated on Jame Gumb, a violent loner whose background and methodology are explored in deeper detail in the novel than in the script: Abandoned by his mother, an alcoholic wannabe-beauty queen, Gumb endures a pained adolescence in foster care before ultimately murdering his grandparents. In his later years, he develops a growing obsession with moths and butterflies—and, as Buffalo Bill, begins hunting women he can kill and flay. "Billy thinks he wants to change," Lecter tells Starling in Harris's book. "He's making himself a girl suit out of real girls. Hence the large victims—he has to have things that fit."

Levine read the passages about Gumb closely; maybe *too* closely. "I drove myself nuts with this character," he recalled. "I lived with this son of a bitch." Before filming, he met with John Douglas at the FBI, watched videotapes of crime scenes, and studied the life of a convicted murderer named Jerry Brudos, a necrophiliac who had killed a series of young women in Oregon in the late 1960s and who had a compulsion to wear women's clothing. Levine's research occasionally went to distressing extremes. "Something that is very consistent with serial killers is they look at a lot of pornography, and I did that too," he said. "That will make you fucking crazy."

In Harris's novel, Gumb's goal is to change genders, though Lecter repeatedly warns Starling not to get lost trying to categorize the killer: "He's not a transexual, Clarice. He just thinks he is, and he's puzzled and angry because they won't help him."

Levine felt the same way. "Male sexuality is a complicated thing, and goes all kinds of different directions," he said of Gumb in the early 2000s. "I met with female impersonators. I went to some very interesting bars looking and talking to people about a side of life that I'm not familiar with. And I came to the conclusion that none of that had anything really to do with [Buffalo Bill]."

Ultimately, the actor saw Jame Gumb (and Buffalo Bill) as "an old glitter rocker," Levine said, "like Iggy Pop if he hadn't become Iggy Pop, or David Bowie hadn't become David Bowie. Here's a guy who imagines himself with this kind of feminine power, you know, this spiritual kind of mother power."

In Demme's version of *The Silence of the Lambs*, Buffalo Bill doesn't show up until more than half an hour into the movie, and is often seen in his labyrinthlike home: a dank, underlit sprawl of squalor decorated with strip club Polaroids, Nazi ephemera, and the remains of Bill's victims. The gnarled body parts were designed by Carl Fullerton and Neal Martz, the film's special makeup effects creators.

The two had met on the set of the 1983 vampire thriller *The Hunger*. In the years afterward, Fullerton would earn an Academy Award nomination for his makeup work in 1985's *Remo Williams: The Adventure Begins*, for which he transformed Joel Grey into an elderly Korean martial arts master. Martz, meanwhile, wound up working on *Manhunter*, where he had helped apply some of Francis Dolarhyde's tattoos and scars. Martz had been on set in the film's final hours of shooting, during the messy showdown at Dolarhyde's home. That was when Mann had approached the young makeup artist with a question. "He walks up to me and goes, 'Can I borrow your shirt?'" Martz recalls. "He liked the color for the cabinets in the kitchen. So I gave it to him." (He eventually got his shirt back.)

For *The Silence of the Lambs*, the two effects artists would be tasked with crafting detailed human remains. Fullerton had real-life experience with cadavers, having visited autopsies to prepare for the 1981 horror film *Wolfen*. "The research is always my favorite part," says Fullerton, who watched as chests were cracked open and faces were removed. "It didn't rattle me. I have a strong science background, and it was purely clinical."

Before shooting began, Fullerton read *Deviant*, a 1989 book about Ed Gein, who, like Gumb, had attempted to create articles of clothing out of human skin. While Gumb's hideous homemade bodysuit would be viewed only fleetingly in the film. Demme gave the makeup artists specific instructions on how the killer's creation should look. "He was fearful it would look like *The Texas Chain Saw Massacre*, where you saw a face mask that was stitched together," says Fullerton.

But when Demme got a first glimpse of the bodysuit, which was made out of polyurethane, it was more realistic than he'd expected. "It looked almost too beautiful," recalled production designer Kristi Zea. "You could see the little goosebumps—it was that sensitive a rendering." Fullerton added different-colored skin, but the director remained unsatisfied. "It's still too nice," he told the creative team. "We don't want anyone to think that this is a great thing to be doing." Finally, Zea said, more color was added to "make it look a little more awful."

Bill's other victims are glimpsed in FBI forensic photos that Starling studies after being assigned the case: lurid pictures of flayed or bloated women lying in mud or water. Some of the pictures were shot near Fullerton's home in Bergen County, New Jersey. That was where a few female actresses showed up to appear in *The Silence of the Lambs*, apparently unaware that they were going to have body casts made. "They didn't know what they were doing there," says Martz. "They had to come to the basement and get naked, and get cast. We were the ones who had to tell these girls they were just a photo in this movie."

Some of the actors were later taken to a series of abandoned areas in New Jersey, where they played dead for the cameras. To ensure that their waterlogged corpses looked accurate, an FBI agent who specialized in washed-up remains examined the resulting images and gave his approval. "We tried to get as close as we could without using a real dead body," Fullerton said.

All of that effort would be hard to notice in the finished film, which contained only a few quick shots of Fullerton and Martz's gory handiwork. Yet there are other signs of Gumb's life of violence around his underground lair, which is decorated with a few American flags—a reminder, notes production designer Zea, that the crimes depicted in the film weren't that far removed from reality. "This country was built on violence," she says. "There's no escaping it."

Early in the film version of *The Silence of the Lambs*, Starling is sent to a rural West Virginia funeral home, where she is confronted with Buffalo Bill's handiwork: the corpse of a young woman who's just been fished out of a river. Her body is covered in brown muck, and her throat contains a death's-head moth pupa.

The victim was played by Chris McGinn, a New York City actor whose experience included some stage work and an episode of *All My Children*. Though her agent worried about her taking the creepy role, and even advised her not to be named in the credits, she was game for whatever the filmmakers wanted. After accepting the part, McGinn says, "I got a call saying 'We'd like to know if you would mind if you're naked when we pull you out of the river.' It was my first movie ever, so I was like 'Oh, okay!' Then they'd call back like a week or two later and say, 'We've changed our minds—we're going to put you on a morgue table, and it's been used, but we'll have a bag underneath you.' I just was like 'Sure, put me on a bag! I don't care what you do!'"

McGinn would eventually find herself lying on a table in front of the *Silence* cast and crew, playing dead for hours, with decaying nails glued to her fingers and dirt adorning her nude body. Foster checked in on her regularly to make sure she was okay, telling McGinn: "If at any point you want to stop and you're afraid to ask, I'll ask for you." When it came time for the scene in which Starling peers into the victim's mouth, a member of the prop department brought over a fake pupa—one that had been made out of a Tootsie Roll, so McGinn wouldn't choke on it.

"Jonathan comes over and says, 'Chris, how far do you think you can take this down your throat?' McGinn recalls. "And the entire set went like dead quiet—it was like one of those E. F. Hutton commercials where everyone went silent. And I said, 'Jonathan, don't you think that's rather a personal question?' And everyone burst into laughter."

That was a not uncommon occurrence on the *Silence of the Lambs* set—despite the grim subject matter. "Everything was a joke," said Brooke Smith, the actor who played Catherine Martin, the kidnapping victim Buffalo Bill keeps captive in a slick-walled basement pit. "On Valentine's Day [Hopkins] gave me a chocolate rose, and said something like Lecter would and just walked away. The crew ate lamb, and made the blueprint of the set into a board game called *The Gumb Game*. The object was to save Catherine."

Smith, then in her early twenties, was a punk rocker turned aspiring actor who'd landed the role with the help of Michelle Pfeiffer, who'd recommended her for the role (Pfeiffer was a client of Smith's mother, the longtime Hollywood publicist Lois Smith). To play one of Gumb's "large victims," the actor had to gain twenty-three pounds in just three weeks. "They installed a refrigerator in my hotel room," she recalled. "It was, like, milkshakes for breakfast! I was aching from it." She also locked herself in a storage room at her parents' home, trying to adjust to life in the dark.

But nothing could have prepared her for the experience of shooting *The Silence of the Lambs*. With the exception of Catherine's brief introductory moment—in which she joyfully sings along to Tom Petty's jangly 1976 hit "American Girl" on her car stereo*—the character spends nearly all of her time in Buffalo Bill's rancid pit. That's where she's tormented by the serial killer, who plans on killing and flaying her once she reaches his ideal weight. To keep her skin supple, he lowers a bottle of moisturizer to her on a rope, commanding her in an almost singsong rhyme: "It rubs the lotion on its skin, or else it gets the hose again."

For days on end, Smith would show up on the set, enter a fake pit through a trapdoor, and then scream and plead her way through Catherine's scenes. "I was doing some kind of mind-fuck thing on myself," she said. "I remember shooting these scenes and seeing the camera guys out there and thinking 'I need help! And not only are they not helping me, they're exploiting me!' Which is crazy [to think]."

When they weren't shouting at each other in front of the cameras, Smith and Levine got along easily, often grabbing dinner together; the young actor became so close to the man playing her captor that Foster gave her the nickname "Patty Hearst." "We had to take care of each other to shoot those scenes," Smith said. "We had to trust each other."

One night, while looking over footage with the crew, Smith got an

---

* "American Girl" was the priciest song to appear in the film, costing about $30,000 to secure. The producers might have saved some money if they'd gone with Smith's suggestion for the scene, and used a track from the legendary New York City hardcore band Bad Brains.

early glimpse at what would become Levine's most enduring *Silence of the Lambs* scene: After applying makeup and donning one of his victim's scalps, Buffalo Bill sets up a video camera and records himself dancing under a disco ball. He then tucks his penis behind his thighs—a move that required Levine to down a couple of tequila shots before filming.

The resulting sequence is scored with a hazy electro-pop track titled "Goodbye Horses," written and performed by singer-songwriter named Diane Luckey, aka Q Lazzarus. Demme had discovered the song in 1986 in a New York City taxi, where "Goodbye Horses" was playing from the front of the cab. Struck by the tune's dreamily propulsive sound, Demme asked the driver what she was listening to—and learned that Luckey, who was behind the wheel, was blasting her own demo on a boombox. The two wound up pulling over for pizza, and Demme had later put "Goodbye Horses" into *Something Wild*.

Demme returned to the song in *The Silence of the Lambs*, where the track's thumping dance beat and keyboard squiggles underscore a moment that's both outrageous and vulnerable: As Buffalo Bill, wearing the scalp of a victim, dances to the bold but wistful tune—"Goodbye horses/I'm flying over you"—it marks the only time in the film where he is comfortable in his own skin, even if it's someone else's. The scene, Levine said, "made this psychotic monster accessible, in a strange sort of way— a strangely gentle sort of way."

Whatever humanity remained in Buffalo Bill could also be found in the scenes in which he took care of his beloved insects, which were overseen by Ray Mendez, credited as the film's "moth wrangler and stylist." Mendez had spent years studying and handling insects at New York City's Museum of Natural History and had worked on a few film projects, including George A. Romero's 1982 horror compendium *Creepshow*, which had found him overseeing twenty-five thousand cockroaches. For *The Silence of the Lambs*, he handled all bug-related matters, from creating the movie's Tootsie Roll pupas to handling hundreds of on-set moths.

In Harris's book, Buffalo Bill imports and cultivates a small army of death's-head moths, which are recognizable by their skull-like markings— and impossible to find in the United States. For the film, they were played by about two hundred tomato hornworm moths, a far more common species that Mendez imported from Virginia to Pennsylvania. To get them to the set, he designed a specially lit cabinet that could be placed on an airplane seat (the insects flew first class, of course). "I put a flap on the side of the cabinet, so the ticket agent could open it up and they could see all the moths sitting inside," Mendez says. "That way, they knew we weren't transporting cocaine or marijuana or whatever."

After the insects landed in Pittsburgh, Mendez and an assistant glued skull-painted fake nails to the moths and then used carbon dioxide to make them drowsy. Whenever the insects were needed for a scene—such as the moment Buffalo Bill gingerly removes a moth from a cage—the warm environment gave them a flutter-ready energy (some of the insects were even fitted with small harnesses to control their movements). "You can't just bring bugs on a set and let 'em go," notes Mendez. "The bugs will do what they're going to do, so part of the job is designing the set so they'll do what you want."

Mendez's moths would play a prime supporting role in the climax of *The Silence of the Lambs*, which finds Starling scrambling in the chaos of Buffalo Bill's lair. It was the ending Tally had once lamented—a scene featuring a woman in a basement with a madman. But Demme wasn't going to stage their confrontation in a conventional way. As Catherine screams for help from the well and moths flap through the air, Starling moves through the dark, her Bureau-issued firearm shaking in her hands. She's unaware that Bill's watching her movements using green-tinted night vision goggles—and that he's close enough to touch her. It's not until he pulls back the hammer of his pistol, his gun making an audible *click*, that Starling whips around and shoots him dead.

Their showdown would be filmed during the last day of principal photography in Pittsburgh—a grueling race to the end that stretched on for more than twenty hours. The cast and crew were exhausted and ready for *The Silence of the Lambs* to be over. "We were going to have a little wrap party, so I ordered a DJ," says producer Saxon. "And by two a.m., he was like 'Are they ever going to come out?' We had champagne on ice—and the ice had melted."

Finally, Foster and the remaining crew emerged from the set, relieved to finally be finished. But the celebration wouldn't last long. Saxon and the rest of the film's creative team had one final task to complete before production would be over for good: They had to let Hannibal Lecter loose into the world.

While working on the initial drafts of his *Silence of the Lambs* screenplay, Tally thought he'd found the perfect send-off for Lecter. In Harris's novel, the doctor is last spotted in his posh St. Louis hotel, where he writes his farewell letter to Starling. That was far too static to work on the screen. So Tally came up with his own ending for the film, one that would find Lecter relaxing on a lounge chair after his escape, disguised in glasses and a beard. He places a menacing phone call to Starling, reminding her that he's never too far away—and neither are her troubles. "Your flock is still for now, Clarice, but not forever," Lecter tells her. "There will always be other lambs, on other nights." After hanging up, Lecter pops an orange slice into his mouth and saunters into a moonlit house. Inside, confined to a swivel chair, is an old nemesis from Lecter's asylum days.

"Well, Dr. Chilton," Lecter says, brandishing a penknife, "shall we begin?"

Demme, upon reading the screenplay's closing words, had a visceral reaction: *Ick*. "We hate Chilton, and he's a slimeball," he told Tally. "But he's a human being. You gotta give him some hair of a chance of being able to get away."

The writer came up with a slightly more tasteful alternative: In the film's new finale, Lecter would still place a farewell call to Starling—only this time, he'd do so from an unnamed tropical location, wearing sunglasses and a suit, and trying to stay hidden underneath a ludicrous blond wig. Before saying goodbye, he watches the frantic-looking Chilton exit a plane, accompanied by a security guard. "I do wish we could chat longer," he tells Starling, "but I'm having an old friend for dinner." He then saunters into a moving crowd, the camera pulling back until he's just a blur in a haze of bodies.

Not everyone was sold on Tally's solution. According to notes from one preproduction meeting, some executives at Orion worried that concluding a dark film in such a sunny locale would be jarring to moviegoers: "We will have scared people too much to make this big tonal shift work." But Demme loved the new ending, partly because it meant that Orion would have to pay for a few days' work in a warm climate. Before the director could sign off on it, however, he wanted to run the idea by the world's foremost Lecter authority. "I was like, I need to clear this with Thomas Harris," Demme said.

By the late 1980s, Harris and his partner, Pace Barnes, were spending their winters at a $1.04 million mansion in Miami Beach, which was where Demme visited the writer for their first in-person discussion. They sat outside and chitchatted over tea until Demme finally got to the point: "Tom, I need to talk to you about a possible change to the ending to the film."

Harris responded by playfully picking up a pair of shears. "I tell you what John," he said, "why don't we go to the rose garden and talk about this." Then he listened to Demme's pitch. It wasn't the ending Harris would have chosen for Lecter; he believed that the doctor would use his newfound freedom to roam the back streets of some old city in Europe—perhaps Florence. But the author *could* see him heading toward a warmer climate—with one caveat: "If he did go to the tropics," he told Demme, "he wouldn't sweat!"

In early March 1990, Demme and a small group of crew and cast members flew to Bimini, a Bahamian island not far from Miami. They'd have just a few days to film Lecter's final scenes, including the closing shot of him slipping casually into the crowd in pursuit of Chilton, all the while never breaking a sweat—or breaking his stride. "I wanted him to be like a cat just moving up the garden path for his prey," the actor said of Lecter's final on-screen moments.

As his costar Heald recalls, "We were told, 'Keep walking until you get the cue to stop.' Well, Bimini's not that long of an island. We were practically walking out to sea by the time a PA came dashing down the road, saying 'Stop!'" After nearly four months, filming was finally over—this time, for good. It was time to turn around, head back to the States, and get the film ready for release.

CHAPTER 17

"I CANNOT BELIEVE I'M ATTRACTED TO HANNIBAL LECTER."

One of the first signs that Hannibal Lecter was finally going to be a big-screen star—and that *The Silence of the Lambs* was destined to be a hit—came in the form of a memo sent to the offices of Orion Pictures in September 1990. It had been six months since production had wrapped, and the studio had recently held test screenings in Chicago and Boston. More than four hundred moviegoers in each city had been asked to give their feedback on the film, and the results had been encouraging: Despite a couple of walkouts, the viewers had loved *Silence*—and they had *especially* loved Lecter. For all of his brutality and bogeyman power, viewers didn't think of him as a villain. In fact, they wanted even more of him. "Some [moviegoers] indicated that they liked the fact that, at the end, the doctor escaped, [and] got revenge," noted the report.

At any other studio, such an across-the-board upbeat response would have been reason to rush *The Silence of the Lambs* into theaters. But by 1990, Orion Pictures was in trouble. The studio had released several commercial hits in the past decade, including *RoboCop* and *Bull Durham*. It had even produced a pair of Best Picture winners in *Amadeus* and *Platoon*. But a rash of costly duds, such as the Roseanne Barr–Meryl Streep comedy *She-Devil*, had pushed the studio toward bankruptcy, and execs were focused on Orion's big movie for 1990: a three-hour-plus western titled *Dances with Wolves*, directed by first-time filmmaker Kevin Costner.

Due to the studio's limited resources, *The Silence of the Lambs* wouldn't hit theaters until Valentine's Day, 1991.

That meant Demme would have nearly a year to fine-tune his film and build up moviegoers' anticipation. Having spent his adolescence cutting out old movie ads from newspapers—and later working as a film publicist—he knew the importance of a good marketing campaign. And it was important that his film stand out from the countless low-budget, high-body-count flicks that had dominated the eighties. "He didn't want it to come across as a slasher movie, like a *Texas Chain Saw Whatever*," says former Orion marketing chief Charles O. Glenn. "He wanted a campaign that said, 'This is a theatrical experience that you do not want to miss. It is formidable. It is *frightening*.'"

On the set of *The Silence of the Lambs* in Pittsburgh, Demme had shown Glenn a haunting piece of art featuring a moth with a skull on its thorax. Looking closer, Glenn had realized that the "skull" was actually made up of seven nude female bodies, inspired by a 1951 portrait of Salvador Dalí by the photographer Philippe Halsman.

A version of that human-formed skull image would find its way to Dawn Baillie, a poster designer who'd been born and raised in Los Angeles. "I used to go to Hollywood Boulevard with my grandma all the time to see movies," Baillie recalls. "Movie theaters were my art gallery. I used to stand and admire the posters, and that's what I wanted to do." By the late 1980s, she'd created striking one-sheets for such films as *Dirty Dancing* and *Indiana Jones and the Last Crusade*.

Earlier in her career, while working at an advertising firm, Baillie had regularly passed a poster for the 1978 serial killer drama *The Eyes of Laura Mars*, featuring a shadowy close-up of Faye Dunaway. That haunting image would help inform her design for the poster for *The Silence of the Lambs*. She was given photos from the film, as well as a copy of Tally's screenplay. Using just those elements for reference—she wasn't able to look at footage—Baillie selected a close-up picture of Foster's face. She then sketched an illustration of Starling's mouth covered by a death's-head moth, effectively silencing her. "There's a simplicity to it," she says of the image. "It conveys horror. But it's elegant, light, beautiful, and a little bit weird."

For the finished image, Baillie set up a photo shoot with a moth rented from the Natural History Museum of Los Angeles County and later drew the human-formed skull on the insect's body. She gave Foster's eyes a Day-Glo orange hue and added the film's title using a bold, almost razor blade–like font called Opti Binder Style, with *The Silence of the Lambs* spelled in all lowercase. "It was my attempt to feminize the masculine font," she says.

Her poster was initially rejected by the Motion Picture Association of America, which worried about the barely visible female nudes appearing on the moth (the image was later replaced by a photo of seven women wearing unitards). But the finished product turned out to be a perfect tease for *The Silence of the Lambs*—evoking the film's solemn tone while revealing zero plot points. In the pre-internet era, full-page newspaper ads in publications such as *The New York Times* and the *Los Angeles Times* were crucial to raising awareness of a film. Soon, Baillie's one-sheet for *The Silence of the Lambs* would be everywhere. "The goal was to come up with an iconic image that would travel with the film," she says.

To further stoke interest in the movie, Lecter made an appearance—at least on-screen—at ShoWest, an annual movie-business confab that by 1990 was drawing thousands of movie theater owners. Glenn asked Hopkins to film a cheeky promotional clip in which he'd talk about the film while in character as Lecter. An early script for the video, written before the film landed its February 1991 release date, played up Lecter's culinary passions: "Hello. I'm Hannibal Lecter. They call me mad, but I'll be out this fall, and coming to your theater . . . I can't wait for you to play our movie, have a little of that popcorn, and maybe soda (slurp, slurp, slurp)."

In truth, moviegoers would be seeing less of Lecter than the filmmakers had originally intended. In the process of putting together the film, Demme and editor Craig McKay had trimmed Hopkins's already scant screen time. Several Lecter scenes were removed, including a sequence in which he drives away in his stolen ambulance, wiping blood from his grinning face.

Demme also made some crucial additions in the editing room. They included composer Howard Shore's patiently brooding orchestral score, featuring none of the synth stabs or discordant noises that had been scary-movie hallmarks throughout the 1980s. Other elements of the film's soundtrack were nearly imperceptible. For the scene in which Starling first encounters Lecter in his cell, Demme gave sound editor Ron Bochar specific instructions for the soundtrack: "This is the bowels of the building," the director said. "Let me hear howling and let me hear bowels."

Bochar added all sorts of near-subliminal animal noises to the soundtrack, including screaming sounds he'd recorded for the 1989 Howie Mandel family comedy *Little Monsters*, which were slowed down and reversed for *The Silence of the Lambs*. No one watching the film would have noticed the extra audio. But "whenever you're down there with Lecter," Bochar said, "there's this element—it's a low tone that rises and then comes down again."

By the fall of 1990, having spent nearly half a year tinkering with the film, Demme was ready to share *The Silence of the Lambs* with others. "We worked it, and worked it, and worked it," he said. "And then we knew we had it." In addition to the test screenings in Boston and Chicago, there was a confidence-boosting fax to the filmmaker from Harris himself. Though he still had no interest in seeing the film, some of the author's friends and family had been invited to an early showing. "They tell me you have made a superb and stunning movie," Harris told Demme. "Congratulations, and every good wish."

The reaction at a New York City screening for the film's cast and crew was similarly jubilant—though Anthony Heald was still unconvinced. "Everybody was saying 'Oh, God, we've got a monster hit!'" he remembers with a laugh. "And I turned to my wife and said, 'They're delusional.'"

On Friday, February 14, 1991, a Connecticut drama teacher named Art Almquist asked a couple of colleagues if they wanted to see the weekend's big new movie: *The Silence of the Lambs*. Almquist worked at a private boarding school, and after a week of dealing with rowdy students, he and his friends needed an escape. "Our school was in this tiny little village," he says. "And getting into a town with a movie theater was a half-hour drive. So it was always a big event."

Almquist was a longtime horror fan. But one of his friends, Mary, was hesitant about tagging along. "She said, 'Oh, God, I don't know. I just have a hard time with movies that have violence against women in them.' And I said, 'I totally get it. But this is Jonathan Demme. *Married to the Mob*, *Stop Making Sense*—these are movies that are progressive and surprising. I'm sure it won't be too much.'"

The three made their way to a packed theater in Torrington for the 7:10 p.m. showing of *The Silence of the Lambs*, which was playing alongside *Home Alone* and the John Goodman comedy *King Ralph*. More than an hour into the film, during a scene in which Buffalo Bill taunts the captive Catherine Martin—a moment that features both characters screaming directly into the camera—Mary got up and headed to the lobby. She was soon spotted by a worker at the concession stand.

"What movie are you seeing?" the employee asked.

"*The Silence of the Lambs*."

"What scene they on?"

"She's screaming in the well, and he's imitating her."

The employee shook her head. "Oh, honey, it just gets *worse*."

In the weeks and months that followed, moviegoers watched *The Silence of the Lambs* with a mix of awe, excitement, and terror. Not long after the film opened, a nineteen-year-old Penn State University student named Shayne Buchwald caught *The Silence of the Lambs* at a small theater in York, Pennsylvania. She was accompanied by her boyfriend, "a big guy who looked like Spencer Tracy," she remembers. "He was probably holding my hand, because he was a bit of a wimp." During a moment in which Starling discovers the deformed head of one of Lecter's ex-patients in a jar, Buchwald's date became so startled that he accidentally elbowed her in the face, causing her nose to bleed. Buchwald quickly grabbed a tissue and kept it plugged in her nose for the rest of the night. There was no way she was going to miss a minute of the film. "It was fascinating and terrifying at the same time," she says.

Buchwald remembers her fellow moviegoers remaining quiet throughout *The Silence of the Lambs'* 118-minute running time—a communal phenomenon that was playing out nationwide. Never before or since has a Valentine's Day–timed film yielded so many stress-packed, romance-free nights. "I haven't heard anything but silence when people walk out of the movie," noted the manager of a Los Angeles theater. "They come out emotionally drained."

Moviegoers heading into *The Silence of the Lambs* had been given fair warning about the film's many shocks. The trailer opened with a few quick shots of Lecter, followed by Scott Glenn as Jack Crawford looking straight into the camera while asking "You spook easily, Starling?"—as if he were daring the audience. But in the prespoiler era, it was possible to buy a ticket for Demme's movie completely unaware of just *how* bizarre and dark the movie would get. And there were plenty of eager audience members lining up for the movie's first weekend, thanks in no small part to critics' reviews of the film, nearly all of them overwhelmingly ecstatic: In *The New York Times*, Vincent Canby called it "pop film making of a high order," while *Los Angeles Times* critic Sheila Benson (who'd been critical of *Manhunter*) described Demme's film as "stunning," and described the first appearance of Lecter as being "as dramatic as the unmasking of the Phantom of the Opera."

That kind of praise rankled the film's few detractors, including Gene Siskel, the *Chicago Tribune* critic who'd become one of the most prominent critics in the country, thanks to *Siskel & Ebert*, the TV show he cohosted with his on-screen antagonist, Roger Ebert. In his thumbs-down review, Siskel derided Hopkins's performance, calling it "way overplayed," and lamented Demme's decision to make "a surprisingly trashy project." The film, he argued, was nothing more than a "star-studded freak show"—one that lacked taste and insight: "I didn't learn a thing about serial killers from this movie." Ebert, for his part, was let down by the film's ending but praised its dialogue and performances. "It worked for me! It worked!" he told Siskel. To which his partner replied tersely, "Well, then you're easy."

But even a widely trusted critic like Siskel wasn't going to keep audiences away. *The Silence of the Lambs* opened at the box office at number one, where it would stay for more than a month. And while Foster was undeniably the film's star attraction—she was profiled by *Rolling Stone* and *The New York Times* and appeared on TV chat shows worldwide—it was Hopkins's turn as Lecter that made the film a cultural event.

By the spring of 1991, the actor's face would be staring back from the covers of both *Newsweek* and *Entertainment Weekly* (which declared him "the scariest man in movies"). Lecter didn't have more than a few pages' worth of dialogue in Tally's script. But many of his bitchy put-downs and asides would become well-known catchphrases. Diane Baker, who played the desperate Senator Martin, would spend decades after the film's release being approached by strangers eager to quote the most cutting line from her scene with Hopkins. "I was in Memorial Sloan Kettering visiting a patient, and there was a nurse pushing a gurney down the hallway with a patient on it, going into an operation," Baker recalls. "She stops, sees me, and says, 'Love your suit.' I looked in horror at the patient. And then she moved on."

Hannibal Lecter had captured the public's imagination—for better or for worse. One New York City psychologist told the press that nearly a third of her male patients wanted to talk about Lecter. "They've lost three or four nights' sleep after that movie," she reported. And Lecter became a frequent topic of conversation at Manhattan power lunches, where high-priced attorneys spoke in trembling tones about watching *The Silence of the Lambs*. "These are people who work on deals worth millions of dollars and it doesn't strike fear into their hearts," noted a lawyer at a large New York City firm, "but for some reason, Hannibal Lecter did."

One viewer who *wasn't* rattled by the film was Harris's mother, who caught *The Silence of the Lambs* at a theater in Memphis. Polly Harris told a reporter she was pleased with the movie, which she hadn't found all that unnerving: "I'm not easily scared," she said.

But she was the exception. Merciless lawyers, seen-it-all movie critics, hardened horror fans—they'd simply never met anybody like Lecter before. The most popular big-screen villains of the 1980s had been blank-masked maniacs and dream-dwelling killers, not to mention various vampires, aliens, ghosts, and gremlins. Lecter was more refined. Granted, he ate people—but he also seemed like a fascinating dining companion. And unlike the coarse killers who'd haunted audiences for the last decade, Lecter was insightful, quippy, and yearning for some sort of connection— all recognizably human traits.

In fact, at least one viewer felt as though he really *had* known Lecter. While watching *The Silence of the Lambs* in the theater, a former Associated Press employee, Tom Kelly, thought of a former coworker. "[Lecter] was so even-tempered, so almost removed from himself," he said. "In some of those scenes, his dry wit made me turn to my wife and say, 'That's Tom Harris.'"

For most moviegoers, though, the only pop culture precedent for Lecter was Norman Bates, the tortured loner made famous by Alfred Hitchcock's adaptation of *Psycho*. In one of the film's most ingenious scenes, Bates pushes a car containing a murder victim into a marsh—only to watch it get stuck. As he looks on nervously, hoping that the car will sink, it's almost impossible not to root for him. From that point on, much of the audience is on the side of Noman Bates—even as he kills again.

But while moviegoers in 1960 rooted for Bates to get away with murder, they ultimately sighed in relief when he was locked up by the film's end. Such a fate wouldn't have satisfied the many fans of *The Silence of the Lambs*. They didn't just want Lecter to survive; they wanted him to be *free*.

And now he was, having fled into popular culture. Throughout 1991, *The Silence of the Lambs* was inescapable, and so was its man-eating main attraction. All you had to do was turn on the TV. Not long after the movie's release, *Saturday Night Live* aired a Lecter sketch starring Jeremy Irons, who had been on an early casting wish list for the Lecter role. On *The Tonight Show with Johnny Carson*, guest host Jay Leno showed off a fake Hannibal Lecter cookbook, titled *How to Eat Friends & Digest People*. NBC even revived Mann's overlooked *Manhunter*, airing the film under the new title *Red Dragon: The Curse of Hannibal Lecter* and promoting it with a growling commercial voiceover: "Hannibal the Cannibal is coming to your house Friday night!"

Everybody wanted to get into business with Lecter. That spring, a merchandiser and part-time actor named Stanley DeSantis, who'd worked on such hot pop culture properties as *The Simpsons* and Spuds MacKenzie, pitched Orion several potential Lecter tie-in products: T-shirts, board games, a video game, even a 1-900 number. DeSantis believed that there were millions of dollars to be made from Lecter swag—provided, he said, that the items were "true to the film and its character, while remaining in good taste." A deal was never struck, though it's unclear if the merch ideas were nixed by studio executives, or by Harris.

A few months later, President George H. W. Bush invoked Lecter while giving a commencement address at the FBI Academy in Quantico. "On my way in, I may have spotted Hannibal the Cannibal in the audience," he told the crowd. "For those parents and others, that's an inside joke that I'm not sure I understand myself."*

When Harris got word of the president's remarks, he sent a joking fax to his agent, Mort Janklow: "Does he have to pay for our material?" The author had kept his pledge *not* to watch the film. When Harris and his partner, Pace Barnes, went to a Miami-area multiplex during the film's release, she opted to see Demme's movie, while he wandered into a different theater. According to the FBI's John Douglas, Harris wouldn't even sit through the movie's trailer.

But the author was nonetheless pleased with how the film was being received. "Splendid!" Harris wrote in a fax to the filmmakers. "My dentist admitted he'd sneaked in free. I took six bucks out of his bill. Raves here, as everywhere. That's some job, gentleman." Harris had plenty to be happy about: The paperback version of *The Silence of the Lambs* had shot to number one on the *New York Times* bestseller list after the film's release—and his film rights deal promised him an extra $10,000 for each week it spent in the top spot.

---

* It's unclear whether the president ever saw *The Silence of the Lambs*, though first lady Barbara Bush was invited to an early benefit screening. In a December 1990 letter to her office, a representative for the film promised Mrs. Bush that, despite the film's dark premise, Starling catches her prey at the end. "So there is a happy ending," the letter noted, "with a twist."

That prompted another fax from Harris. "I have two reasons to celebrate: Your brilliant picture, and the new readership it has brought me," he wrote to Demme from Miami. "All I needed was a really swell bottle of champagne." By then, Harris could afford entire crates of bubbly. There was plenty of money coming in thanks to *The Silence of the Lambs*. "He and Pace are having so much fun," a friend said a few months after the film's opening. "They just bought this crazy fifties house with a pool, and he drives a big Jaguar."

The response to *The Silence of the Lambs* also thrilled many within the FBI, particularly the women who'd been working in the Bureau for years, awaiting recognition and respect. With Starling, they had an onscreen hero—brainy, nervy, and averse to men's bullshit—who could be claimed as one of their own. "The first time I went to see it," Athena Varounis wrote in a letter to the producers, "I was accompanied by a group of female Special Agents. . . . You would not have found a more critical audience anywhere! In the end, after some intense discussion, you were voted a 'four and a half guns' out of a possible five." When Mary Ann Krauss caught the film, she was struck by how expertly it portrayed the nuts-and-bolts aspects of FBI fieldwork. But what *really* struck her was Foster's twang. "I was like 'Holy moly—was she recording me?'" Krauss says. "A southerner can pick up on an accent like that. And I felt like she did a good job."

The raves for the film extended throughout the Bureau. "The FBI people are very pleased with the professional portrayal," special agent Walter B. Stowe, Jr., wrote in a congratulatory letter sent to Demme during the film's opening weekend. "It never hurts to see the organization we all care about and know to be good well-depicted on the big screen."

Such a depiction was a public relations victory for the FBI. *The Silence of the Lambs* made working for the Bureau seem thrilling and purposeful. Shayne Buchwald was already interested in true crime and psychological thrillers when she watched the film with a bloody nose in that small Pennsylvania theater. But not long after that night, she realized that she wanted to join the Bureau and began researching serial killers and profiling. "Lecter fascinated me, but it was Clarice who really held my attention," she says. "I admired how quick and clever she was, as well as how honest she was with him . . . she knew how to get what she needed."

Buchwald joined the FBI Academy in 2002 and went on to spend more than two decades with the Bureau, with a focus on violent crime. At one point early on during her Bureau career, she was commuting regularly on a red-eye flight from California to Maryland. When crew members learned what she did for a living, they gave her a fitting nickname. "They'd say, 'Clarice, do you want some more water?'" She rewatched *The Silence of the Lambs* every year, and after she retired from the Bureau in 2023, she had an image of the film's death's-head moth tattooed on her left arm.

No one at the FBI could have predicted the long-term effect that *The Silence of the Lambs* would have on the Bureau's reputation. The film's biggest beneficiary, however, was Hopkins. Suddenly he was one of the most recognizable actors in the world, not to mention a middle-aged sex symbol. Women approached the fifty-three-year-old star and shyly told him that he'd been in their dreams (sometimes as Lecter). And when he appeared on *The Tonight Show*—still sporting Lecter's slicked-back hair—in March 1991, several audience members "oohed and aahed as if he were Mel Gibson," according to a *Newsweek* account. As one of Hopkins's admirers told a reporter after meeting the actor in person, "I cannot believe I'm attracted to Hannibal Lecter."

A month into the long theatrical run of *The Silence of the Lambs*, Hopkins was a guest on *The Mark & Brian Show*, a popular Los Angeles radio program. The actor did a few impressions, including one of his idol and former neighbor Richard Burton—and answered questions from overheated listeners.

CALLER: I am shaking.
HOPKINS: What's your name?
CALLER: My name's Karen.
HOPKINS [AS LECTER]: Hi, Karen.
CALLER: It sends chills up my spine when you say, 'Hello, Clarice.'
        Would you say that for me?

HOPKINS [AS LECTER]: Hello, Clarice. I'll help you catch him, Clarice. Hi, Clarice. Where do you live, Karen?

CALLER: You know, I hope there is a sequel, because I will be first in line to see it.

Just a few years before portraying Hannibal Lecter, Hopkins had all but given up on being a Hollywood movie star. Now he had the attention of the entire film industry. Not long after *The Silence of the Lambs* opened, he found himself on a long, contemplative drive—much like the one that had taken him from the Utah desert to the film's Pittsburgh set. This time, he was cruising down LA's Sunset Boulevard, an area known for its towering movie advertisements. "I always used to feel resentment at seeing someone else's name up on the big billboards," Hopkins said. But this time, he spotted a massive poster for *The Silence of the Lambs*, featuring the words ANTHONY HOPKINS. "I just pulled over and looked at it. And it made me laugh. Did I feel any different? No, I feel exactly the same. I realize now it's all a game, and next month, there'll be someone else up there."

But Hopkins wouldn't be going away anytime soon—and neither would Lecter.

CHAPTER 18

"THAT'S WHEN THEY GASPED."

With each week *The Silence of the Lambs* stayed atop the box office, there were growing concerns that the film, for all its artistic virtues, represented a new high—or maybe a new low?—in pop culture bloodshed. "Yes, the picture is tactfully made, but the question remains, why make it at all?" wrote Stephen Farber in the *Los Angeles Times*. Describing *The Silence of the Lambs* as "thoroughly morbid and meaningless," he lumped the film in with recent releases such as *Goodfellas* and *The Grifters*, all part of what he described as "a long line of super-violent, repellent movies to inspire critical hosannas."

Farber wasn't alone in noting the country's ever-rapacious appetite for blood and gore. "Movies, Music, Books—Are There Any Limits Left?" asked the April 1991 cover story of *Newsweek*, which featured a close-up image of Lecter's unblinking eyes underneath the headline "VIOLENCE GOES MAINSTREAM." The magazine's essay argued that Demme's film was relatively restrained—especially when Lecter's rampage was compared to what the magazine described as "an appalling accretion of violent entertainment." As proof, the magazine cited the recent shoot-'em-up films *RoboCop 2* and *Die Hard 2*; Bret Easton Ellis's gory new novel, *American Psycho*, about a Wall Street–prowling sadist named Patrick Bateman; and Aerosmith's MTV hit "Janie's Got a Gun," which follows a victim of sexual abuse who kills her father. Hannibal the Cannibal, RoboCop,

Patrick Bateman, Steven Tyler—they were all responsible, *Newsweek* argued, for creating "the sense that things have gotten out of control."

According to some critics, Demme's film threatened to make things even worse. "I hated *The Silence of the Lambs*," said author Anne Rule, who'd documented her time with Ted Bundy in the best-selling *The Stranger Beside Me*. "It made Dr. Lecter seem to be a hero. I could see unbalanced people leaving theaters all over the country, thinking, 'I could do that. I could fool the police.'" And the FBI's Robert Ressler, who'd assisted Harris with research for both Lecter novels, was disappointed by the movie version of *The Silence of the Lambs*. "I don't think that was a very healthy, accurate, or responsible portrayal of a violent offender," he said a few years after the film's release. "The audience is clapping, pulling for this monster."

But pop culture hadn't invented violence. And anyone drawn to Hannibal the Cannibal's face on that *Newsweek* cover would also have spotted the much smaller headline running across the top: "APOCALYPSE IN IRAQ." On January 17, 1991, the United States, as part of a multicountry coalition, had began dropping bombs over Baghdad in response to a series of aggressive moves by the country's leader, Saddam Hussein. For more than a month, Operation Desert Storm was broadcast on live TV, making it possible to watch warfare from thousands of miles away. Some of the battle footage was captured using night vision lenses, the same fuzzy, green-tinted technology with which Buffalo Bill tracks his prey. But the explosions and missile drops being beamed directly from Iraq by CNN were way more visceral and definitely more upsetting than anything Hollywood could dream up. At a time when the world seemed to be turning scarier and deadlier, spending a couple of hours with Hannibal Lecter felt like an escape from reality—or, perhaps, a safe way to process it.

The country's growing familiarity with violence, and the general sense that "things have gotten out of control," would be reinforced that summer when police discovered the remains of eleven bodies in the Milwaukee, Wisconsin, apartment of a thirty-one-year-old named Jeffrey Dahmer. While living a seemingly mundane life, Dahmer had killed seventeen men, many in their teens or twenties, over the course of thirteen years. Authorities deemed the condition of some of the remains to be "not inconsistent with cannibalism." And one report claimed that Dahmer had "fried a victim's bicep in vegetable shortening" before eating it.

At the time of Dahmer's arrest, *The Silence of the Lambs* was still in theaters across the country and only starting to roll out worldwide. The media was quick to connect the film to Dahmer. *People* magazine ran a photo of Dahmer on its cover next to a headline describing his crimes as "a Real-Life *SILENCE OF THE LAMBS*." And a *New York Times* editorial noted that Demme's film had suddenly "burst from flat-screen fiction into inescapable 3-D reality."

Columnists and critics would spend the next few months linking the two cannibals: one real, one imaginary, both newly famous. There was even concern that Lecter's on-screen behavior could incite off-screen acts of cruelty. "I worry a lot about people like Jeffrey Dahmer," fretted one film professor. "I wonder how crazies are affected by things like [*The Silence of the Lambs*]."

It didn't matter that their crimes had little in common. (Vegetable oil? Hannibal the Cannibal would *never*.) Lecter and Dahmer had become the decade's first superstar serial killers, their exploits followed by millions. In the fall of 1991, Harris's *Silence of the Lambs* novel began winding down its lengthy run on the bestseller charts—just as a trio of quick-turnaround paperbacks about Dahmer's crimes was arriving in stores. That included *The Milwaukee Murders: Nightmare in Apartment 213: The True Story*, which would later be reprinted with a cover line promising "The twisted story of the real-life 'Hannibal Lecter.'"

If Dahmer had eclipsed Lecter's fame, it was only temporarily. As the year ended and *The Silence of the Lambs* found itself on numerous best-of lists, it was becoming clear that the filmmakers and their cast were headed to the Oscars. But in the lead-up to the awards, Demme would be forced to confront a series of controversies that had been gathering momentum for months. And for once, the dust-up had nothing to do with Lecter.

Unlike Hannibal the Cannibal, whose smarts and occasional charm al-lowed many moviegoers to overlook his crimes, Buffalo Bill is an unredeemable monster, one who physically and verbally abuses his female prisoners before cutting up their bodies and dumping them in the wild. And not long after the film's release, he became a target of public scorn.

Thanks in part to the recent release of Ellis's *American Psycho*, which finds Patrick Bateman menacing girlfriends and sex workers alike, there'd been an increasing awareness of books and movies featuring violence against women. And Bill's cruel acts in *Silence*—part of what one critic described as the film's "sick pornography of butchery"—depressed some viewers, who wondered if the film had had to reach such extremes. "Why do we have to go through women portrayed as objects to be murdered and skinned to be able to have a portrayal of one woman as competent?" asked one female psychotherapist. And Kathleen Carlin, a prominent women's rights advocate, told a reporter that after watching *Silence*, she had called her daughters and warned them, "*Don't go outside ever again. Don't be nice to anybody.*" "This movie touches on what every woman knows," Carlin said. "We are always prey in this society."

Demme agreed. In fact, it was a key reason he'd decided to make *The Silence of the Lambs*, which he defended in the press as "anti-violence." "We don't want to be titillating and fun and a slasher movie," he said. "We want to be harrowing—and really, just as appalling and threatening as this whole subject is."

The director had a harder time managing the *other* outcry over Buffalo Bill, one that had begun in gay publications such as *OutWeek* and *The Advocate* before finding its way to newspapers nationwide. In a February 15, 1991, story for the *Miami Herald*, the journalist Ryan Murphy, who in later years would cocreate such hit TV shows as *American Horror Story* and *Dahmer – Monster: The Jeffrey Dahmer Story*, noted the backlash against Buffalo Bill in the gay community. Here was a character who'd murdered a male former lover; who dreams of being a woman; and who owns a poodle named Precious. "They couldn't have made him more stereotypically gay and evil if they tried," *Advocate* critic David Ehrenstein told Murphy. "Once again, our old friend the gay monster is on grand display."

The "gay monster"—the queer-coded big-screen murderer—had been a film trope for decades, recently showing up in movies such as *Cruising* and *Dressed to Kill*. As *The Silence of the Lambs* opened in theaters, the recently formed Gay & Lesbian Alliance Against Defamation, or GLAAD, called for a boycott of the film over its handling of Gumb, claiming that the movie promoted homophobia. Members of GLAAD had attended early screenings, and had seen Buffalo Bill's effect on moviegoers. "They were watching it with a presumably largely straight audience," says Richard Jennings, then the executive director of GLAAD's Los Angeles chapter. "And despite the flayed bodies on the screen, what really elicited the biggest reaction was when people saw his nipple ring—that's when they gasped."

The activists weren't just angry about Gumb; there was also resentment toward Foster, whose sexuality had been the subject of public speculation and private conversations for years. (The actor wouldn't publicly allude to being gay until 2007 and didn't formally come out until 2013.) That she was now starring in a film perceived to be homophobic rankled some gay activists. Around Manhattan, posters were hung up featuring Foster's photo under the words "ABSOLUTELY QUEER."

Demme had foreseen controversy over the Buffalo Bill character, and even tried to get ahead of it. Before the film's release, he told reporters that Jame Gumb wasn't "portrayed as gay." Instead, the director said, Gumb is "someone with a gender problem—he's not someone with a sexuality that draws him to men." That argument didn't sway critics such as *The Village Voice*'s Stephen Harvey, who felt that Gumb was "endowed with all the fag cliches homophobes have doted on for decades: bleached locks, whiny voice, frilly glad rags, and, choicest of all, the love of a teensy white poodle named Precious."

As anger about Buffalo Bill began earning more press, Demme knew he had to respond. The film publicist turned director wrote a letter to the gay magazine *Guide*, acknowledging that the controversy had "opened my eyes to a couple of things." He noted the plague of "cowardly violence" directed at homosexuals in America, as well as the lack of positive gay characters on-screen. And though he reiterated his belief that Buffalo Bill wasn't gay, the director "[shared] the outrage" over the country's rampant homophobia, saying he was glad that the movie "unwittingly provided a public touchstone for the issues raised."

Levine, meanwhile, noted that he didn't want to play Gumb as a cli*chéd* "mincing homosexual." Instead, he saw the character as "an acutely homophobic heterosexual man doing that mocking thing." He added, "There was a lot of flack about him being gay. I never played him as being gay."

The Silence of the Lambs left theaters in the fall of 1991, having grossed more than $130 million in the United States alone. Yet the film maintained its cultural momentum throughout the end of the year: On Halloween, a small town in Indiana invited local kids to run through a homemade attraction titled "Hannibal Lecter's Escape." During the Christmas holidays, the VHS became one of the most rented cassettes in the country. And by New Year's Day, the movie had picked up several year-end awards, including New York Film Critics Circle wins for Best Film, Best Director, Best Actress, and Best Actor.

It would have been a sweep, had Ted Tally not been shut out in the Best Screenplay category. Not long afterward, he hired a personal publicist to help his awards odds. "I thought, 'Nobody's going to rattle my own drums,'" he says. "And I didn't want people to think this movie was born in a FedEx envelope on the way to Jodie Foster's house."

When Academy Award nominations were announced in February 1992, it was clear that the voters had gotten Tally's message. His script was in the running for Best Adapted Screenplay—one of seven nominations for the film. Demme, Foster, and Hopkins all landed on the ballot. So did editor Crag McKay and sound team members Tom Fleischman and Christopher Newman. And to no one's surprise, the film became part of a competitive Best Picture race, where *The Silence of the Lambs* was considered a long shot. It wasn't the most nominated film in the category—an honor that went to the Warren Beatty Mob odyssey *Bugsy*. Nor was it the most commercially successful: Disney's *Beauty and the Beast* had been the studio's highest-grossing animated film to date. And the year's other two Best Picture nominees, Barbra Streisand's sentimental *The Price of Tides* and Oliver Stone's frenetic *JFK*, had recently opened in theaters, meaning that they were still fresh in voters' minds.

The Silence of the Lambs had earned plenty of praise, not to mention money. But it wasn't the kind of film the Academy of Motion Picture Arts and Sciences liked to reward. Recent Best Picture winners had been mostly limited to sweeping foreign-set epics (*Out of Africa, The Last Emperor*) and PG-rated domestic dramas (*Terms of Endearment*). It was hard to see how a classy yet unsavory thriller such as *The Silence of the Lambs*, with all its face biting and penis tucking, would win over the same voters who, just two years earlier, had swooned over *Driving Miss Daisy*. In an essay for *New York* magazine, the Oscar-winning screenwriter William Goldman polled several anonymous Academy members about *Lambs'* chances. "A dazzling film about a nut who *eats people*?" one of them said. "Remember the age of the Academy."

Still, while *The Silence of the Lambs* was framed in the media as an Oscar underdog, it was also a mass audience hit with a beloved lead character—all of which was good news for Academy Awards show host Billy Crystal. The comedian had opened the previous year's ceremony by striding onto the stage atop a horse—a nod to his forthcoming film *City Slickers*, as well as the kind of knowingly groan-yielding gag that set a breezy tone for the entire broadcast. For the 1992 show, Crystal and his writers wanted to top that with something even more ambitious.

"We were looking for an entrance for him," says writer Bruce Vilanch. "And we sat in the room and said, 'Well, *The Silence of the Lambs* is the biggest thing. It's the movie with the most resonance.'" Vilanch had seen the extent to which the film had infiltrated mainstream culture: A few months earlier, when the injured Detroit Pistons center Bill Laimbeer had begun wearing a plastic mask on the court, some observers had nicknamed the player "Silence of the Laimbeer." "It had gotten so deep that sports people were joking about it," Vilanch says. "So we knew it was really encased in the culture."

As Vilanch prepared a *Silence of the Lambs* spoof for the telecast, he and the rest of the Oscar team got word that a coalition of gay rights activists, including members of the groups ACT UP and Queer Nation, planned to protest the ceremony. Though there was still lingering frustration about *Silence*'s portrayal of Buffalo Bill, Demme's film wasn't the agitators' only target: After months of prerelease outrage, the thriller *Basic Instinct*, about an ice pick–wielding bisexual murderer, had just arrived in theaters. And *JFK* was drawing complaints about its multiple gay criminals and conspirators. With the AIDS epidemic claiming tens of thousands of lives a year, and so few positive queer stories to be found on-screen, Hollywood homophobia had become a ripe target for attack. "We're telling them we don't want any more negative portrayals of us," one activist said. "We're not slashers . . . we don't skin women." Another promised that the protest would be "as disruptive as possible."

Vilanch understood why the Oscars had been singled out: "The show was the biggest billboard in the world, after the Super Bowl," Vilanch said, "so if you were going to make a stink, that was the perfect place to do it." But he'd never agreed with the complaints about Demme's film. "At the time, I was writing a column for *The Advocate*—because I'm a gay icon, so I get to do stuff like that," he says with a laugh. "And I was sort of befuddled by the controversy, because this character was a psychotic serial killer. He wasn't gay; he was *weird*. He affected many different postures, and I always thought, 'You're embracing *him*? You're deciding *he's* gay?' I was amazed we would take him as one of our own. But I was a lone wolf."

Finally, on the afternoon of March 30, streams of limos began arriving at Los Angeles's Dorothy Chandler Pavilion, where the sixty-fourth annual Academy Awards was set to begin. Across the street, protestors stood behind a police barricade, carrying signs that included "Worst Picture: Silence of the Lambs" and "Quick, get out of the closet, there's a big moth in there" (a taunt presumably aimed at Foster). As the red carpet became crowded with attendees such as James Cameron—some wearing red ribbons to raise awareness of AIDS—they could hear the crowd's shouts of "Burn, Hollywood, burn!"

It didn't take long for things to get more chaotic. A group of protestors soon pushed through the barricade and into the street, where they sat down and linked arms, prompting police to ride in on horseback. At least ten people were arrested, and while the 44 million viewers watching the ceremony didn't see any images from the protest, the mood inside the pavilion was uneasy. "They were all panicked that someone might get in and do harm," notes *Silence of the Lambs* star Diane Baker. Adds Tally, "We worried somebody was going to interrupt the program. It was in the back of our minds."

It was up to Crystal to calmly reassure the nearly three thousand audience members—which he did by entering the stage dressed as the year's most cherished monster: Hannibal Lecter. As Howard Shore's *Silence of the Lambs* main theme played, the host was wheeled out on a hand truck, wearing a tuxedo and a replica of Lecter's mask. Bette Midler and Brad Pitt looked on as Crystal walked straight to Hopkins's seat and shook his hand. "I'm having some of the Academy over for dinner," he said. "Care to join me?"

"Yes, anytime," Hopkins replied.

That wasn't Crystal's only riff on Lecter. As part of the show's opening musical medley, he sang a few lines from Hannibal the Cannibal's perspective, to the tune of the 1960s hit "The Shadow of Your Smile" ("Look inside my pot, Clarice, and see/A guy who looks a lot like Chef Boyardee").

Before the show began, Tally and Hopkins had talked about the odds of *The Silence of the Lambs* winning Best Picture. The screenwriter figured that they had a fifty-fifty shot. But after Tally watched Crystal's *The Silence of the Lambs* song-and-dance number, "I thought, 'This is going to be our night.'"

The host would drop numerous references to the film throughout the broadcast, at one point suggesting potential spin-offs, such as *Miss Thigh-Gone* and *The Flesh Prince of Bel-Air*. Later, he paused the show to perform an impression of Lecter if he'd been voiced by the frog-voiced Massachusetts politician Paul Tsongas, who was running for president at the time.

The *Silence of the Lambs* team would have to wait through nearly two and a half hours of jokes and speeches before the film won its first award of the night, for Best Adapted Screenplay. Tally thanked Harris for "graciously [lending] me his brilliant novel" and concluded his remarks with a quote from Lecter: "All good things to those who wait."

After leaving the stage, Tally was told to meet with the press. But he wanted to stay and see if Hopkins would win Best Actor. "That was the only question mark: whether people thought it was too short of a part," he says. A few minutes later, Hopkins—who was up against Warren Beatty, Robert De Niro, Nick Nolte, and Robin Williams—heard his name called. The actor received a standing ovation as he held his statue up to the crowd. "My God," he said, looking genuinely surprised. "I can't believe it. This is really unexpected." The actor maintained his composure behind the podium with the help of an old theater trick. "I had put some tooth-paste on one of my shoes," Hopkins said, "so that I could focus on a white mark and relax myself."

After Hopkins left the stage, *Bugsy*'s star and producer, Warren Beatty, turned around in his seat and gave a bittersweet prediction to a few nearby Orion execs: "It's going to be a sweep," he told them. In quick succession, the remaining *Silence of the Lambs* nominees were called to the stage and handed their awards. First, there was Best Actress winner Foster, who expressed her gratitude to the FBI's John Douglas and acknowledged her costar. ("The reason that I'm here—Anthony Hopkins. Quid pro quo, Doctor.") She was followed by Demme, whose Best Director speech touched on Orion's financial troubles—the studio had recently filed for bankruptcy protection—and praised Harris's "extraordinarily moral and amazing book." The night ended with presenter Elizabeth Taylor making a joke about "cannibal indigestion" before announcing *The Silence of the Lambs* as Best Picture.

Against all odds, the night had turned into a coronation for the film—a "'Lamb'-slide,'" as one headline noted. Even the riskiest Oscar prognosticator wouldn't have bet on the film's taking the night's top five categories. Only two other movies had managed such a feat: Frank Capra's 1934 comedy *It Happened One Night* and the 1975 drama *One Flew over the Cuckoo's Nest*.

Yet it wasn't just the number of statuettes earned by *The Silence of the Lambs* that shocked many Hollywood observers; it was the fact that a horror thriller would prove irresistible to the humdrum-loving Academy voters. In recent years, several tough but worthy films, including *Goodfellas* and *Mississippi Burning*, had been passed over for Best Picture in favor of softer dramas. By choosing *The Silence of the Lambs*, the Academy members were breaking with snoozy tradition. "Dear Jonathan," read a letter sent to the director after the ceremony, "This year the best film actually won! Congratulations." The well-wisher didn't sign his full name, but it was printed at the top of the stationery: Steven Spielberg.

The Silence of the Lambs would find even more admirers in the decade ahead. In the mid-1990s, years after the film's release, a fiftysomething man turned on his TV, hoping for a quick weather update. Instead, he landed on a cable network airing the film—a movie he'd been trying to avoid. "The dialogue was very familiar," he later said. "So I sat down and watched it. And it was a wonderful movie."*

At that point, Tom Harris had spent almost half a decade working on his next Lecter novel. He would not be rushed.

---

* Harris told this story to *The New York Times* in 2019. It contradicts a (very brief) interview he gave *New York* magazine in 1991, in which he claimed he'd watched *The Silence of the Lambs* upon its release, and thought it was "a great movie."

PART 3
GROWING PAINS

Hannibal (1999, 2001)

Red Dragon (2002)

CHAPTER 19

"HE'S OUR ROCK-SOLID LUNATIC."

Throughout the early 1990s, Anthony Hopkins would hear the same question over and over again from reporters and fans: *When is Hannibal Lecter coming back?* The actor was as intrigued as anyone about Lecter's fate. "I'd like to know what happens to him," he said.

Hopkins had long expressed interest in starring in a sequel to *The Silence of the Lambs*—so long as he was comfortable with the material. "We have seen so many nasty things like the Jeffrey Dahmer case," he said shortly before his Oscar win. "I don't want to do anything which might glamorize that." Jonathan Demme and Jodie Foster were also eager to make a new Lecter film. But no one was sure when Harris would return with a new book. The author had been working on his fourth novel since at least 1988. That was when Mort Janklow had announced that the rights to Harris's next two books were up for grabs—and that they wouldn't come cheap. *The Silence of the Lambs* had just spent months on the best-seller list, giving Harris back-to-back-to-back hits. It was time to cash in.

Janklow announced that the auction would start at $1 million and warned prospective bidders that they'd have to give Harris approval over every aspect of the book, from its jacket copy to its publicity campaign. According to one report, the buyer would also have to agree not to "change a single comma" of his writing. Those were tough terms. But as one book industry insider told the press, Harris was "hot, hot, hot." As soon as the auction got under way, Janklow watched the country's five major publishing houses battle over which would write Harris the largest check. "The numbers kept getting bigger," he said. "I set off one against the other."

The winning bid came from Dell Publishing Company, which agreed to pay Harris $5.2 million—and, as part of the deal, gifted Harris a pair of Abyssinian kittens. It was one of the last mammoth book deals of the 1980s, leading some publishing insiders to wonder if Dell had overpaid. After all, Harris wasn't exactly known for his speedy output. "His books come as they will, not as he wills," noted *Silence of the Lambs* editor Tom McCormack, who had backed out of the auction after the price got too high.

But Carole Baron, the president and publisher of Dell, had no problem accommodating Harris's unpredictable timetable: "Those were the days when we worked on gut, not analysis," she says. And by nabbing Harris, she'd locked down the author responsible for *The Silence of the Lambs*—which had just spent months on the bestseller list—as well as *Black Sunday* and *Red Dragon*, both of which had millions of copies in print. "After a certain point," she says, "you're just going for a writer, and you don't really care how much you pay."

Harris's fourth novel was originally expected to arrive some point in late 1991—a date that quickly came and went. Janklow then predicted that the book would arrive in 1993 . . . or maybe 1994. When *those* deadlines passed, some fans began wondering if Harris and his best-known creation were coming back at all. "Why is it taking Hannibal Lecter so long to return to the screen?" asked a reader of *Parade* magazine's popular "Personality Parade" section in 1995. The answer was simple: Until a new book was finished, Lecter was on hiatus. "We can't begin to think of the things Hannibal says," producer Ed Saxon told *Parade*. "That's Tom Harris's job."

Lecter may have been one of the most quoted and most duplicated pop culture figures of the late twentieth century, but he'd remained elusive to audiences. And each year that the character was in limbo, he became all the more intriguing. "Did they ever really decide why Hannibal Lecter liked to eat people?" asks one of the teenage killers in the 1996 slasher classic *Scream*. "Don't think so! See, it's a lot scarier when there's no motive."

As the 1990s went on, "everyone wanted to know when we would have the new Thomas Harris book," Baron says, "and I assured them that it was coming." But Lecter's newfound fans weren't going to wait. They'd spend the decade seeking out bloodshed in countless movies, books, and TV shows about unapologetic serial killers—some imagined, some terrifyingly real.

A few years after he'd given away the role of Hannibal the Cannibal in *Manhunter*, Brian Dennehy got the chance to play a very different sadistic slayer: John Wayne Gacy. "Oh, mister policeman—don't you know a clown can get away with *murder*?" taunted the actor, his face covered in makeup, in the 1992 miniseries *To Catch a Killer*. The movie initially aired less than a year after *The Silence of the Lambs* hit theaters and drew millions of viewers—including Gacy himself. "Sorry you would participate in this fraud," the convicted murderer told Dennehy in a letter from prison. "You've always been one of my favorite actors. As for the 33 bodies that were discovered, lots of people had access to that crawl space."

Gacy might have given a thumbs-down to *To Catch a Killer*, but he was in the minority. In the years ahead, TV viewers and moviegoers would become hooked on a lucrative (and often ludicrous) genre: the serial killer drama. Hollywood had always been interested in tales of mass murderers, going all the way back to the 1920s and '30s, when revered filmmakers such as Alfred Hitchcock (*The Lodger*) and Fritz Lang (*M*) had gotten their start telling tales of ruthless killers. In later years, serial killers were chronicled in everything from low-budget sleaze epics (1963's *Blood Feast*) to big-studio dramas (1971's *Klute*) to tough indie dramas (1986's *Henry: Portrait of a Serial Killer*).

But after the phenomenon of *The Silence of the Lambs*, filmmakers and studio executives raced to put as many stalkers and sickos as possible in front of the cameras. "A big-screen onslaught is on the way," declared a 1992 *New York Times* article, accompanied by a photo of a grim-faced Hopkins as Lecter. "Meet the serial killer—popular culture's villain of the 1990's."

The impact of *The Silence of the Lambs* could be spotted right away in theaters, where films such as *Jennifer 8* (1992), *Blink* (1994), and the brazenly titled *Copycat* (1995) arrived in rapid succession.[*] All were tales of cunning mass murderers being undone by a determined young woman. And all would be compared, often unflatteringly, to *The Silence of the Lambs*, with one critic describing *Copycat*'s menacing baddie as "Hannibal Lecter lite." More serial killer thrillers would arrive in the years ahead, clogging cable TV lineups and video store shelves: *Kalifornia*, *Sliver*, *Switchback*, *Striking Distance*. There were even spoofs such as *Serial Mom* and *So I Married an Axe Murderer*. By the mid-1990s, the genre was so robust that *Henry: Portrait of a Serial Killer* director John McNaughton claimed he was receiving three to four prospective serial killer scripts *per week*.

While some of the modern murderamas performed well, only one came close to matching *The Silence of the Lambs*, both in terms of both notoriety and bankability: *Seven*. Directed by MTV auteur David Fincher, and released in September 1995, the movie starred Brad Pitt and Morgan Freeman as police detectives racing to find a killer who chooses victims who violate the seven deadly sins. Sleek looking and greasy feeling, Fincher's film owes a debt to the entire Lecter enterprise: Much like *Manhunter*, it's a crime thriller in which high-tech forensics provides clues. And just as Demme skimped on the gore while making *The Silence of the Lambs*, Fincher keeps most of *Seven*'s most heinous acts off-screen. In its final moments, Pitt's character discovers that his young wife's head has been lopped off and placed in a box. For years afterward, Fincher would be harangued by viewers who were outraged by his decision to depict a woman's lopped-off head: "You have no right," they'd tell him. In fact, her remains are never visible on-screen. *Seven* was so convincingly grim, so soaked in the *suggestion* of violence, that viewers imagined a horror that wasn't there.

---

[*] Those films' respective lead actors—Uma Thurman (*Jennifer 8*), Madeleine Stowe (*Blink*), and Holly Hunter (*Copycat*)—had all appeared on *The Silence of the Lambs* casting director Howard Feuer's list of potential Clarice Starlings.

After opening at number one, *Seven* stayed atop the box office for a month. From that point on, *any* on-screen story featuring serial killers—including prime-time procedurals such as *Profiler* and *Millennium*—would be compared to *The Silence of the Lambs*, *Seven*, or both. Audiences were so needy for gory stories of mass murder and mind games that in 1998, the old-school slayer Norman Bates returned in a remake of Hitchcock's *Psycho*. The original film had traumatized audiences back in 1960. But by the time the updated version arrived, the story of a quiet loner who kills just a *handful* of people was apparently not so scintillating. Moviegoers were uninterested in the new *Psycho*, and critics were unimpressed, with one reviewer damning the film by describing it as "quaint."

By the 1990s, it turned out, even a knife-wielding maniac like Bates had lost his edge. He'd been snuffed by a literal murderer's row, including many drawn from real life. Throughout the decade, the true-crime industry would enjoy newfound visibility, if not respectability. There were prime-time TV movies such as *Overkill: The Aileen Wuornos Story*, starring Jean Smart as the notorious sex worker turned murderer. On daytime television, the syndicated tabloid shows *A Current Affair* and *Inside Edition* regaled viewers with tales of serial killers from across the country, with segments such as "The Ghoul of Gainesville." And bookstores devoted entire shelves to tell-alls such as *A Father's Son*, a memoir written by Lionel Dahmer about his cannibalistic offspring (the elder Dahmer had been paid a $150,000 advance for the book, which was promoted on network TV). It was even possible to study serial killers at sea: By 1994, the same year Robert Ressler derided Demme's film as irresponsible, the now-retired former FBI agent was hitting the cruise ship circuit, giving a talk titled "The Silence of the Lambs: Myth and Realities."

The fact that death and suffering made for good business troubled some true-crime practitioners. "This is—let's face it—a tacky genre," an anonymous publisher of serial killer books told a reporter in 1994. But if consumers had qualms about buying salacious paperbacks with titles such as *The Milwaukee Murders* ("His den of death was a human slaughterhouse!"), they could assuage their guilt by knowing that they weren't alone. Through a perverse combination of affection and repulsion, real-life serial killers had become *cool*. And their fans had an insatiable appetite for grist and gristle—the nastier, the better.

"We want as much salacity as we can get," noted the British columnist Laurie Taylor in 1994. "We want our new celebrity criminals to resemble legendary rock stars like Jim Morrison and Sid Vicious and Kurt Cobain. They should ideally be loners, people whom no one else has ever properly understood, and who are driven towards self-destruction by some personal vision of the world."

In the 1990s, no true-crime superstar fit that description like Charles Manson. As the decade started, he was safely behind bars in California, serving multiple sentences for first-degree murder. Yet he'd managed to retain his yearslong hold on the public imagination. To the young Gen Xers who'd hadn't been born when his acolytes had gone on their 1969 Los Angeles killing spree, "Charlie" was an ironic icon. *Spin* magazine put the madman on its cover. Guns N' Roses singer Axl Rose regularly wore a Manson T-shirt, and his band covered one of Manson's songs, an acoustic ditty titled "Look at Your Game, Girl." A Philadelphia clothing store even used a photo of Manson in its advertising, with the tagline "Everyone has the occasional urge to go wild and do something completely outrageous."

That level of pop culture infamy enraged some observers, especially those old enough to remember the 1960s. "You can't glorify somebody like Charles Manson," a middle-aged postal worker complained to the *Reno Gazette-Journal*. But Vincent Bugliosi, the prosecutor who'd helped put Manson away decades earlier, understood why the criminal's perpetual rebelliousness might appeal to teenagers and twentysomethings. "Manson's come to symbolize anti-establishment hatred," he said in 1994. "Other killers killed individuals; he struck out at society as a whole."

There was another reason for Manson's unlikely lionization: He hadn't personally killed anybody in those 1969 attacks; instead, he'd commanded his followers to do his bidding for him. His distance from the crimes, however slight, made him a more palatable monster to his fans. Plus, he'd been around for decades—and few things breed celebrity like longevity. "No matter who you are, no matter what your age, you *know* Charles

Manson," *The Boston Globe* noted in 1994. "He's our rock-solid lunatic in this mixed-up, topsy-turvy world."

Wearing a Manson T-shirt could be explained as a low-effort act of nineties rebellion. It was harder to grasp the celebrity of more recent monsters, such as Dahmer. He wasn't some aging menace whose crimes were decades in the past; he was a modern-day abomination whose various offenses, such as performing amateur lobotomies on his victims, had been covered in excruciating detail in the press (sample *New York Post* headline: "Little Body Shop of Horrors"). Yet the lurid accounts of his activities didn't prevent him from becoming a cult figure. The same Philadelphia store that had used Manson in its ads also created a poster featuring Dahmer (its tagline: "Go a little insane now, not a lot insane later"). The cannibal was so inexplicably alluring that during his 1992 jury selection, a pair of teenage girls were spotted outside the courtroom, having skipped school to get Dahmer's autograph. "We just want to see him," one girl explained. "He is famous."

Serial killers had become the bad boys of the 1990s. It was a phenomenon that director Oliver Stone would examine in his coarse, kinetic 1994 road-trip film *Natural Born Killers*. The movie, which began as a screenplay by Quentin Tarantino, starred Woody Harrelson and Juliette Lewis as Mickey and Mallory Knox, a pair of oversexed underdogs who go on a murder spree. As the young lovers kill their way across the country, their escapades become must-see TV for millions of home viewers.

Stone, who greatly reworked Tarantino's script, originally envisioned *Natural Born Killers* as a wild satire. But as he edited the film in early 1994, the filmmaker saw real-life murderers being lionized on network television. That winter, Manson was interviewed by Diane Sawyer, and Dahmer appeared on *Dateline NBC*. Suddenly a film about sadists becoming celebrities didn't seem quite so far fetched. As Warner Bros. pointed out in the film's press notes, "Killers are the hottest media draws in town."

It was a glib proclamation—but as Stone pointed out, it was true. "The world is violent, and we're swamped in it this century," he said before the film's release. "I'm making the point that the killers had been so idealized and so glorified that the media became worse than the killers."

In its first weekend, *Natural Born Killers* dominated the box office, knocking the gentle *Forrest Gump* from the top spot. It stayed in theaters for months and was so much in demand that in the United Kingdom, drug dealers began peddling bootleg copies of it long before its release. By year's end, the rappers Dr. Dre and Ice Cube had released a gory homage titled "Natural Born Killaz" (sample lyric: "I'ma pulla fuckin' Jeffrey Dahmer/Now he's suicidal, just like Nirvana").

Stone had intended *Natural Born Killers* to be a critique of Americans' love affair with violent offenders. But nobody got the joke. Instead, Mickey and Mallory became America's latest superstar killers. And to some viewers, the duo's violent acts were uncomfortably *relatable*. "The most pacifistic people in the world said they came out of this movie and wanted to kill somebody," the director said.

In the 1990s, the thin dividing line between those who commit awful crimes and those who obsess over them became all the more visible. The same year Stone unleashed *Natural Born Killers*, the novelist Joyce Carol Oates wrote an essay for *The New York Review of Books* about Americans' fixation on serial killers. She noted that the big-screen success of *The Silence of the Lambs* had heralded a new era, one in which mass murderers had become the country's "debased, condemned, yet eerily glorified Noble Savage." And Oates argued that the intense interest in Dahmer, Bundy, and Ed Gein was partly due to "our uneasy sense that such persons are forms of ourselves, derailed and gone terribly wrong."

Yet that fascination/revulsion with killers had its limits. At a certain point, all celebrities lose their luster. On May 10, 1994, a few months after Oates's essay was published, John Wayne Gacy was scheduled for execution by lethal injection at a maximum-security facility in Joliet, Illinois. For hours beforehand, gatherers stood outside the prison walls, some wearing T-shirts proclaiming "No tears for the Clown." One bystander even dressed as an executioner.

Gacy had spent the past fifteen years as one of America's most recognizable killers. He'd been the subject of several books, and his clown paintings had recently fetched thousands of dollars on the open market. Anyone who'd bothered to learn about Gacy, however, would quickly realize that he wasn't some alluringly misunderstood outsider. He was a cruel, sad-sack monster who'd ended the lives of dozens of boys. The success of *The Silence of the Lambs* may have convinced some people that serial killers were geniuses with grand ambitions and compelling world-views. But Manson, Dahmer, and Gacy were not brilliant rebels worthy of fandom—even ironic fandom. They'd simply found a new way to be famous: murder.

In his final moments, Gacy told a prison official that he had a final message for the world: "Kiss my ass." Not long afterward, he was led into a chamber and placed on a gurney, where a cocktail of drugs was injected into his arms. Due to a clog in a tube, eighteen minutes passed before Gacy died.

It was an ugly scene all around, a reminder that for all of the cultural elevation of serial killers in the 1990s, their notoriety was the result of man-made brutality. It was almost enough to make one pine for fictitious madmen—like Hannibal the Cannibal. His evil seemed so much cleaner, so much more *civilized*, than that of his real-world counterparts. Yet throughout the decade, Lecter was nowhere to be found. And neither was his keeper.

CHAPTER 20

"HANNIBAL LECTER, WHERE ARE YOU?"

In early 1992, FBI special agent Athena Varounis visited Harris in Miami Beach. She'd stayed in touch with the author for years after their initial meeting at the cafeteria of the J. Edgar Hoover Building. When *The Silence of the Lambs* swept the Academy Awards, Varounis called the author to congratulate him.

"Ain't that something!" she told Harris.

"Ain't that something!" the author repeated back.

In Miami, Harris could enjoy all the spoils of fame—and none of the hassle. He sped around town in his black Porsche Carrera, a set of knives stored in the trunk just in case he was asked to help out at a friend's dinner party. And he roamed freely around his favorite Miami Beach stores, knowing that he wouldn't be recognized (a bakery clerk at a high-end food market Harris frequented knew him simply as "the bearded guy"). Few people realized that a best-selling millionaire was living in their midst. When Harris had reported for jury duty in a local murder case in 1992 and identified himself as a writer, the judge had asked if he'd published anything of note. The court was stunned by his sheepish response: "Yes—*The Silence of the Lambs*."

Yet for all the privileges the novel had granted Harris, he told Varounis that *The Silence of the Lambs* had become both "a blessing and a curse." She took notes during her visit, capturing Harris's mindset at the time:

"It's brought a great deal of attention upon him, but he can't begrudge its success. He has an office he goes to write but he hasn't done near as much as he should. It's a lot of pressure to try to top the previous book."

Perhaps as a response to those outsized expectations, Harris spent much of the decade wandering the world, his travels a mix of business and leisure. In the mid-1990s, he could occasionally be found in Paris, taking culinary classes at the famed Le Cordon Bleu. He also spent time in Florence, one of Lecter's favorite cities and the home of a ferocious serial killer, *il Mostro di Firenze*, "the Monster of Florence," who was suspected of murdering sixteen people between 1968 and 1985. Harris befriended the investigator leading the case, and in 1994 was spotted at a hearing for the man accused of being *il Mostro*. "He refused to say much," a reporter wrote of Harris, "except that he found the case fascinating and the trial boring."

There'd be other research trips in the years ahead, including visits to a convention of homicide detectives in Orlando, Florida. At those gatherings, Harris often sat in the back of a makeshift classroom, scribbling in his notebook as he listened to profilers and forensic experts lecture on topics such as DNA evidence, blood spatter, and the preferences and peccadilloes of various serial killers. After the day's sessions had wrapped, he might meet up with the speakers, asking them questions over drinks and dinner. "I never saw him look happier than when he was eating a good fish sandwich," noted one police academy instructor who got to know the author over time.

Harris had also made law enforcement connections in his home city of Miami, sometimes consulting with David Rivers, a sergeant with the Miami-Dade Police Department's homicide Bureau. "He's a hoot," said Rivers. "If you didn't know who he was, you'd think he's just a little old guy from Mississippi. He's not impressed with himself, or anybody else."

Those new sources would come in handy, as Harris's relationship with the FBI had changed. Several of the agents he'd spoken to for *Red Dragon* and *The Silence of the Lambs* had retired by the early 1990s. Some had gone into the private sector, while others, including Robert Ressler and John Douglas, had written their own books about catching serial killers: Douglas's 1995 memoir *Mindhunter: Inside the FBI's Elite Serial*

Crime Unit would later serve as inspiration for the Netflix series *Mindhunter* (several episodes were directed by *Seven*'s David Fincher). As a result of those retirements and departures, "Harris lost contact with us," notes one BSU veteran.

The author still had at least one key FBI source: Varounis. By the early 1990s, she was in Washington, DC, working as a technically trained agent and dealing with the latest tapping and tracking devices, which she demonstrated for Harris. During their meetings, the two discussed what Clarice Starling's post-Lecter career in the FBI might look like. Harris wanted to know how a young female agent might be treated once she was in the field. "The men would be insanely jealous," Varounis told Harris. "They would be satiated only once they destroyed her." She shared a maxim she'd adopted during her long career with the Bureau: "Don't fall in love with the badge—the badge will never love you back."

When Harris returned to Miami after his various sojourns, he holed up in an office near his home and tried to write. As always, the work was torture. At one point he took a break from book duties and visited the set of the Demi Moore comedy *Striptease* (Harris's motion picture literary agent, Bob Bookman, also worked with the film's director, Andrew Bergman). A fan spotted the author and asked about the status of his next novel. "Let me tell you about my day," Harris reportedly said. "I get up at eight in the morning. I leave the house at 8.30 and I arrive at my office at 8.37. I stay in the office until two in the afternoon. And between 8.36am and 2pm, I'm doing one of three things: I'm writing; I'm staring out the window; or I'm writhing on the floor."

Still, he managed to publish at least one short work in the mid-1990s: an essay for a teen magazine called *Mouth2Mouth*. The publication was the creation of Angela Janklow, the daughter of Harris's agent, Mort Janklow. As she was putting together *Mouth2Mouth*'s premiere issue, she began dreaming up contributors who could help get the magazine some attention. "I was thinking 'Who's an iconic, intelligent, unusual person who's difficult to access—the J. D. Salinger of this moment?'" she says.

Janklow got her father's help in wrangling Harris, whose assignment was straightforward: He was to create his dream syllabus for a ninth-grade

English class. "What I expected was 'Tom Harris's 10 Books That Everybody Should Read as a Freshman,'" Janklow says. "Instead, I got something that was poetry in motion."

Harris's article appeared in *Mouth2Mouth*'s spring 1994 issue, which featured Cindy Crawford and Shaquille O'Neal on its cover. The author seemed to realize that he was an uneasy fit for a magazine featuring stories about Adam Sandler and Sonic the Hedgehog. "A world odd enough to put me in charge of educating ninth-graders," he wrote, "would also rotate end over end, I think, with the Western Hemisphere forever dark." His proposed English class syllabus no doubt perplexed *Mouth2Mouth*'s teen readers. It included such works as Alexandre Dumas's *Grand dictionnaire de cuisine*, the poetry of Pablo Neruda, and the lyrics from Willie Nelson's 1975 album *Red-Headed Stranger*. Harris also suggested that the students do some cooking projects every once in a while. His essay took up just half a page, accompanied by the phrase "How different we'd all be if he'd been our teacher."

If that brief cameo led readers to believe that Harris might soon reemerge with another novel, their hopes would be short lived. By the late 1990s, there was no sign that the author was making progress. "Tom tormented himself about how hard it was to write," recalls Bob Bookman, the agent who'd brokered the film rights for *Silence* and who was one of many waiting for Harris's follow-up. "I once asked, 'What did you do today?' and he said, 'I basically writhed around on the floor.'"

Dino De Laurentiis, who had dibs on the film rights for the next Lecter book, sent his personal pasta chef to cook for Harris in Miami, reportedly in the hope that the food would speed up the writing process. It had been more than a decade since the *Manhunter* producer had passed on making the film version of *The Silence of the Lambs*—and then watched it become a worldwide hit. "In a way it vindicated Dino, because he was right all along that there was something to the Lecter character," says his daughter Raffaella De Laurentiis. "On the other hand, it disappointed him, because *The Silence of the Lambs* was not his movie. But, Dino being Dino, he wanted to make another Hannibal movie."

As producers, publishers, and filmmakers awaited Lecter's return,

Harris's fans lamented the author's absence on the newly emerging internet. That was where rumors about his next novel—supposedly titled *The Morbidity of the Soul*—were shared in defeated tones. "He always takes his time," one reader wrote in a 1997 message forum post. "3 books in almost twenty years! Clarice will be a senior agent in the sequel. Or probably retired. ;-)"

But murder junkies could take comfort in the rows of serial killer novels filling airport bookstores and library spinner racks in the 1990s. Bret Easton Ellis's startling *American Psycho* was the most prominent example—a book so fussed and fought over that it had become hard to ignore (even if some grossed-out readers likely had to put it down after a few pages). The decade also found serial killers stalking prey in such hit novels as Caleb Carr's *The Alienist*, Susanna Moore's *In the Cut*, and James Patterson's *Kiss the Girls*, as well as in the comic book writer Alan Moore's trippy Jack the Ripper saga *From Hell*. Even Joyce Carol Oates, a Princeton professor who by the mid-1990s had earned numerous literary honors, would get grody: In 1995, she published the Dahmer-inspired *Zombie*, a faux journal of an ice pick–wielding murderer who conducts experiments on his victims. An early version of Oates's lurid tale was published in the highbrow *New Yorker* (sample entry: "There was a gush of blood and I came, I lost control and came, so hard I kept coming and coming like a convulsion.").

As the decade wound down, it had become nearly impossible to flip through the cable TV lineup or browse a bookstore without coming face-to-face with a grinning murderer. It was overkill in every way possible. Yet audiences were still seeking the cannibal who'd made it all possible. In 1997, a newspaper columnist wrote an essay complaining about a lack of compelling pop culture villains. The story's pleading headline: "Hannibal Lecter, Where Are You?"

He was closer than people realized. By that point, Harris had begun meeting semiregularly with his editor, Carole Baron. During summers, the two would dine at one of Harris's favorite Sag Harbor hangouts: the restaurant at the American Hotel, known for its high-end menu and thousand-plus-bottle wine list. Over their meals, they would debate the latest movies and discuss Lecter's whereabouts. Baron had spent the decade patiently waiting for Harris to finish his latest novel. But she knew he couldn't be rushed, and refrained from asking him when it might arrive. "Tom would talk about the book or hand me pages," she says. "I would stick 'em in my bag, and eagerly go home and read them and respond."

Finally, in March 1999, Baron got a phone call from Harris. "Are you busy?" he asked before telling her that a six-hundred-page manuscript was en route, one with a succinct title: *Hannibal*.

When Baron broke the news of Harris's return to her staff at Dell, "I practically got a standing ovation from our sales team," she says. "And I got flowers from the buyer at Barnes & Noble." Eleven years had passed since *The Silence of the Lambs* had arrived in hardcover—a far longer delay than anyone could have anticipated.

Lecter would be back just in time to bid adieu to the bloody decade he'd helped invent. In his absence, it seemed as though the world had become more violent than ever: The twenty-four-hour news cycle pumped out ghastly images of destruction, while the bustling true-crime industry sustained itself on a constant supply of real-life killers. Harris would respond to such late-twentieth-century savagery with a novel more ghastly, more *corrosive*, than anyone could have expected—even himself. "I dreaded doing *Hannibal*," he confessed, "dreaded the personal wear and tear, dreaded the choices I would have to watch."

CHAPTER 21

"YOU ARE A WARRIOR."

Despite the novel's title, it takes more than a hundred pages for Hannibal to show up in *Hannibal*. The book's early sections instead focus on Clarice Starling, who's clearly become the doctor's favorite unofficial patient. It's been seven years since she killed Buffalo Bill and graduated to the FBI, where her career has floundered—partly because of her flinty attitude and partly because of intra-Bureau politics and sexism. She's become, in Harris's words, "a rising star that stuck on the way up," reduced to a thankless churn of serving warrants and bugging telephones. (*Don't fall in love with the badge—the badge will never love you back.*)

Starling's profile within the Bureau gets an unwanted boost during *Hannibal*'s vigorous opening scene, which finds her taking part in a drug raid near a crowded fish market. The mission goes disastrously wrong, with Starling killing a dealer as she cradles a baby—a moment captured on live TV. The botched mission is the latest PR fiasco for the FBI, which Harris depicts in *Hannibal* as impotent at best, corrupt at worst. In the years since the author had taken his Quantico classes, the Bureau had been under increased scrutiny due to a pair of fatal standoffs: the 1992 siege of a family cabin in Ruby Ridge, Idaho, and the 1993 destruction of the Branch Davidian compound in Waco, Texas. Both incidents are mentioned just briefly in *Hannibal*, yet they loom over the novel as reminders of the real-world destruction to which America was becoming accustomed, and as motivation for the embroiled FBI to cast the now-controversial Starling aside.

Yet she still has the support of her most avid fan, who writes to Starling after her public debacle, sending well-wishes on a letter enclosed in his trademark mauve envelope:

> *You are a warrior, Clarice. The enemy is dead, the baby safe. You are a warrior.*
>
> *The most stable elements, Clarice, appear in the middle of the periodic table, roughly between iron and silver.*
>
> *Between iron and silver. I think that is appropriate for you.*
>
> *Hannibal Lecter*

In the years since escaping the police in Memphis, *Hannibal* reveals, Lecter has lain low and lived large. After having his extra finger removed during a trip to Brazil, he has settled in Florence, Italy, where he's disguised himself as a historian named Dr. Fell, and replaced the head curator of Palazzo Capponi, a centuries-old palace with an extensive library. "He has found a peace here that he would preserve," Harris wrote. "He has killed hardly anybody, except his predecessor." Lecter's journeys in Florence take up more than a hundred pages in *Hannibal*, with Harris documenting the city's various architectural, cultural, and sociopolitical histories in rich detail. Reading the novel, it's hard to tell which enigmatic visitor had more fun stalking the city's palazzi in the 1990s: Hannibal Lecter or Tom Harris.

In the world of *Hannibal*, Lecter's long disappearance has only added to his mystique. He's the most famous serial killer in the world, so much so that his old personal items, such as his copy of Dumas's *Grand dictionnaire de cuisine*, command five-figure sums on the black market. One law library has even set up a Hannibal Lecter Collection, so that scholars can study his crimes. And of course there are countless amateur obsessives trading Lecter trivia online:

In cyberspace at least, interest in Dr. Lecter remained very much alive. The damp floor of the Internet sprouted Lecter theories like toadstools and sightings of the doctor rivaled those of Elvis in number. Imposters plagued the chat rooms and in the phospho-rescent swamp of the Web's dark side, police photographs of his outrages were bootlegged to collectors of hideous arcana.

Those outrages, Harris reveals, include Lecter's near destruction of Mason Verger, a gazillionaire pedophile who had once been under the doc-tor's care. In the years before he was caught by Will Graham, Lecter had fed Verger a cocktail of hallucinogenic drugs—and then encouraged the pa-tient to peel off his face and feed it to his dogs. Verger had survived, though his face had not: "Noseless and lipless," Harris wrote, "with no soft tissue on his face, [Verger] was all teeth, like a creature of the deep, deep ocean."

Even for Harris, who'd sired the likes of the Tooth Fairy and Buffalo Bill, Verger was an absurdly obscene creation. He keeps a giant eel, known as a "Brutal Moray," near his bedside. He brags about his days hanging with Idi Amin. And he drinks chilled martinis garnished with the tears of poor foster children. Verger lives in pursuit of "hard-core fun," and he's come up with a delicious plan for getting revenge on Lecter: With the help of some Sardinian kidnappers, he will abduct Hannibal and feed him feet-first to a ravenous army of specially bred wild boars—creatures "capable of lifting a man on their great ripping tusks."

After learning of Verger's scheme, Lecter escapes from Italy, leaving a trail of bodies in his wake. Though he's now on the FBI's Ten Most Wanted list, he has had just enough surgery that he can slip undetected into the United States in the hope of finding Starling. He crosses the border by joining a Canadian tour group, forcing him to confront what must be, for him, an unimaginable horror: flying coach. Stuck in a middle seat, where he's "rebreathing the farts and exhalations of others in economically re-processed air," the anguished Lecter does his best to fit in:

Like many others scattered throughout the cheapest seats, Dr. Lecter wears a bright yellow smiley-face badge with CAN-AM

TOURS on it in big red letters, and like the tourists he wears faux athletic warm-ups. His warm-ups bear the insignia of the Toronto Maple Leafs, a hockey team. Beneath his clothing, a considerable amount of cash is strapped to his body.

While in flight, Lecter gives out a sudden, short scream. His thoughts had momentarily turned to a figure never mentioned in Harris's previous novels: Mischa, his long-dead younger sister. Despite the doctor's claim in *The Silence of the Lambs* that he was a man without a past—"You can't reduce me to a set of influences"—*Hannibal* reveals that Mischa has haunted and driven him for decades. The two siblings were born in Lithuania, only to be orphaned during World War II, when their parents were killed by Nazi bombs. Left to fend for themselves, the Lecter children were found by a group of deserting soldiers. Desperate and ravenous, the troops eventually ate Mischa, leaving Lecter with an indelible memory: the sight of his sister's baby teeth lying in the soldiers' stool pit. He was six years old at the time, and the image has never left him.

But Lecter has a plan to bring Mischa back—one inspired by the work of Stephen Hawking. "Dr. Lecter wants time to reverse," Harris wrote, adding that Lecter has "a desperate wish to make a place for Mischa in the world, perhaps the place now occupied by Clarice Starling." Lecter wants Starling to be a stand-in for his long-dead sister. And given the agent's plight after she's been punished by the FBI, Lecter thinks he may be able to draw her close. In his mind, he'd free her from her doomed existence at the Bureau, and she'd relieve him of the pain of his youth. Another quid pro quo.

Lecter's psyche-scarring childhood wasn't the only new bit of information Harris divulged in *Hannibal.* There's a tossed-off reference to his cousin Balthus, the real-life Polish-French artist known for his carnally charged paintings. *Hannibal* also digs into Lecter's "memory palace," a vast cognitive library where he keeps detailed recollections of everything from blueprints to patient interviews. It's one of the many near-superhuman powers he has accrued by the time of *Hannibal.* His always strong sense of smell is now powerful enough to sniff out the faintest odors. And despite his extravagant diet, he is fit and powerful, capable of pulling one victim's lungs out through his back. "Size for size," Harris wrote, "he is as strong as an ant."

Hannibal also catalogs the doctor's rarefied tastes—his penchant for carbon-steel kitchen knives, white truffles, and $3,600-a-case Bordeaux. This is a guy who even while on the run finds time to maintain a vintage black Jaguar Mark II and play an eighteenth-century Flemish harpsichord. "His face may have changed, but his tastes did not," *Hannibal* notes, "and he was not a man who denied himself."

Lecter also has his more ignoble pursuits: At one point in the novel, he satisfies himself by quietly sneaking into Starling's car, taking a giant sniff, and licking the steering wheel, moving his mouth "as though he savored wine." His obsession with the agent is equal parts pervy and paternal; he really *does* admire Starling, and wants her to see herself as he does. "Did you ever think, Clarice, why the Philistines don't understand you?" he writes Starling. "It's because you're the answer to Samson's riddle: You are the honey in the lion."*

In *Hannibal*, Harris slowly teases out the similarities between Lecter and Starling: Both are isolated, misunderstood orphans who can't play nice or fake their feelings, making them outcasts among their peers. It makes for an unseemly bond, one that would reach an unsavory climax in *Hannibal*'s shocking last chapter, which was certain to arouse readers' ire—or just arouse them, period.

That graphic climax was destined to be spoiled on the internet, which may be why, in early 1999, Harris wanted to get *Hannibal* into bookstores as quickly as possible. After turning in his manuscript to Baron that March, he told her that he wanted the book to be in readers' hands that summer—a remarkably speedy turnaround time. "People said it wouldn't work," Baron recalls. "But for *Hannibal*, they made it work."

• • •

---

* The riddle appears in Judges 14:14. "So he said: 'Out of the eater, something to eat; out of the strong, something sweet.'"

With *Hannibal* slated for a June release, the publishing industry hustled to make room for Lecter. More than a million copies of *Hannibal* would be sent to retailers, as would hundreds of thousands of new paperback copies of *Red Dragon* and *The Silence of the Lambs*. A rival publisher even rejiggered its release calendar, to ensure that certain books wouldn't get lost in the *Hannibal* hoopla.

In the media, Lecter's return was treated as a fait accompli success. *Entertainment Weekly* raced to publish a cover story featuring Lecter on the cover under the jubilant headline "He's Back!" Excitement for Harris's novel was so high—and online speculation about its subject matter so rampant—that copies were kept in safes in the publisher's offices. To further safeguard against leaks, Baron opted not to send any early copies to reviewers. "Everyone would read the book at the same time," she says.

The hype surrounding *Hannibal* was surpassed only by the clamor over the year's *other* returning antihero: Darth Vader. Harris's novel would arrive shortly after the release of *Star Wars: Episode I—The Phantom Menace*, the franchise's first film in more than a decade. Lecter and Vader were both arrogant, irritable loners with a cool taste in masks. They'd also long maintained a sense of mystery. But on the internet, books and films were being exhumed and examined 24/7, with fans analyzing even the most minuscule plot point. As a result, audiences had come to loathe obscurity. When it came to their favorite characters, they demanded that every missing year be accounted for, and every villainous act be justified or explained—as if that were even possible.

Not surprisingly, Harris wanted nothing to do with the feeding frenzy around *Hannibal*. Before its release, a *Washington Post* reporter called Janklow and asked to speak with Harris, who was sitting in his agent's office at the time. Janklow refused to hand over the phone. "No interviews," he told the *Post*. "No signings. No nothing. It'll just be the biggest book of the year without all that." And though Harris showed up for a celebratory cocktail party at Delacorte Press's Manhattan offices on June 8, 1999—the day of *Hannibal*'s release—the author kept his appearance brief. "He was very gracious and thanked everybody," said Baron. "And then he disappeared."

Harris's refusal to promote *Hannibal* wasn't a problem, given the book's built-in star power. "Hannibal is back," noted a display at a Barnes & Noble in Santa Monica, California. "Are you ready?" Retailers were certainly well prepared: At some bookstores in the United States and United Kingdom, the owners stayed up late so they could sell copies at midnight. One shop hired a Lecter impersonator and gave away glasses of Chianti, while another handed out pizza with all-meat toppings. Within the first twenty-four hours of *Hannibal*'s release, many retailers ran out of stock, forcing them to frantically order more copies. "It's just going straight out of the shops," reported an employee of *Hannibal*'s UK publishing company.

As if Harris's fans needed an extra reason to rush out and buy *Hannibal*, *The New York Times* ran an ecstatic review by Stephen King, whose love of *Red Dragon* had helped make that novel a must-read in 1981. "The readers who have been waiting for 'Hannibal' only want to know if it is as good as 'Red Dragon' and 'The Silence of the Lambs,'" he wrote. "It is a pleasure to reply in the negative. No, not as good. This one is better." Lecter's time away from the spotlight, he noted, had only made Lecter all the more powerful: "In a late-century literary landscape where most psycho-villains are little fellows in rubber masks, armed with knives and burdened with cumbersome sexual kinks, Dr. Lecter casts a long shadow indeed. . . . If Hannibal Lecter isn't a Count Dracula for the computer-and-cell-phone age, then we don't have one."

King's rave was explicit, emphatic, and slightly confusing. (Lecter lacked kinks? Had King missed the bit about Hannibal running his tongue along Starling's steering wheel?) The review was also emblematic of the initial goodwill toward *Hannibal*. Critics declared the novel "vast, pungent, pulpy, terrifying" (*Entertainment Weekly*); "a Grand Guignol romp" (*The Nation*); and "deliciously frightening" (*Newsday*). Such endorsements appeared right around the time *Hannibal* debuted at number one on the *New York Times* bestseller list. The book stayed atop the chart for nearly two months before Lecter was dethroned by Europe's *other* all-knowing, seemingly immortal academic: Harry Potter.

Throughout the summer of 1999, *Hannibal* dominated vacation discussions and clogged library wait-lists. But as more readers found their way to the end of Harris's morbid 486-page travelogue, a slow-brewing backlash began. In *Talk* magazine, the novelist Martin Amis described *Hannibal* as "on all levels, a snorting, rooting, oinking porker, complete with twinkling trotters and twirlaround tail." An admirer of Harris's previous novels, Amis attacked *Hannibal* with the ferocity and frustration one would use to skewer a former lover. "Martin loved books that were being billed as literary and cultural events, to sharpen his irony on," says *Talk* founder Tina Brown. "And when I realized the release of 'Hannibal' was going to be the book of the month, I knew he would, forgive me, eat it up!"

Virtually every aspect of the novel offended Amis, from Harris's syntax to Lecter's sins. "I got through the thing in the end," he wrote, "with many a weary exhalation, with much dropping of the head and rolling of the eyes, and with considerable fanning of the armpits."

Other readers bemoaned *Hannibal*'s gore—an odd gripe about a book about a cannibal, but an understandable one: While *Red Dragon* and *The Silence of the Lambs* had featured their fair share of blood and guts, *Hannibal* reveled in its ripeness. One character is hung with his bowels hanging out, leaving him with a postmortem erection; another loses his face to a man-eating pig, leaving behind "a bloody dish." A frustrated reader told the press that *Hannibal* "reeks of snuff." And one critic closed out his review with a single-sentence, frowny-faced dismissal: "Yuck."

Some readers wondered if *Hannibal*'s go-for-Baroque violence and vile supporting characters were Harris's way of criticizing his increasingly bloodthirsty audience. On an internet thread that started less than a week after *Hannibal*'s release, a fan asked, "Does anyone else think that Harris . . . is deliberately punishing the summer beach-book crowd and movie audiences who turned his awful serial killers into pop icons (namely Lecter)?"

Yet most of the discussion about *Hannibal*, whether online or in print, had to do with the book's ending, which takes place in Lecter's makeshift hideaway near the Chesapeake Bay. By that point, Verger's scheme to feed Lecter to the superswine has failed—in part because some of the pigs "smelled no fear" in Lecter and refused to eat him. Meanwhile, Verger has faced his own gruesome demise: First, his bodybuilder sister, who needs a suitable heir to inherit the family fortune, uses a cattle prod to collect his sperm. Then she stuffs his killer eel into his mouth, drowning him with blood ("Wiggle, wiggle, Mason," she coos).

With Verger out of the picture, Lecter is in the clear, allowing him to spend quality time with Starling. He takes her to his retreat, where he pumps her full of mind-bending drugs and subjects her to long, drowsy therapy sessions. At one point, he presents Starling with the bones of her dead father, which he'd had the foresight to dig up earlier. His goal? To get her to address the grief and anger she feels about her dad's untimely demise:

> "Clarice, I'm going to leave you here with the remains. Remains, Clarice. Scream your plight into his eyeholes and no reply will come." He put his hands on the sides of her head. "What you need of your father is here, in your head, and subject to your judgment, not his. I'll leave you now. Do you want the candles?"

It all makes for the wildest literary therapy session since *The Bell Jar*. What happens next in *Hannibal*, though, would cause some readers to scream their plights into whatever eyeholes they could find. After weeks of therapy, Lecter leads Starling to the dining room, where she's seated near her archenemy Paul Krendler, a slick and slimy Department of Justice operative who's long thwarted her Bureau career (he'd once referred to her as "cornpone country pussy" after she'd rejected his advances). Lecter has abducted and lobotomized Krendler so the crooked flunky can join Starling and the doctor for a private dinner. Among the exotic menu items: grated fresh black truffle, whole caper berries—and slices of Krendler's prefrontal lobe. ("All we ask," Lecter tells Krendler before digging in, "is that you keep an open mind.")

In a shocking turn, Clarice Starling, the upright FBI agent who strived to do everything by the book, happily dines on her tormenter's brains. If that's not unthinkable enough, she then submits to Hannibal the Cannibal, offering him a wine-dappled breast. *Hannibal* next flashes a few years into the future, with the couple living in Buenos Aires, where they attend the opera and make love with impunity: "Their relationship," Harris wrote, "has a great deal to do with the penetration of Clarice Starling, which she avidly welcomes and encourages."

It was a truly salacious send-off, turning Hannibal Lecter and Clarice Starling into man-eating lovers on the run. Online, Harris's fans debated the finer points of the novel's last few pages: Had Lecter forced the zombified Starling to hand over her affections—or had he merely unlocked her long-sunken desires? Had Starling found in Lecter a surrogate father, in the way Lecter viewed her as a replacement for his sister? Oh, and: Has *any* bestseller ever featured a phrase as clunky and unsavory as "the penetration of Clarice Starling"?

Those questions would linger for decades. At the time of *Hannibal*'s release, though, the sight of straight-arrow Starling going full cannibal upset many of the agent's fans. Art Almquist, the drama teacher who'd taken friends to see *The Silence of the Lambs* on its opening weekend in Connecticut, had spent the subsequent years rewatching and studying Demme's film—even making it the subject of his graduate thesis. He read the early sections of *Hannibal* with excitement: "I thought, 'This is cinema gold. I can't wait for the movie.'" But when he got to the ending, he was aghast: "Harris abandoned everything we love about these characters."

Many *Silence of the Lambs* fans took the final pages of *Hannibal* as a personal betrayal. "Simply no excuse," complained one critic. "The ultimate discourtesy," griped another. On a message board thread devoted to the book's final sequence, a commenter described Starling's cannibalism as "completely unbelievable. It'd be like having Sherlock Holmes consumed by cocaine, behead Watson and eat his brains." Even Varounis, Harris's longtime friend and fan, was put off by *Hannibal*. "I didn't like it," she says. "I was a little troubled by it."

The *Hannibal* pile-on grew so vocal, especially online, that Harris ultimately pushed back. In early 2000, after *Entertainment Weekly* ran another Lecter cover story—this one noting *Hannibal*'s shortcomings—the author fired off an angry letter to the magazine. "For the sake of your own critical faculty, let me suggest something," Harris wrote. "Give *Hannibal* a close and independent reading, and then tell me from your heart—who has dumbed down, Clarice Starling, or her critics?"

Still, even Harris seemed to understand why many readers struggled with the book's ending. In an essay written around the same time as his diatribe to *EW*, he acknowledged how hard it had been to watch the agent and the cannibal become a couple: "[I] feared for Starling," he wrote. "In the end, I let them go, as you must let characters go, let Dr. Lecter and Clarice Starling decide events according to their natures."

Their increasingly simpatico natures *did* make a certain amount of sense by the final moments of the book—at least to those who shared Harris's increasingly glum worldview. The novel arrived at the twilight of a decade in which serial killers had become celebrities and warfare had become prime-time entertainment. In one especially provocative moment, the author paused the narrative to acknowledge the unpleasantness of the times—and to wonder what norms were left to break. "Now that ceaseless exposure has calloused us to the lewd and the vulgar, it is instructive to see what still seems wicked to us," Harris wrote. "What still slaps the clammy flab of our submissive consciousness hard enough to get our attention?"

In a novel full of kidnappers and creeps, sell-outs and schemers, pornographers and pedophiles—a book in which nearly *every character* has either compromised their beliefs or never held any in the first place—Lecter comes to seem almost respectable by comparison. He grants Starling the care and respect her colleagues can never seem to provide her. And at least Lecter's urges come with *some* self-imposed limits. "He told me once that, whenever it was 'feasible,' he preferred to eat the rude," one character recounts in *Hannibal*. "'Free-range rude,' he called them."

For all the complaints readers had with *Hannibal*'s loony ending, Harris's novel solidified Lecter as a perfect antihero for an imperfect time—a monster, sure, but one with purpose and passion, not to mention a curious charm. As the world around him coarsened, Lecter only became more refined. And while readers may have felt an unhappy ripple in their guts as they paged through Harris's novel, many couldn't wait to see *Hannibal* on the big screen.

CHAPTER 22

"WHEN THE POPE-A DIE, WE CREATE A NEW POPE-A"

Ted Tally would always remember when he received his early copy of *Hannibal*. The screenwriter had waited years to learn where Harris would take Lecter. But by April 20, 1999, the day Harris's manuscript finally appeared, Tally's attention was elsewhere. That morning two armed students had entered Columbine High School in Columbine, Colorado, where they killed more than a dozen students and teachers—at the time, the deadliest school shooting in US history.

The incident hung over Tally as he confronted the ultraviolent *Hannibal*. "It definitely influenced my reaction to the book," he says. It wasn't just the book's grisliness that turned him off; he also blanched at the novel's treatment of Starling. "I thought, 'I love Tom Harris and owe him my entire career. But I can't see how to make this work as a movie. I can't see liking *this* Clarice as much as we came to love her from the other book.'"

Demme, meanwhile, read *Hannibal* while vacationing in the Caribbean. "It absolutely broke my heart," he said. Like Tally, the director was troubled by the book, especially the ending. "Tom Harris, as unpredictable as ever, took Clarice and Lecter's relationship in a direction that just didn't compute for me. Clarice is drugged up and she's eating brains with him. And I just thought, 'I can't do this.'"

When *Silence of the Lambs* coproducer Ed Saxon read *Hannibal*, he was equally disappointed. "It wasn't a sequel to the movie we made," he says. "Tom's Gothic predilections took over." And while Saxon was initially game to turn it into a film—"You don't give up a tentpole, even just for financial reasons," he says—he would soon be out as well.

By that point, Dino De Laurentiis had already bought *Hannibal*'s film rights for $10 million. But it soon became clear that De Laurentiis would have to make a sequel to *The Silence of the Lambs* without that film's Oscar-winning director, screenwriter, and producers.* "We would have had a huge payday," remembers Tally. "But Jonathan said, 'What are we going to do—get up in the morning and say, 'Let's do a really great flaying scene'? We both had young children at the time. And I didn't want to put that into the world."

For Demme, walking away from the sequel to *The Silence of the Lambs*—a movie he'd been waiting to make for nearly a decade—was devastating: "I had to tell Tom it was a journey I couldn't take." The news of his departure shocked many in Hollywood, where a *Silence of the Lambs* reunion was all but a "foregone conclusion," Demme said. But when the director's agent called De Laurentiis to inform him that Demme was passing, De Laurentiis took the news in stride. "When the Pope-a die, we create a new Pope-a," he said. "Good luck to Jonathan Demme. Good-bye."

De Laurentiis was determined to make *Hannibal* no matter what; he just needed the right director. In 1999, he was working on a film on the island of Malta, not far from where the filmmaker Ridley Scott was shooting his sword-and-sandals epic *Gladiator*. Scott's filmography included horror hits (*Alien*), thrillers (*Someone to Watch over Me*), and tales of passionate yet complex relationships (*Thelma & Louise*). Much like Harris's novels, the director's films tended to be ornate and precise, often alternating between classy and mischievous. He seemed a natural fit for the unnatural *Hannibal*. But when De Laurentiis handed him a manuscript, the director balked at the book's title. "Dino, I don't want to do elephants coming over the Alps," he said. "I'm doing a Roman movie now."

---

* In addition to Saxon, *The Silence of the Lambs*' Oscar-winning producing team included Kenneth Utt, who passed away in 1994, and Ron Bozman.

After finally getting around to reading *Hannibal*, Scott quickly signed on to direct the film version, which would be a coproduction of Universal Pictures and MGM—the result of complicated, long-running legal wrangling over the rights to Harris's creations. With Tally out of the picture, the studios recruited the famed playwright and screenwriter David Mamet to work on a *Hannibal* adaptation. Mamet had created the hustling real estate salesmen of *Glengarry Glen Ross* and the desperate thieves of *American Buffalo*.

Yet a purported version of his script, which circulated among movie fans in 2000, downplayed much of Lecter's ferociousness. Instead, Mamet's *Hannibal* portrayed Lecter as a specially bred wild bore. At one point in Mamet's *Hannibal* draft, Lecter abducts Starling, only to realize that she's been equipped with a tracking device:

LECTER

Oh, no. Oh, NO. They've put a beeper on you. How careless of me. How finally careless, Do you think? [*sic*] Have I erred on Purpose? Eh? Or am I just unlucky? Could one not say that's the essential question of Philosophy . . . ?"

It was a far cry from the days of Lecter having an old friend for dinner. Mamet's script caused some consternation among the bigwigs at Universal and MGM, who saw *Hannibal* as a shot at a lucrative franchise (one exec even believed that Lecter could be "the James Bond of serial killers"). Audiences didn't want to see their favorite cannibal bemoaning his various existential hang-ups, and Mamet was soon replaced by Steven Zaillian, the Oscar-winning writer of *Schindler's List*. Zaillian's immediate task was coming up with a suitable ending for *Hannibal*, as Scott had no interest in bringing the book's Lecter-Starling romance to the screen. "I just couldn't buy that," the director said.

To devise a new finale, Scott turned to Harris, who was invited to help the filmmakers come up with a new third act for *Hannibal*. The author wasn't thrilled to learn that the book's final moments wouldn't make it to the screen. "I grieved about that," he said years later. "The moviemakers did not trust the audience to understand the ending. I'm sorry about that." And he wasn't too keen to get any closer to Hollywood, telling Scott that he was hesitant to be involved with the *Hannibal* film: "I don't really do this, you know?"

Despite his reservations, he flew to Los Angeles and holed up with Scott and Zaillianin in a suite at the Beverly Hills Hotel, where they hammered out a less contentious conclusion to *Hannibal*. "After four days of sitting around the table,' Scott said, "his comment was, 'This has been really fun. I'll do this again.'" As the *Hannibal* script came together, De Laurentiis worked on getting *The Silence of the Lambs'* Oscar-winning costars to commit to the sequel. Hopkins wasn't an immediate yes. In the near decade since he'd starred as Lecter, he had banked a couple of big-studio films a year, often playing icy functionaries (*The Remains of the Day*), impulsive eccentrics (*The Road to Wellville*), or both (*Nixon*). He'd finally found a home in Hollywood—and in the United States, where he'd become a citizen in early 2000, leading one British newspaper to dub the actor "Hannibal Defector."

Hopkins had plenty of screen work to keep him busy. And though he'd waited years for Harris to deliver *Hannibal*, he found the book "bizarre," and was disappointed when Demme dropped out. Still, there was little doubt that he would eventually join Scott's film. The actor was permanently etched in millions of viewers' minds as Lecter; passersby asked him to quote the cannibal on the street, while restaurant chefs sent liver and fava beans to Hopkins's table. It was impossible to separate Hopkins from Hannibal—so much so that when the actor had dated the celebrity homemaker Martha Stewart after *The Silence of the Lambs*, she'd had trouble getting past the idea of dining with the man who'd played Hannibal the Cannibal. "I have a big, scary house in Maine that's way by itself on a hundred acres in a forest," Stewart explained, "and I couldn't even imagine taking Anthony Hopkins there. I couldn't because all I could think of was him eating, you know . . ."

De Laurentiis was confident that he'd eventually get Hopkins to agree to make *Hannibal*. In the meantime, the producer worked on Foster, who was proving much harder to convince. Throughout the summer of 1999, as Harris's book sat atop the bestseller lists, she remained mum on whether she'd play Starling again. Her wavering irritated De Laurentiis, who began telling the press that he didn't actually *need* the actor, whom he sometimes referred to as "Judy Foster." "The only thing that matters is a good director and a good story," he said. "With those two things, *I* could play Starling. Within two minutes the audience will forget all about Jodie Foster—I promise you."

Foster never responded to such slights. In fact, it would take months for her to publicly express her doubts about starring in *Hannibal*. "I stand to make more money doing that sequel than I've ever made in my life," she said. "But who cares, if it betrays Clarice—who is a person, in some strange way, to me. The movie worked because people believed in her heroism. I won't play her with negative attributes she'd never have."

By year's end, Foster had officially turned down *Hannibal*. At the time, she blamed scheduling conflicts, though she later acknowledged that she hadn't wanted to "trample" on Starling. Upon hearing the news, De Laurentiis—finally free of dealing with the star—bid a sanguine farewell to Foster's agent: "Give my love to Judy Foster. Goodbye." But the actor's decision caused panic in the offices of Universal and MGM. What had once been a sure-thing sequel now looked as though it might not happen at all, unless they found a suitable replacement—and quickly.

The question of who'd take over for Foster became a monthslong guessing game, one that played out in public, especially on the internet, where comments boards and reader polls lit up with suggestions. An *Entertainment Weekly* online survey yielded more than ten thousand votes, 80 percent of which went to *X-Files* star Gillian Anderson.[*] She wasn't in the running, though Scott met with several other well-known twenty- and thirtysomething stars, including Angelina Jolie, Gwyneth Paltrow, Hilary

---

[*] "They haven't contacted her, but she's perfect," Anderson's manager told the magazine. "When they were casting *The X-Files*, they said, 'What we want is Jodie Foster from *The Silence of the Lambs*.'"

Swank, and Cate Blanchett. In the end, it was Julianne Moore, the gutsy star of such 1990s dramas as *Short Cuts* and *Boogie Nights*, who was found to have the vulnerability (and availability) to play Starling. Like Foster, she'd prepare for the role by attending classes at Quantico, where the actor learned how to use handcuffs and shoot two-handed. "This movie was the first time I actually had to fire a gun and look like I knew what I was doing," Moore said.

Her participation was enough for Hopkins to finally commit to doing *Hannibal*, which would land him a career-high payday of more than $10 million. "It's a bit of a gamble doing a sequel," he said at the time. "I don't want to think about it. I learn my lines, show up, make sure the check's in the mail."

Even Harris approved of the casting switcheroo for *Hannibal*, sending a handwritten dispatch to *Entertainment Weekly*: "Julianne Moore is perfect to play Clarice Starling. I couldn't be more pleased. Sincerely, Thomas Harris." The note was concise and polite, with Harris's words expressed in a graceful longhand. The only way it could have been more elegant was if it had been written on mauve stationery.

Production on *Hannibal* began in May 2000 in Florence, where the filmmakers were greeted with outrage. Apparently, some local politicians didn't want Hannibal Lecter hanging around the neighborhood. "This will add nothing to Florence's prestige in the world," noted their angry letter to Florence's mayor. If *Hannibal* were to shoot in the city, the protesters noted, Florence would forever be known as a place full of "morbid thrills and vulgar horror."

For the filmmakers, the outcry was nothing more than free publicity. Not that the $80 million movie needed more attention; *Hannibal*'s every move was being documented by the global press, who trailed Hopkins from the moment he stepped off his plane in Italy. At a kickoff press conference for the film, Hopkins joked about eating fava beans, while Scott declared his goal of making the definitive Lecter film. "I'm very competitive," the director said. "So it may even be more interesting than *The Silence of the Lambs*."

Unlike Demme's film, which had been shot in relative seclusion, the production of *Hannibal* was chronicled on a near-daily basis, with constant updates (some legitimate, some invented) appearing on the internet. Even Harris got swept up in the press frenzy. In May 2000, reporters spotted him in Florence, where he had his first meeting with Hopkins. While in town, Harris picked up a custom-made replica of *Il porcellino*, a famous bronze wild boar statue he'd spotted during his *Hannibal* research trips (according to local lore, the statue granted the owner good luck).

Hannibal would be shot around Florence for more than a month, during which time photos emerged of Hopkins dressed as Lecter, wearing a white panama hat and black sunglasses, looking like a murderous Truman Capote. After finishing in Italy, the cast and crew moved to a series of locations in the United States. That included Montpelier, James Madison's massive eighteenth-century Virigina estate, where Hopkins could sometimes be found doing Lecter impressions for Moore's young son or reading a copy of the true-crime hit *Perfect Murder, Perfect Town*, about the 1996 murder of the child beauty queen JonBenét Ramsey.

Even now, in his second run-through as Lecter, the actor didn't quite understand the cannibal's appeal. "The reaction to Lecter has always puzzled me," he said. "It's odd. The man is *completely crazy*." To get the old scent back, Hopkins popped a copy of *The Silence of the Lambs* into a VCR before working on *Hannibal*. He had mellowed in the decade since Demme's film, and he believed that Lecter had, too. "I thought, 'Do I repeat that performance, or do I vary it?'" he explained. "Ten years had passed, so I changed it a bit. Because I've changed."

The Lecter of *Hannibal* would be notably different from the cool, coiled doctor audiences had fallen for years earlier. In Scott's film, Lecter is so mellow that he practically purrs, at one point waltzing around his Florence palazzo in black pajamas, looking as though he'd just wandered into the library of the Playboy Mansion. He's also far more playful, littering conversations with the occasional "okey-dokey" or "goody-goody" and winking at one of his victims in midthreat. "I'm giving very serious thought . . . [*long dramatic pause*] . . . to eating your wife."

Those comical moments would be balanced out by *Hannibal*'s morbid thrills and vulgar horror. In the post-*Seven* era, moviegoers wanted their slicing and dicing as up close and personal as possible. And there'd be plenty of hands-on violence in *Hannibal*. When Lecter disembowels the Italian police officer who is on his trail, the man's intestines land on the ground with a wet *slap*. Later on, as Lecter cuts open Paul Krendler's head—an effect achieved with the help of a $70,000 puppet built to resemble the head of actor Ray Liotta—the doctor's shown peeling away the sack covering Krendler's brain (a neurosurgeon was on set during filming to make sure Scott got the details of the scene correct). "It made me gag," Liotta said of the scene. "But then I realized it's Anthony Hopkins, as *Hannibal Lecter*, eating me! That is so fuckin' cool!"

Scott, a fan of Michael Mann's *Manhunter*, didn't want to rely on gross-out imagery alone. *Hannibal* was constructed as a cat-and-mouse thriller, one that found Lecter trying to stay incognito at a time when cell phones, the internet, and ever-present security cameras were increasingly making it hard to hide. In *Hannibal*, Lecter's face is displayed on the FBI's Ten Most Wanted website alongside those of such real-life criminals as Olympic Park bomber Eric Robert Rudolph, crime boss James "Whitey" Bulger, and Al Qaeda leader Osama bin Laden—whose mug shot would be appearing on screen, albeit briefly, just a few months before the attacks of September 11, 2001.

Such real-world elements didn't mean that *Hannibal* would be as grounded, or as sobering, as Demme's version of *The Silence of the Lambs* had been in 1991. *Hannibal* would arrive on the heels of the Clinton-era slasher-flick revival, which had seen the launch of numerous franchises: *Scream*, *I Know What You Did Last Summer*, *Urban Legends*. Moviegoers, especially *young* moviegoers, had come to expect their horror movies to feature plenty of carnage and a little bit of camp.

Scott would have to make some tricky tonal decisions while approaching *Hannibal*: Was it a winking madman-on-the-lam horror film? A high-strung law-and-order procedural? Both? Ultimately, *Hannibal* would be an amalgam of contrasts: between wide-screen vistas and grubby surveillance footage; between bustling city streets and darkened government offices; between operatic violence and *Fangoria*-friendly blood and guts.

Those colliding sensibilities were evident in *Hannibal*'s ending, which did away with many of Harris's original ideas while retaining his novel's innate ghastliness. The film's final scenes find the injured Starling in the arms of Lecter, who's escaped the clutches of Mason Verger and is once again on the loose. He takes the agent to the home of her longtime foe, Paul Krendler, where she's sequestered and sedated. When she awakens, she's seated at a table and watches groggily as Hannibal dines on the bureaucrat's brains. Unlike in Harris's novel, she refuses to join in.

After a confrontation, Lecter forces a kiss upon Starling, who handcuffs him while he's distracted. It would appear that Hannibal the Cannibal has *finally* been cornered—but before the police arrive, Lecter cuts off his hand and escapes into the night. He's last spotted on a plane, dressed in blue leisurewear. As he heads off to an unknown destination, he reaches into his neatly arranged carry-on lunchbox—which sports a Dean & DeLuca logo—and offers a young passenger a piece of Krendler's brain. ("It is important," Lecter tells the child, "always to try new things.")

It was a sufficiently shiver-inducing ending, one that hinted at Lecter's amorous tendencies while avoiding the whole "penetration of Clarice Starling" aspect. Scott was confident that audiences would go for it—and that *Hannibal* would be a hit. After filming wrapped, the director was spotted at recording sessions for the *Hannibal* score at a studio in London. He entertained guests by giddily spitting out a verse from what he called "the Hannibal rap": "Hannibal! Face eater! Cop killah! Muthafucka!"

Not long before Scott's version of *Hannibal* was slated to hit theaters, Harris received a letter from an old friend, one he'd stayed in touch with throughout the 1990s. "I hope things are going splendidly with *Hannibal*, as I'm sure they are," Jonathan Demme wrote. "Guess who's going to be the first person in line when that flick opens?"

After an assaultive monthslong marketing campaign—including a trailer that asked "How long can a man stay silent before he returns to the thing he does best?"—*Hannibal* had its US premiere at Manhattan's Zieg-feld Theater in February 2001. The guest list included Muhammad Ali, Lauren Bacall, and Regis Philbin, as well as Jennifer Love Hewitt and Alec Baldwin, both of whom were spotted leaving before the movie was over. Even some of those who stayed to the end struggled with the film's gore. During *Hannibal*'s bloody final moments, one high-profile guest sat in the Ziegfeld with his eyes covered. Apparently, the sight of Lecter eating a man's brains was too much for Donald Trump—though his future wife, Melania, didn't flinch.

When *Hannibal* was released a few days later, it earned $58 million in its first weekend—more than the next fifteen films combined, and the highest-ever opening-weekend haul for a horror movie. Despite the film's unpleasant action and hard-R rating, squeamish moviegoers showed up in force, including some who had barely been alive when *The Silence of the Lambs* had opened. "That was a little weird," said one twelve-year-old after watching *Hannibal* with her mom on opening weekend. "It wasn't really what I was hoping for."

Most reviewers agreed. "A lot can happen in 10 years," noted Kenneth Turan in the *Los Angeles Times*. "An actor can misplace a character, a story can lose its connection to an audience, and a highly anticipated sequel can forget why anyone was interested in it in the first place. All of which happened to the unfortunate *Hannibal*."

That was emblematic of the many glum assessments of Scott's film, which ranged from disgust to disappointment. "I saw *Hannibal*," Foster whispered to a reporter a few years after its release. "I won't comment." Some naysayers found Moore's take on Clarice to be chilly, lacking the spark between Foster and Hopkins. Others seized upon the film's para-dox: By making Lecter *bigger*—with more screen time, more one-liners, more near-superhuman strength—they'd reduced his ability to be fright-ening. In *Manhunter* and *The Silence of the Lambs*, he had been a not-so-secret weapon, deployed only when absolutely necessary before being sent back to the shadows. But in *Hannibal*, he's on the loose and so om-nipresent that he loses his shock value. "I liked Lecter when he was more mysterious," Brian Cox said right before *Hannibal* hit screens. "That made him infinitely more frightening."

Like Freddy, Jason, or Michael Myers, Lecter had become a cartoon killer, spouting would-be catchphrases while *always* managing to avoid capture (despite the film's constant reminders of the twenty-first-century surveillance state). To those who remembered Lecter as the iconically laconic villain of *The Silence of the Lambs*, the over-the-top Lecter of *Hannibal* was hard to take seriously. "When Lecter has a scene with Clarice in his arms," Elvis Mitchell wrote in a *New York Times* review, "you expect him to belt out an Andrew Lloyd Webber song."

None of the criticisms of *Hannibal* bothered Lecter's fans. The movie stayed at number one at the box office for a month, and by the end of its run, it had made more than $350 million around the globe—more than *The Silence of the Lambs*. In his years away from theaters, Lecter had only grown more powerful. "He's as big a star as Tom Cruise," De Laurentiis said, beaming.

In fact, *Hannibal* had transformed Lecter into something even bigger. "It's like Batman or Superman," one studio executive said. Lecter, against all odds, had become a superhero. And like all superheroes, he'd never be allowed to die.

CHAPTER 23

"I HAD NO DESIRE TO BE FAVA BEAN MAN AGAIN."

During the frenzy over *Hannibal*, Dino De Laurentiis received an unexpected gift: a new Lecter screenplay, one that would reunite the cannibal with Clarice Starling. The script finds the FBI outcast living in San Francisco, where she's recovering from a nervous breakdown. She has somehow escaped from Lecter. But she still sees him in her dreams (and, she thinks, on the street). One night, Starling awakens and realizes that she's been handcuffed to her bed. Sitting in the corner of her bedroom, smoking a cigar, is Lecter. "Hello, Clarice," he says.

That was how Anthony Hopkins wanted Lecter's next chapter to begin. In the early 2000s, the actor wrote a *Hannibal* sequel, which he presented to De Laurentiis. Nothing ever came of Hopkins's effort, as the producer had his own idea for Lecter's next on-screen adventure—an idea that was, in fact, decades old. "Everybody asks me, 'Dino, we need to know what, when, where, who arrests for the first time Hannibal Lecter,'" he said. Lecter's capture had already been detailed in *Red Dragon* and *Manhunter*, of course. But twenty years had passed since *Red Dragon* had been published. And though *Manhunter* had found a worshipful home video audience since its 1986 release, few noncinephiles had seen it.

De Laurentiis was no snob when it came to dusting off old ideas; after all, he'd once brought King Kong back to life. And by the early 2000s, Hollywood was knocking out new versions of such vintage hits as *The Planet of the Apes* and *Ocean's Eleven*. For De Laurentiis, the easiest way to get Lecter back into theaters was to resurrect *Red Dragon*. And he wanted to do so fast, while the character was experiencing so much post-*Hannibal* momentum.

He started by hiring Ted Tally, whose *Silence of the Lambs* script had become a model of page-to-screen precision—one that was studied by screenwriters and academics alike. Tally had since moved on to tackling other high-pedigree adaptations, including Cormac McCarthy's *All the Pretty Horses*. He initially wasn't keen on returning to the dungeon of Lecter's mind. "After *Silence of the Lambs* I was offered 500,000 serial-killer things, and the last thing I wanted to do was another one," he said. But knowing that Harris took years between novels, he figured that it was his best shot at adapting a Lecter story again.

De Laurentiis's next task would be to convince Hopkins, now in his midsixties, to agree to go back in time, playing a younger, livelier Lecter in a story set before *The Silence of the Lambs*. Despite the actor's attempts to write his own Hannibal screenplay, he was iffy about taking on the character yet again. "I told my agent, 'Are you sure this is a good thing? Three in a row?'" he recalled.

If the actor passed on remaking *Red Dragon*, De Laurentiis had devised a backup plan, which he'd pitched to Tally. "We open in a plastic surgery in Brazil," the producer told him. "And when they take the bandages off, he looks a lot like Kevin Spacey." (Recalling the moment later, Tally added, "I don't think he was really joking.")

But audiences wouldn't go for any such switcheroo. To tens of millions of moviegoers, Hopkins *was* Lecter. Even the iffy reviews for *Hannibal* couldn't prevent it from becoming a hit on home video, where the film earned an additional $125 million (at one point in late 2001, the two best-selling DVDs in the country were *Hannibal* and a rereleased version of *The Silence of the Lambs*). And in the wake of Scott's movie, several polls would name Lecter as the greatest film villain of all time, over the likes of Norman Bates, Darth Vader, and the shark from *Jaws*.

Hopkins didn't deserve *all* the credit for Lecter's infamy. But despite several film executives' hope that Hannibal could become a 007-like character—one who could be interpreted by numerous other performers—there was no way *Red Dragon* would work without Hopkins. "You have more leverage than any actor I can think of in Hollywood," Conan O'Brien had told the actor after *Hannibal* was released. "If you give them a hard time and ask for a lot of money, they can't go to William Shatner."

Luckily for De Laurentiis—and unfortunately for Shatner—Hopkins's resistance to *Red Dragon* proved to be short-lived. It helped, of course, that the gig promised to come with yet another gigantic paycheck: Hopkins would receive at least $20 million for his work, a salary that would put him into the same league as Tom Cruise and Julia Roberts.

But the actor also wanted assurances that this time around, there'd be none of Lecter's quips, winks, or "goody-goody"s. In public, he happily played up the character's more cartoonish side. In 2001, while receiving the Man of the Year Award from Harvard University's Hasty Pudding Theatricals group, Hopkins entertained students by eating blood-colored ice cream out of a mannequin's head and delivering Lecter-like impressions of Jack Nicholson and Richard Nixon. But *Hannibal* had clearly exhausted the actor's sense of humor. "I'd done the cutesy stuff twice, and the jokes had worn thin," he said. "I wanted to move on. I had no desire to be Fava Bean Man again."

For *Red Dragon*, the actor wanted to play Lecter with "more menace, more danger, much more rage," he said. "I also wanted to reveal to the audience that behind the mask of this charming man is this killer. I wanted to show that vicious, really horrifying side of him."

Reestablishing Lecter's bad-guy bona fides would require giving him plenty of screen time in *Red Dragon*—a challenge for the filmmakers, since Hannibal appears in person in about a dozen pages of Harris's novel. If Tally wanted to keep Lecter-obsessed moviegoers happy, he'd have to greatly expand the cannibal's role. "Tom Harris was the first one who saw that," Tally recalled. "He told me, 'You have to have Hannibal in the movie early and often.'"

The screenwriter added a handful of additional Lecter scenes to *Red Dragon*, some of which flash back to the doctor's upper-crust, preasylum days: At a local symphony performance, Lecter grows irritated by a flutist's bum-note performance, so he chops up the musician and serves him as an *amuse-bouche* at a fancy dinner party. Later in the film, Graham comes to the grim realization that Lecter—whom he'd treated as a colleague and confidant—is in fact the serial killer he's been hunting. That leads to a tussle in which Lecter sticks a stiletto into Graham's chest. "I don't want you to feel any pain," he says before promising to eat Graham's heart.

As he worked on *Red Dragon*, Tally stayed in touch with Harris via email and fax. "I would send him rough drafts of new scenes that were not in the book, for his comment," Tally says. "He was very supportive. He's *always* been supportive—which made me feel guilty about not doing *Hannibal*."

Once Tally's *Red Dragon* script was completed, it was time to find a director who wouldn't be daunted by the prospect of taking on a suddenly thriving franchise. Online rumors that *Pearl Harbor*'s bombastic Michael Bay would direct the film came and went. De Laurentiis even reached out to Michael Mann to see if he'd be interested in tackling *Red Dragon* again ("We never heard back," noted Dino's wife, Martha De Laurentiis, one of the film's producers).

Executives at Universal eventually landed on Brett Ratner, a film-maker with zero experience in the world of horror. Ratner, still in his early thirties, was a New York University film school grad who'd shot music videos for Mariah Carey and Jay-Z before transitioning to features. He was a devout scholar of Hollywood history, one who'd been mentored by the legendary Robert Evans, and who worshiped older auteurs such as Hal Ashby and Roman Polanski. To some in the industry, Ratner repre-sented a Gen-X spin on old-school Hollywood hustle and bluster. To oth-ers, he was a walking, talking tracksuit—a guy who dropped all the right names and copped all the right frames. "I'm true to myself," Ratner said. "Whether you like it or not."

Still, even Ratner's haters couldn't argue with his box-office record, which included the *Rush Hour* series, starring Chris Tucker and Jackie Chan as mismatched crime fighters, as well as the hit Nicolas Cage hol-iday drama *The Family Man*. The director was a wiz at pleasing needy stars and capricious moviegoers, and the studio figured he'd be a good fit for *Red Dragon*—which surprised Ratner. *I'm not a dark guy*, he thought when he got the offer. *I don't make dark movies, I do comedy.* But Ratner loved Tally's script. And he wasn't worried about comparisons to *Manhunter*. "Nobody knows that film," he said. "The Michael Mann film had nothing to do with the book. My movie is a true interpretation of Thomas Harris's novel."[*]

When Ratner's hiring for *Red Dragon* was announced, some movie fans reacted with disbelief: *That guy? Really?* The director shared their concerns. He sought counsel from Harris, visiting the author in Miami to make sure he had a proper enough grasp on the novel. Even with that guidance, Ratner wondered if he'd gotten too big for his britches. "I was hearing the voices," he said. "You know: 'You're not as good as Jonathan Demme.' 'You can't compare to Ridley Scott.' 'You suck compared to Michael Mann.'"

But De Laurentiis had faith in Ratner. The producer, now in his early eighties, was deeply invested in *Red Dragon* being a hit, both financially and emotionally. He accompanied the director on several location-scouting trips, including to Darlington, Maryland, where the filmmakers found a gorgeous eighteenth-century house that could double as Dolarhyde's lair, which is set ablaze in the movie. There was only one problem: The homeowners didn't want flames near their historic property. De Laurentiis told them not to worry about damage. "We give you some money," he said, "we burn [the house], it falls down, and you create a new beautiful, modern house." (The owners declined the offer.)

"Every morning, when we would get to the Universal lot to shoot, Dino would be there before anyone else," says the filmmaker Kevin Krakower, who documented the production of *Red Dragon*. "He would just stand in front of the soundstage and wait: 'Where's Brett? Where's Brett?' He was this giant presence in this little body. He was like King Kong."

De Laurentiis and Tally weren't the only behind-the-scenes forces

---

[*] "He *said* that?" Mann responded when told of Ratner's put-down in 2002. "He's just talking."

making a return to Lecter's world. To help assuage his fears about directing the film, Ratner assembled a sort of Hannibal Lecter superteam, hiring *Manhunter* cinematographer Dante Spinotti and *Silence of the Lambs* production designer Kristi Zea. He also used the film's lofty profile (and its more than $80 million budget) to lure a prestigious cast, including *Fight Club*'s Edward Norton as Graham; *The English Patient*'s Ralph Fiennes as the crazed Francis Dolarhyde; and *Breaking the Waves* breakout Emily Watson as Dolarhyde's girlfriend, Reba. The trio of actors had extensive stage and screen credits and numerous Oscar nominations—as did Hopkins. They were all more established and more respected than Ratner. And the director knew it. "I don't think Edward Norton was saying, 'God, I gotta work with the guy who did *Rush Hour*,'" Ratner said.

Those differences would lead to tensions on the *Red Dragon* set. And years later, Hopkins would publicly question whether he should have kept playing Hannibal Lecter at all. But before filming began, he seemed eager to step back into Lecter's cell. At the first cast get-together, he reunited with *Silence of the Lambs* star Anthony Heald, who'd be reprising his role as the slimy Dr. Chilton.

"He saw me from across the room," Heald recalled. "And he came dancing across the floor, waving his arms, saying 'We get to do it again! We get to do it again!'"

A casual visitor to *Red Dragon*'s Los Angeles set in early 2002 would have been forgiven for thinking that it was a laid-back production. On any given day, Hopkins might be spotted in Lecter's cell, playfully doing impressions of Marlon Brando. In between takes, Ratner could be seen giving the cast and crew excitable feedback—"fucking great," "fucking awesome"—and heard humming Michael Jackson's "Smooth Criminal" (an apt homage to *Red Dragon*'s pair of cerebral killers). At one point, the King of Pop, a close buddy of the director, actually showed up to watch the proceedings, hanging out with Ratner behind the camera as Francis Dolarhyde menaced Reba.

But despite such occasionally chilled-out moments, Ratner would spend much of the shoot in a state of mental exhaustion. "I got yelled at by a different actor every week," he recalled. *"Brett, what the fuck are you doing?"* He found himself in long, tense conversations with Norton, an actor who was not shy about giving creative feedback, regardless of whether or not it was solicited. "I was always bickering with Ed," Ratner said. "He was trying to direct the movie; he was trying to write the movie." The filmmaker also fielded constant questions from Philip Seymour Hoffman, who'd been cast as the scheming tabloid reporter Freddy Lounds, and who flinched at Ratner's requests to redo scenes over and over again: "Why?" the actor asked. "Just tell me *why*."

At times, Hopkins also bristled at Ratner's approach. The actor had accumulated years of experience, not to mention several awards, playing Lecter in the past. So he wasn't thrilled when Ratner pestered him to do numerous takes or pulled him aside for on-set conversations about how to play Lecter ("My eyes tend to glaze over" during such talks, he said). "Demme and Ridley were of a certain generation: no nonsense, 'Let's get down to it,'" notes Rick Nicita, Hopkins's agent at the time. "*Red Dragon* didn't have that alchemy. It wasn't a great experience."

Ratner, though, was unapologetic about pushing the film's biggest star to his limits. "When in my whole life am I going to shoot Anthony Hopkins as Hannibal Lecter again?" he said. "I'm going to enjoy this. But I was also thinking that it was very important to make something that you haven't already seen."

In many ways, though, Ratner's version of *Red Dragon* would be a return to the world of *The Silence of the Lambs*. With Zea's help, the crew had carefully reconstructed her original asylum set from Demme's film, meaning that Lecter's underground home looked just as dank and dour as it had in 1991. And though Hopkins wasn't as thin as he'd once been— he carried some noticeable heft, despite having dropped twenty pounds for the film by dieting and lifting weights—just the sight of Lecter in his old blue jumpsuit and slicked-back hair would be good enough for most viewers.

Yet *Red Dragon* also unveiled a side of Lecter that, while always present in Harris's novels, had been just briefly glimpsed in previous movies:

his arrogant ferality. In the film version of *The Silence of the Lambs*, he seems resigned to his life behind bars. And Scott's version of *Hannibal* had found Lecter laid back and loose. In *Red Dragon*, though, Hannibal the Cannibal is deeply enraged: at Graham, the man who put him away; at the doctors and lawyers in charge of his care; and at the world, with all its contemptible "poor dullards," as he calls them. His rancor animates his every exchange in *Red Dragon*. During a sequence that Tally invented for the film, Lecter takes his weekly exercise by walking around an asylum gym, his hands chained to the ceiling. As he fields questions from Graham about the Tooth Fairy, he alternates between showing off his smarts—he quotes a poem by William Blake—and showcasing his fury. At one point, he lunges at Graham with his teeth bared and gnashing.

Ratner would describe Hopkins's performance as having "a Charles Manson anger and bitterness." And Hopkins had prepared for the film by watching the cult leader's prison interviews. The two madmen couldn't have been more different: One was a seething intellectual who preferred to work solo, the other a rambling oddball who let his acolytes do his bidding. But in *Red Dragon*, Lecter seems more rageful and more desperate than he'd been in *Hannibal*. Here was a larger-than-life monster, finally knocked down to size. The question was: Would audiences care about Hannibal Lecter when he was pent up and pissed off—when he wasn't having any fun?

On an early-fall evening in 2002, a group of shadowy figures crept quietly into New York City's Ziegfeld Theater. More than a thousand Lecter fans had gathered for a preview screening of *Red Dragon*, and at the last minute, De Laurentiis had convinced Hopkins and a few others to drop by and see how the film was playing. "We came in for the last twenty minutes," Hopkins said. "I thought I could just sneak out."

As soon as the credits rolled, an audience member spotted the actor walking to a nearby limo. Within minutes, he was being pursued by a mob. "It was a weird scene," Tally recalled. "People were swarming around him, trying to touch him, shouting and cheering and applauding, and trying to get autographs. He was like a rock star. And I thought, 'This guy is a can- nibalistic serial killer—what are you doing?'"

The clamor over Hopkins, a newspaper noted at the time, was further proof that Lecter had become "the Elvis of screen villains." And at the *Red Dragon* premiere—as well as its many after-parties—in Manhattan that September, it was clear that the cannibal could still draw a crowd: Among the attendees were Sean "Puffy" Combs, Val Kilmer, former first daugh- ter Chelsea Clinton, and several early-2000s peak celebrities, including Jewel and Katie Holmes. Even Harris appeared at one of the celebrations, posing for photos with De Laurentiis and Ratner. The author was evi- dently pleased with *Red Dragon*, which had maintained his novel's orig- inal ending, featuring the showdown between Graham and Dolarhyde at the former agent's Florida home. Harris even sent a note to Ratner ex- pressing his approval. "He said, 'Here's all the *R*s for reassurance,'" the director claimed, "and he put, like, 100 *R*s on the letter."

Critics were far less emphatic in their evaluations of *Red Dragon*, which were evenly split. Nearly all agreed that the film went down eas- ier than the way-too-ripe adaptation of *Hannibal*. And there was a sense of surprise that Ratner had delivered a thriller that at least *aspired* to Hitchock-like moodiness. A few even thought that *Red Dragon* was pretty great: *Time* declared the film to be "darkly seductive, flawlessly acted." And in the *Chicago Sun-Times*, Roger Ebert granted *Red Dragon* three and a half stars—the same grade he'd given *The Silence of the Lambs* more than a decade earlier. The film, he wrote, was a "sure, stylish" reminder of Lecter's appealing intelligence: "In these days of movie characters who obediently recite the words the plot requires of them, it's a pleasure to meet a man who can hold up his end of the conversation."

Other reviewers felt that Lecter was even less fearsome than he'd been in the previous year's *Hannibal*. "By now [Hopkins] propels the character with his ocular muscles, like a bored athlete looking to amuse himself," wrote *Entertainment Weekly*'s Lisa Schwarzbaum. "Every synapse of the collective audience memory bank is receiving Hopkins' performance based on what we already want and expect from Our Hannibal." That overfamiliarity, noted *The New York Times*' Elvis Mitchell, had robbed

Hannibal of his ability to scare or surprise. "Lecter is such a huge presence at this point that he capsizes the picture's narrative," he wrote, adding "Mr. Hopkins excels at this Grand Guignol comic relief, though it's tiresome because we've heard it before."

When *Red Dragon* opened in October 2002, it became the third Lecter film in a row to open at number one. By the end of the year, it had made $93 million in the United States alone. That was a healthy figure, but it was little more than half of *Hannibal*'s domestic haul. And the sense among moviegoers—and many movie executives—was that the Lecter series had run its course. "Look, I wanna be honest with you," De Laurentiis told a reporter right as *Red Dragon* was hitting theaters. "Everybody in my [company] says, 'It's over.'"

Lecter's other caretakers felt the same way. "I like the idea of a trilogy, and if it ends here, it will end gracefully," Tally said upon *Red Dragon*'s release. "I would hate to see this become *Hannibal Lecter XIII*."

As for Hopkins, he'd now starred as Lecter more times than Bela Lugosi had been on-screen as Dracula. And while he had made plenty of money playing Hannibal, the creative rewards had diminished. "Nobody will entice me to do it again," he said.

More than a decade later, the actor appeared to regret having extended Lecter's on-screen life at all: "Made the mistake of doing it twice—three times," he said in 2016. "'The Silence of the Lambs' is okay. It was a good film."

But even a pair of second-tier sequels wouldn't diminish Lecter's fearsomeness. And the character would follow Hopkins for the rest of his life, no matter where he went.

In one of *The Silence of the Lambs*' most tense scenes, Lecter fakes out the authorities by placing the body of a dead police sergeant on top of an elevator and making it appear as if it's his own corpse. Long after the film's release, Hopkins found himself in an impressive steel elevator in Los Angeles. A woman got on with her preteen son, not noticing the actor as they all started traveling down.

"What does this remind you of, this elevator?" the woman asked.

"Hannibal Lecter," the boy replied.

Hopkins stood behind them, saying nothing. When the passengers finally turned around—and met the same cold, unblinking eyes that had once stared back at them from the screen—the boy jumped and his mother scremed. No matter where Hopkins went for the rest of his life, Hannibal Lecter would be by his side.

PART 4
DEATH

Hannibal Rising
(2006, 2007)

CHAPTER 24

"I DON'T WANT TO LOSE THIS FRANCHISE."

Before *Red Dragon* opened in late 2002, Dino De Laurentiis made a promise: If the film earned a billion dollars, he'd find a way to bring Hannibal Lecter back. *Again.* "I would be crazy not to do another one," he said.

The film's earnings didn't come anywhere close to that goal. But De Laurentiis charged ahead with a sequel anyway. Thanks to his original *Red Dragon* deal in the 1980s, he owned the film rights to Lecter. And he was determined to squeeze out as many Hannibal the Cannibal stories as he could: "Dino would say things like, 'We do four more! We do 20 more!'" Hopkins recalled.

It was an absurd notion, one that ignored why Lecter was so beloved in the first place. From the moment he'd been introduced in Harris's *Red Dragon* novel, he had always functioned best as a vaporous scene stealer; the less people saw of him, the more they feared him. That went not only for Will Graham and Clarice Starling but for the millions of readers and viewers following the Lecter saga. He had to stay in the background for long stretches in order to regain his powers. And for all the griping about Harris's slow output, his fans had come to accept Lecter's frequent absences. The wait made his inevitable return all the more exciting.

In just three years, though, audiences had been treated to a *Hannibal* novel, a *Hannibal* film, and a new *Red Dragon* adaptation. It was Lecter overload. If De Laurentiis rushed out another film too quickly, he would risk alienating moviegoers—or, even worse, angering them. "Aw, gee *whiz*, no, no!" Demme said about De Laurentiis's plans to keep bringing Lecter to screens. "Gosh, nothing good can happen anymore without it being exploited until every single centime has been milked out of it."

But milking past successes, even if they were in danger of expiring, was a Hollywood tradition. Sequels, prequels, and remakes had been a key part of the big studios' strategies for decades—and they'd become even more important in the early 2000s. With movie theaters facing competition from video games, the internet, and television, film executives were increasingly looking for stories with built-in followings. For many producers, owning the rights to Spider-Man, Harry Potter, or *The Lord of the Rings* was more valuable—financially *and* socially—than winning an Oscar.

That made Lecter a prize asset for De Laurentiis. The producer was now in his mideighties, making him one of the last old-school showmen—a Hollywood survivor who'd weathered bankruptcy and bombs. And while he was no longer the big-screen titan he'd been decades earlier, when he had been working with the likes of Fellini and King Kong, he still owned one of the most bankable bad guys of all time. He needed Lecter alive. "I don't want to lose this franchise," he said.

In the early 2000s, he and his wife, the producer Martha De Laurentiis, began developing a new Lecter story—though technically, he was still plundering Harris's previous work. In *Hannibal*, the author had dug into the cannibal's past, detailing Lecter's childhood in Lithuania with his late younger sister, Mischa. "Maybe we should do a movie about the young Hannibal," De Laurentiis said, "and see what happened to him, why he became a monster."

The producer approached Harris with the idea—though it's perhaps more accurate to say that he *attacked* Harris with the idea. "I say to Thomas, 'If you don't do it, I will do it with someone else,'" the producer recalled. Harris said no, prompting De Laurentiis to make it clear that he was serious: "I said, 'I *will* do it with somebody else.' And then he said, 'Let me think about it.'"

Harris wrote an outline for what would become his fourth Lecter story. It spanned the early 1940s to the early 1950s, following Lecter from childhood through adolescence. During those years, the young boy experiences a series of unspeakable tragedies: His parents are killed in war-torn Lithuania, leaving the brilliant young Lecter and his sister, Mischa, all alone in a snowbound lodge. That's where the children are discovered by a group of outcast Waffen-SS soldiers, who grow so desperate for food that they dine on Mischa. Lecter escapes, eventually relocating to France, where he lives with his Japanese aunt by marriage, Lady Murasaki. She encourages the teenage Lecter's pursuits: studying cadavers as a medical student, and hunting down Mischa's killers.

Harris's new tale would end with Lecter, having become a murderous wunderkind, heading toward America. It was an open-ended fate, and one that would ostensibly allow De Laurentiis to make years' worth of new Lecter films. Not long after Harris submitted his outline, De Laurentiis made two bold announcements. The first was that he'd green-lit a new Hannibal film, and given it a regal title: *The Lecter Variation: The Story of Young Hannibal Lecter* (it was an homage to Bach's *Goldberg Variations*, one of Lecter's favorite compositions). The second big reveal was that Harris was going to handle the movie's screenplay as well as an accompanying novel—tasks that the famously slowpoke author planned on tackling *simultaneously*.

To anyone who'd followed Harris's career, the prospect of him knocking out both projects within even a semireasonable time frame seemed laughable. He was a writer who retained complete editorial control over his work and who toiled over every comma—traits that were seen as all but heretical in deadline-driven Hollywood. But it wasn't just the projects' demanding logistics that baffled Harris's loyal readers. For years, the author had remained quiet about Lecter's origins. He was a character who existed in a narrative vacuum. ("Nothing happened to me, Officer Starling. *I* happened.") And while *Hannibal* had dribbled out details of Lecter's haunting childhood, they'd made up only a small part of the novel. Now Harris was suddenly going to reveal all.

Years later, Harris's fans would wonder what had compelled him to write the fourth Lecter book (which, like the film, would eventually be titled *Hannibal Rising*). Harris had been Lecter's careful steward for decades—working on the novels at his own unhurried pace, having final say on every editing and marketing decision. Had he actually jumped at the chance to write *Hannibal Rising*? Or had he been pushed by De Laurentiis, in an arrangement *Entertainment Weekly* described as "friendly blackmail"?

As usual, the author didn't provide much in the way of explanation. "[De Laurentiis] could have done whatever he wanted to," Harris said of *Hannibal Rising* years after its release. "He had a lot of enthusiasm for a movie, and it was contagious, I suppose."

Whatever his motivation, Harris would soon accomplish a feat that neither Jack Crawford, Will Graham, nor even Mason Verger had been able to pull off: He was going to kill Hannibal Lecter.

Harris worked on *Hannibal Rising* for much of the early 2000s. During that time, horror movies underwent a notable shift. The A-list bogeymen who'd dominated the 1980s and 1990s suddenly seemed less fearsome. "Both Freddy and Jason are so last century," noted a *New York Times* review of 2003's *Freddy vs. Jason*, a team-up that marked both characters' final on-screen appearance for several years. They weren't the only slasher-flick stars to experience a downturn in the 2000s. It was the decade in which Chucky from *Child's Play* bottomed out at the box office and the *Scream* saga all but shut down. The lovably nasty pop culture slayers who'd spent years being killed off and resurrected had finally gone to the grave for good—at least for the time being.

In their place came a new kind of big-screen monster. Starting in the early 2000s, the United States had been confronted by round-the-clock images of real-world violence in the form of terrorism, televised wars, and mass shootings. The devastation of the September 11, 2001, attacks had been followed by a litany of aftershocks: the fatal anthrax attacks of 2001, the DC sniper murders of 2002, and too many school and workplace shootings to count. Increasingly, otherworldly figures such as Freddy and

Jason didn't seem anywhere near as scary as our fellow humans. "The nation and the world experienced this collective trauma," notes Bryan Fuller, the creator of TV's *Hannibal* and a longtime horror fan. "Everybody got a little harder, a little dumber, a little more lizard brained."

Hollywood responded with a series of nauseating films about killers armed with sharp weapons and brutal desires. Hits such as *Saw* (2004) and *Hostel* (2005) kicked off lucrative franchises in which victims were often assaulted physically *and* emotionally, with each new installment getting more and more bloody. At the same time, classic scary movies from the past were dusted off and injected with new blood, resulting in bleak remakes such as *The Texas Chainsaw Massacre* (2003) and *The Hills Have Eyes* (2006). It was the Abattoir Age, with moviegoers seeking out shocking tales of revenge and retribution.

"People were paying to see people get tortured," Fuller says. "All of the fear and acrimony that they were experiencing—all the extremities of humanity that were hard to look at and experience—were manifest on-screen. Maybe that was some form of therapy."

Meanwhile, the serial killer dramas that had flourished in the years after *The Silence of the Lambs* would grow more sophisticated. Audiences still wanted pulpy thrillers about bold agents and brainy madmen, of course. But the country's appetite for true crime had become all the more insatiable, thanks in part to the internet, which made it possible to spend days or weeks examining crime-scene photos or exhuming Ed Gein's handiwork. At the same time, amateur manhunters who'd once gotten their serial killer kicks from tawdry tabloid shows or quick-fix TV films were turning to more grounded tales of murder. In 2002, the newcomer Jeremy Renner starred in the haunting biopic *Dahmer*. A year later, Charlize Theron played the serial killer Aileen Wuornos in the surprisingly empathetic *Monster*, a film that would earn her an Academy Award. And in 2007, *Seven* director David Fincher returned to the serial killer genre with *Zodiac*, in which the yearslong pursuit of the Zodiac Killer is depicted as an elegant, patient procedural inspired by *All the President's Men*.

It was hard to see where Hannibal Lecter fit in during those strange times. He was too talky, too *thoughtful*, to satisfy the more extreme gore hounds. Yet he was also too fantastical for true-crime fans, who wanted their serial killer stories drawn from the headlines. If Harris wanted to keep Lecter from becoming a relic, he would have to come up with something as urgent, and as unprecedented, as *Red Dragon* had felt upon its release in 1981.

And he'd have to do it *fast*. De Laurentiis wanted to get the *Hannibal Rising* movie into theaters in time to capitalize on the Lecter-mania that had boosted the recent *Hannibal* and *Red Dragon* films. The producer quickly settled on a director: Peter Webber, a British filmmaker in high demand, thanks to his 2003 Oscar-nominated period drama *Girl with a Pearl Earring*. Webber was soon whisked to Miami, where he met Harris at his home. "He lived in this rather glamorous house that looked over the water, with very expensive Chinese rugs," Webber says. "And he had a butler who looked after him."

One night, Harris took Webber out for dinner so they could discuss *Hannibal Rising*. "When we came back, his butler fixed the strongest cocktails I've ever had in my life," the director says. "I wasn't a great drinker, and after a couple of his very dry martinis, I was quite toasted." The two made their way to Harris's garden, where they smoked cigars and chatted. "I asked him, 'So tell me about Hannibal Lecter: 'Where'd you get the idea? Who was it based on?' And he told me in great detail who he was, exactly how he'd come across him—all of this stuff."

The next morning, Webber woke up in a fog. "I couldn't remember any of it. It's something that kind of plagues me to this day. I had the keys to the kingdom—to really understand exactly who Lecter was based on and what the story was. I almost got the impression he only told me 'cause I was drunk and he knew I wouldn't remember."

Webber stayed in touch with Harris as he labored on the *Hannibal Rising* screenplay, burning through numerous revisions. For a longtime solo act like Harris, the process of writing a screenplay, which requires a deft mix of collaboration and confrontation, proved frustrating. "Leave me alone," he'd tell the filmmakers when they checked on the script's progress. "Let me finish the book." He had good reason to be fed up: Every day spent on *Hannibal Rising* (the screenplay) was a day he had to put down

Hannibal Rising (the novel). He'd committed to an unforgiving workload, and sometimes the strain showed. "At one point," Webber recalls, "he wrote and said, 'I don't want to do another draft. I've written enough to keep a small Korean touring theater company going for fifty-five years. That's enough.'"

Finally, in 2005, Harris handed over his final *Hannibal Rising* screenplay to De Laurentiis. That fall, the film's cast and crew headed to Prague to start filming. Webber had met with several young stars for the role of Lecter, including Tom Hardy and James McAvoy, before settling on the French actor Gaspard Ulliel, a handsome twenty-one-year-old who'd starred in a series of European period dramas. *Hannibal Rising* would be the most sizable role of Ulliel's career, which was cut short when he died in a skiing accident in January 2022 at the age of thirty-seven. "He had a magic and mystery the others didn't," says Webber, who enrolled Ulliel in anatomy lectures at a Prague medical school, where the actor handled a body during an autopsy. ("It's not that shocking," Ulliel said. "You don't have any blood—the only liquid you have is the grease. It's a bit like an omelette.")

In *Hannibal Rising*, Ulliel portrays Lecter with a combination of adolescent insecurity and teenage rage; sometimes he's borderline emo, other times he comes off as flip. He's also notably horny, as evidenced by his *very* intimate relationship with his aunt, Lady Murasaki, played by *Memoirs of a Geisha* star Gong Li. And while Webber's film doesn't get anywhere near as gory as some of its circa-2000s contemporaries, *Hannibal Rising* finds Lecter beheading, torturing, and slicing up multiple victims (one is even drowned in a vat of embalming fluid).

Yet the film's creepiest moment arrives toward the end, after Lecter captures a vile ex-soldier named Grutas, played by the Welsh actor Rhys Ifans. It was Grutas who'd led the effort to eat young Mischa. Before dying, Grutas explains to Lecter how the young man's cannibalistic career had started. "You ate her, half conscious," Gustav tells Lecter, "your little lips greedy around the spoon." *That* was Lecter's original sin—his unwitting role in the tragedy that would shape the rest of his life. (Lecter, upon hearing Gustav's confession, then carves several scarlet *M*'s on the man's body.)

Hannibal Rising completed shooting in early 2006. In the months that followed, it became clear that executives at the Weinstein Company, one of the studios handling the film's release in the United States, were anxious about the movie's box-office prospects. Early test screening results had been mixed. And there were concerns that moviegoers were so loyal to Hopkins that they might not give a new big-screen Lecter a chance. "I remember sitting in with the marketing people," Webber recalls, "and they said, 'We'd have a much easier job marketing this movie if it was about a young serial killer who *wasn't* called Hannibal Lecter.' That baggage can help, but it can also hinder you. It's such a singular character, and people have this sense of ownership."

None more so than Harris, who'd finally see *Hannibal Rising* at a private Manhattan theater in 2006. After so many years, and so many adaptations, this would finally be *his* Lecter movie. Harris had been irritated by Michael Mann's handling of *Red Dragon*. And despite the author's involvement with the *Hannibal* screenplay, he was disappointed by Ridley Scott's decision to change the novel's dark original ending. But with *Hannibal Rising*, he'd had the chance to wrest back control of the character he'd created a quarter century earlier.

Which made the author's reaction to the film more disheartening. After *Hannibal Rising* ended, "he just sat in there and didn't come out," Webber says. "I think he was rather shocked. He clearly didn't like it at all. That was the last time I saw him."

If Harris had been disappointed by the latest Lecter film, at least he could take comfort in the fact that his publisher, Delacorte Press, planned an extensive rollout for the *Hannibal Rising* book. The novel would appear on shelves right before the 2006 holidays, and Delacorte had committed to sending out 1.5 million hardcover copies, Harris's largest print run to date. With the film version of *Hannibal Rising* arriving in theaters just two months later, the hope was that Lecter's latest comeback would attract both moviegoers and book buyers. "Millions of readers in 25 languages have wondered how Dr. Lecter developed his particular appetite for evil," noted *Hannibal Rising* publisher Irwyn Applebaum. "This novel will satisfy their curiosity."

But the first wave of reviews made it clear that *Hannibal Rising* was anything but satisfying. Harris had always enjoyed a surplus of critical goodwill: Even *Hannibal*, for all its naysayers, had received numerous rhapsodic reviews. But *Hannibal Rising* could muster only the faintest of praise. "Although this isn't a terrible novel," Terrence Rafferty wrote in *The New York Times*, "it never feels like a necessary one: what it most resembles is a deluxe collection of deleted scenes on a special-edition DVD."

That was one of the kinder notices. *Hannibal Rising* was seen by most book critics as unnecessary at best, insulting at worst. "You know that creepy face mask Hannibal Lecter sports in *The Silence of the Lambs*?" asked *USA Today*'s Deirdre Donahue. "Well, the reading public should imprison author Thomas Harris in it, because he is ruining one of the great villain franchises of all time." Her complaint, echoed by several others, was that by tying Lecter's homicidal future to his traumatic past, Harris was trying to humanize a character readers loved for his inhumanity. Nobody wanted to read about Lecter mewing over his dead sister. They wanted him dining on other people's minds, outwitting the world from the confines of a cell. "We like him fine as a monster," Donahue wrote.

Harris was also criticized for *Hannibal Rising*'s stiff prose, particularly in the more heated moments between young Lecter and Lady Murasaki. A sample exchange:

Her eyes cleared and she was in the present. She smiled at Hannibal. "I see you and the cricket sings in concert with my heart."

"My heart hops at the sight of you, who taught my heart to sing."

Such passages had been inspired by Murasaki Shikibu's *The Tale of Genji*, an eleventh-century Japanese work often cited as the world's first novel. Though Harris cited *The Tale of Genji* in the acknowledgments of *Hannibal Rising*, it's doubtful that readers noticed—that is, if they even made it that far in the book.

The complaints piled on. Harris's fourth Lecter outing, according to critics, was "ham-handed and choppy," not to mention too "effete and European." One reviewer decried it as "a novel a parodist could deliver." Such takedowns weren't enough to fully sink *Hannibal Rising*'s commercial prospects. Hannibal was still an attractive brand, as was Harris. The book spent three months on the *New York Times* bestseller list—though according to one report it sold 300,000 copies in hardcover, a steep decline from *Hannibal*.

The news didn't get any better when the film version of *Hannibal Rising* hit theaters in February 2007. Webber had expected a fair amount of resistance toward his film. "I know that some people will say, 'How dare you?' as if we've sinned against the Church of Lecter," he noted before it opened. But he was taken aback by the hatred toward the film. "It's surely the most hated of all the Hannibal films," he says. "The reviews were so vitriolic."

Some movie critics had the same issue with *Hannibal Rising* that book critics had with the novel: Namely, there was too much Hannibal—a character who "should only exist in the margins," noted a review in *The New York Times*, which accused *Hannibal Rising* of having been "conceived in the clamor of the marketplace." Added *Newsday*, "Rationalize Lecter's brand of pure, irrational evil, and you take all the fun out of it." Moviegoers were apparently equally uninterested in diving into Lecter's past: *Hannibal Rising* was bested in its opening weekend by the comedy *Norbit*, featuring Eddie Murphy in a fat suit. In the months that followed, the film had little box-office traction, making less than $30 million in the United States.

Hannibal Rising would find a following in the months and years ahead: It became a surprise bestseller on DVD, debuting at the top of the sales chart. And over time, Webber would hear from younger fans who connected with the anguish and anger of young Lecter. "There are a lot of sensitive teens who feel like they don't quite belong in this world," he says. "And the film speaks to them. That made me feel better about it all. Because otherwise, for a few years it was an episode I just wanted to forget about."

In many ways, *Hannibal Rising* never had a chance. To mainstream audiences, it was a historical drama with no A-list stars. And to horror fans, it felt like a relic. *Hannibal Rising* had the bad luck of arriving at a time when scary-movie fans were desperate for new blood, resulting in a wave of inventive horror flicks: Throughout 2007, there'd be upsetting existential thrillers such as *The Mist* and *28 Weeks Later*; deftly made found-footage flicks such as *REC* and *Paranormal Activity*; and future cult classics such as *Trick 'r Treat*. And anyone looking for a serial killer thriller could just stay at home and watch prime-time shows such as *Dexter* and *Criminal Minds*. The audience for a throwback like *Hannibal Rising* had moved on.

Following the film's box-office failure, even De Laurentiis admitted that the Hannibal franchise needed to take a break. "It was disappointing," he said after *Hannibal Rising*'s opening weekend. "We haven't talked about another movie." *Hannibal Rising* would be one of De Laurentiis's final films; he died in 2010, at the age of ninety-one. Harris, meanwhile, had no apparent plans to write another Lecter novel. After five books and four films, it was clear that readers and moviegoers wanted a break. "The audience had had enough of it," Harris's agent, Mort Janklow, said years after the release of *Hannibal Rising*. "He had exhausted the character. As my grandmother used to say, 'Too much is plenty.'"

Harris wouldn't publicly address *Hannibal Rising* for more than a decade. "I did that for myself, as much as anything," he finally said in 2019. Whether that meant he'd written *Hannibal Rising* to reclaim the character from Hollywood—or simply to indulge in his love of eleventh-century Japanese literature—is impossible to know. But he was now free of the burden of having to write another Hannibal Lecter novel. A character who loved nothing more than fun and chaos had died from the most boring cause imaginable: indifference. It was time for Lecter to go away—to retreat back into the darkness, where he was at his most menacing. Where he could wait to strike again.

PART 5
REBIRTH

Hannibal
(2013–2015)

CHAPTER 25

"WE FEEL MURDEROUS THINGS IN OUR LIVES."

In early 2009, some of the most famous monsters of filmland—or at least the actors who'd played them—gathered in a Hollywood photo studio. Sharon Stone was there, clutching the ice pick she'd wielded as the killer novelist Catherine Tramell in *Basic Instinct*. She was joined by Louise Fletcher, who'd starred as the cruel Nurse Ratched in *One Flew over the Cuckoo's Nest*, as well as Malcolm McDowell, dressed in part as *A Clockwork Orange* thug Alex DeLarge. According to *Entertainment Weekly*, which had commissioned the rogues' gallery, the mood in the room was lively: The actors chatted and exchanged phone numbers, and at one point, McDowell playfully recreated the nihilistic song-and-dance number he'd immortalized in *Clockwork* nearly four decades earlier.

In the middle of it all was Anthony Hopkins, wearing a tie adorned with tiny cartoon lambs and holding the original greenish brown Lecter mask he'd donned for *The Silence of the Lambs*. It had been nearly two decades since he had first played Hannibal the Cannibal. Yet he was still constantly fielding questions about his most infamous role: What made Lecter so scary? Why did moviegoers love him so much? He didn't mind such inquiries—"It's part of who I am," he explained—but he didn't have a good answer for them. For years, whenever he was asked to analyze Lecter's appeal, Hopkins often gave the same response: "I have no idea," he'd tell people. "Ask a sociologist or psychoanalyst why Lecter's become this cult figure."

But by the time of that 2009 photo shoot, the actor's understanding of Hannibal the Cannibal had evolved. Hopkins was now in his early seventies, and his familiarity with humanity had deepened with age. "We feel murderous things in our lives, and anyone who denies it is a liar," he said. "We're taught as children to repress all that stuff: Don't be jealous, don't be greedy, don't be angry. We bury the feelings alive, and they never die." What Lecter offered audiences, he said, was a sort of secondhand catharsis—a chance to experience, from afar, dark desires long kept hidden. "When you project on screen an arch-villain [like] Hannibal Lecter, it gets something to respond in us," he said. "It's making us acknowledge that we have those parts of ourselves."

Hopkins's realization—that nothing is more unsettling than our own battened-down urges—was one that many Americans shared. The terrors that had made Harris's *Red Dragon* so urgent back in 1981 had come to seem almost passé. Serial killers still existed in the twenty-first century, of course, but sadly, they'd become so commonplace that few, if any, came close to achieving the mono-monikered infamy of Dahmer or Bundy.

Instead, the tabloids of the 2000s focused on murderers who were "just like us"—but deadlier. The new A-list monsters were neighbors, co-workers, and fellow parishioners: Andrea Yates, the suburban mom who drowned her kids in the bathtub; Scott Peterson, the smiling husband accused of dumping his pregnant wife's body in a bay. Their actions—and the nonstop attention they generated—spoke to the rising fear that with enough provocation, *anybody* could be a natural-born killer.

That notion would underline the most intricate and grotesque Lecter story yet, a cerebral and gonzo TV series that would serve as the doctor's unexpected comeback. The show had a simple title: *Hannibal*. In its brief lifetime, the series would unite Thomas Harris's menagerie of murderers into a long-running, phantasmagoric swirl—one that was hypnotic, violent, and nearly impossible to define.

• • •

In the 1990s, Bryan Fuller was living in Los Angeles, hoping to make it as a film director. But after he began watching the hit series *Star Trek: Deep Space Nine*, he realized that he'd rather work on TV scripts. *I could do this*, he thought "I kind of saw the matrix," Fuller said. "I was like 'Oh, *that's* how they tell the story."

Fuller submitted a spec script to the show's producers that eventually landed him work on both *Deep Space Nine* and *Star Trek: Voyager*. He wasn't the only aspiring moviemaker to migrate to TV in the late 1990s and early 2000s. Thanks in part to the success of HBO's operatic crime saga *The Sopranos*, the medium was entering a commercial and creative zenith, similar to what the Hollywood film studios had experienced in the 1970s. Many of the new TV dramas were more sophisticated, more intense, and more *adult* than they'd been in the past. That was especially true on cable television, where lax restrictions on sex and violence meant that storytellers could play around with bold, sometimes uncomfortable ideas. Shows such as *Six Feet Under*, *The Wire*, and *The Shield* won big awards, earned near-unanimous critical acclaim, and helped make cable TV subscriptions a must-have for tens of millions of Americans.

In 2003, the cable network Showtime, hoping to compete with HBO, debuted Fuller's first original series, *Dead Like Me*. It was a vibrant fantasy drama about a group of earthbound grim reapers. The show treated death not as a grim specter but as an inevitability—and, perhaps, an opportunity for reinvention. It was a notion that would animate much of Fuller's work. He wasn't freaked out by dying: As a child growing up in Clarkston, Washington, he had attended many family funerals. "There were a lot of older uncles and great uncles and cousins," he says. "And it was the seventies, so people weren't quite up on their prostate examinations. Death was a common event."

Dead Like Me lasted just two seasons, with Fuller departing the show early in its run following battles with the studio producing the show. In the years ahead, he'd establish a reputation as a headstrong, sometimes unyielding collaborator, one who wasn't afraid to feud with executives. "I live in active terror of mediocrity," he later explained. "Usually I'm the last one standing with the dukes still raised when other more diplomatic folks would say, 'Okay, it's good enough.'"

Fuller went on to create a handful of other original shows, including the critically beloved *Pushing Daisies*, about a pie maker who can revive the dead. The series didn't last long, but it earned a devoted audience, turning Fuller into a TV industry rarity: a showrunner with a cult following. In 2010, not long after *Pushing Daisies*' cancellation, he was on a plane to New York City, where he hoped to catch a few Broadway shows. During the flight, he bumped into Katie O'Connell, the CEO of the production company Gaumont International Television. As they talked on the flight, O'Connell mentioned that Gaumont was developing a series about Hannibal Lecter. "Do you think there's a show here that's worth exploring?" she asked.

Fuller was intrigued. He'd been a horror aficionado for decades, killing time at some of those childhood funerals by listening to his cousins describe the plots of essential 1970s scare flicks such as *Jaws* and *Shivers*. In later years, he had used his babysitting money to buy a VCR and begun studying decades' worth of slasher classics, from *Psycho* to *Black Christmas* to *Angel*. After watching *Manhunter*, he'd picked up the novel that had inspired it—and had been hooked by *Red Dragon*'s combination of police work rigor and pure fright. "People interpret Thomas Harris's books as crime thrillers," he says. "But they're actually horror stories."

But those stories had been interpreted and reinterpreted for the screen so many times that they'd lost some of their power. "I love *The Silence of the Lambs*, I love *Manhunter*, I love *Red Dragon*, and I love Ridley Scott's *Hannibal* movie," Fuller said. "Then *Hannibal Rising* came along, and the character sort of died. Everybody lost interest in him because they are like, 'You showed him with his pants down and we didn't like his underwear." As a result, he said, the Lecter brand had been "oversaturated, overexposed, and de-fanged."

Fuller wasn't the only one wondering if Hannibal might have been cannibalized by his own success. After Dino De Laurentiis's death in 2010, his producing partner and wife, Martha, took over the Lecter franchise. Dino had been trying to get a Lecter TV show off the ground since at least the early 2000s. By the time she revived the idea, De Laurentiis knew that the villain had lost some of his cool. "Everybody in the world, when they would hear 'Hannibal for television,' they'd [think], 'Back to the well *again*?'" she said. Her concerns were echoed by Harris, who was nervous about handing off Lecter to another creator: "He said, 'You know, Martha, I'm afraid somebody's going to fuck it up. I don't want it to be fucked up.' And I said, 'I don't want it to be fucked up, either.'"*

She was reassured after having dinner with Fuller, who saw Lecter not as some purely vengeful blood-lusted maniac, but as a refined intellectual curious about human behavior—and how he can shape it. If Lecter was going to work on TV, "he's got to be hypersane, as opposed to insane," Fuller said. "He's not a psychopath, because he experiences regret. He's not a sociopath, because he experiences empathy. He's a work of fiction. Serial killers don't think like Hannibal Lecter, which is partly why we're so fascinated with him. He is this grand wonder that defies categorization."

Fuller also knew that Lecter couldn't support an entire TV series by himself. He was a character who came most alive while playing with and preying on others. For the series, Fuller wanted to pair Lecter with the man who'd eventually put him behind bars: the troubled FBI profiler Will Graham. "I always felt like there was so much more between the lines of Will Graham on the page than had ever been seen in the way that he was presented on screen," said Fuller. He'd once planned on becoming a psychiatrist, and he was drawn to Graham's many neuroses and his ability to relate to murderers: "I thought, 'God, if you have an empathy disorder and you're putting yourself in the minds of serial killers to catch them, how damaging and traumatizing that would be.'"

A devious serial killer and an antisocial investigator: Only a decade or so earlier, the idea that two pitch-black antiheroes could propel their own network series would have seemed impossible. But there was good reason

---

* The *Hannibal* TV series would be one of Martha De Laurentiis's final projects. She died of brain cancer in 2021, at the age of sixty-seven.

to believe that a Lecter TV show could succeed. After all, he'd helped create the modern small-screen landscape.

In the decades since *Manhunter* and *The Silence of the Lambs* had reimagined the find-the-freak crime procedural, their influence could be seen all over prime-time programming. In 2000, CBS had debuted *CSI: Crime Scene Investigation*, about a team of forensics specialists specializing in investigating unorthodox deaths. An immediate ratings hit, *CSI* owed a considerable debt to *Manhunter*. The show recruited William Petersen for a leading role, finally turning him into a megastar. It also shared some of *Manhunter*'s creative DNA: brooding investigators, brightly lit crime labs, and quick-moving conversations about fingerprints.

CSI would eventually inspire a number of spin-offs, including *CSI: Miami* and *CSI: NY*, all of which featured serial killer subplots. So did other 2000s small-screen hits such as *Law & Order: Special Victims Unit*, *NCIS*, *Criminal Minds*, and *Cold Case*. Their creative methodologies varied. And none of the shows would sire a killer as renowned as Lecter. But all of them owed a debt to Harris's combination of somberness and suspense. "Thomas set the bar," Martha De Laurentiis said of the crime-time glut. "Pretty much everything afterwards has been an imitation."

After getting the okay from Martha De Laurentiis, Fuller mapped out the show that would become *Hannibal*. It would be set in the period prior to the events of *Red Dragon*, when Graham is still a top FBI profiler, and Lecter is still a highly respected forensic psychiatrist. The two are brought together in the film's pilot, which follows Graham as he investigates the murders of several young women, some of whom have been cannibalized. Given Graham's fragile emotional state, FBI boss Jack Crawford asks Lecter to keep tabs on his star profiler. In subsequent *Hannibal* episodes, Lecter subjects Graham to a series of ad hoc therapy sessions in which the cannibal tries to earn the patient's trust and gain entry into his mind:

LECTER: Ever have any problems, Will?

GRAHAM: No.

LECTER: Of course you don't. You and I are just alike: Problem-free. Nothing about us to feel horrible about. You know,

Will—I think Uncle Jack sees you as a fragile little teacup. The finest china used only for special guests.

GRAHAM: How do you see me?

LECTER: The mongoose I want under the house when the snakes slither by.

Though Lecter and Graham would be *Hannibal*'s leads, they'd be part of a wide ensemble. Fuller didn't have the rights to *The Silence of the Lambs*, meaning that he couldn't pull Clarice Starling or Jame Gumb into the world of *Hannibal*. But he had a free hand when it came to *Red Dragon*, *Hannibal*, and *Hannibal Rising*. Over the course of *Hannibal*'s three seasons, characters and storylines from those novels would blur and collide. "I've always described the writing staff as mash-up DJs," he said. "We're spinning tracks from *Red Dragon* with lyrics from *The Silence of the Lambs*."

Some figures from Harris's novels would be radically transformed for *Hannibal*, including Dr. Alan Bloom, a forensic psychiatrist with a small role in Harris's novels. In Fuller's show, Dr. Bloom would become Dr. *Alana* Bloom, a prospective love interest for both Graham and Lecter, played by Caroline Dhavernas. Fuller would also incorporate characters mentioned passingly in Harris's novels, such as Garrett Jacob Hobbs, aka the serial killer known as the "Minnesota Shrike," and provide them with episodes-long story arcs. (Fuller never learned how such changes sat with Harris, as the two never spoke: "I would have loved to have a conversation with him about cannibals or about lilacs in the garden or about whatever. But it never came to pass.")

Throughout the series' run, Fuller would nudge Harris's creations past the parameters of the page—and of reality. *Hannibal* would amplify some of the more rococo elements of Harris's novels, dropping the writer's investigators and murderers into an environment that felt somewhere between a nightmare and a wet dream. "When I sat down to the script," he remembered, "I was very consciously saying, 'What would David Lynch do with a Hannibal Lecter character? What sort of strange, unexpected places would he take this world?'"

That wasn't Fuller's only cinematic touchstone for the show. He wanted *Hannibal* to recall atmospheric horror classics such as *Rosemary's Baby*, *The Shining*, and *The Hunger*, films that were equal parts stylish and unsettling, with occasional bursts of violence as well as an underlying sense of existential ennui—elements that were becoming commonplace on TV by the 2010s. In the decade since *The Sopranos* had pushed boundaries and upended expectations, a new wave of adventurous dramas had emerged. Hits such as *Dexter*, *Mad Men*, and *Breaking Bad* were beautifully shot, delicately structured, and populated with realistically (and relatably) damaged lead characters. "Everybody's fucked up now on TV," Martha De Laurentiis noted. "It's great, because we *all* have problems."

Still, when *Hannibal* was given the green light in early 2012, some industry observers were surprised to learn that the show would be airing not on some nervy cable network but on NBC. At the time, the network was mostly playing it safe with shows such as *Betty White's Off Their Rockers* and Donald Trump's *The Apprentice*. Such programs were reliable but hardly radical. If NBC was going to stay relevant, it needed shows that could compete with those on HBO, whose viewers were tuning in to steamy, grisly series such as *True Blood* and *Game of Thrones*. "Networks are hemorrhaging viewers," Fuller noted after *Hannibal* was announced. "They have to start adopting more of a cable model and a cable attitude."

But network TV shows were still being built around recognizable, likable, *welcoming* stars, which meant that Fuller would have to find an actor who could play Lecter with enough charm to seduce not only Will Graham, but the millions of viewers who'd be invited to relax on the doctor's couch.

While growing up in a working-class district of Copenhagen, Denmark, Mads Mikkelsen heard tales of a famous local serial killer. The murderer's victims were all women, and before their deaths, a mysterious female voice could be heard singing the same eerie tune.

The story was made up. But it was well known in Denmark, thanks to a famous Danish radio program titled *Mordets melodi*, or *Melody of Murder*. It was one of the crime shows Mikkelsen's father listened to in the family home. Mikkelsen and his brother were enthralled by such tales and by those who performed them. But a life in the arts seemed like a faraway fantasy. "There were no actors, opera singers, or ballet dancers in my family," he said. "We never dreamt of being actors."

Instead, Mikkelsen trained as a gymnast, eventually discovering dance as a teenager. "I was a working-class little boy," he said, "almost like a Billy Elliot story." In the 1980s, he earned a scholarship to study at the Martha Graham Dance Company and temporarily relocated to Manhattan. "Everything was just like the movies," he said. "There were even kids playing from this fire hydrant that was broken. I got myself some roller skates, and that's how I transported myself."

After a couple of summers in New York City, Mikkelsen returned to Denmark, where he appeared in stage shows such as *Chicago* and *West Side Story*. In 1996, when he was in his early thirties, he finally made his first big-screen appearance, playing a street rat in the drug dealer tale *Pusher*. Making the film, Mikkelsen said, felt like "pure rock 'n' roll." So he became conflicted when, a few years afterward, he signed on for a mainstream TV procedural titled *Unit One* (*Rejseholdet*). It turned him into a national star, prompting one Danish women's magazine to anoint him "The Sexiest Man in the World."

In Hollywood, though, executives and filmmakers weren't quite sure what to make of Mikkelsen's straight-lined smile and sunken eyes. And the actor didn't seem particularly interested in commercial films, instead choosing indie projects such as 2002's *Open Hearts*, a stark relationship drama created using the rules of the avant-garde filmmaking manifesto Dogme 95. It wasn't until 2006 that he jumped into the world of big-studio franchise movies, playing a menacing genius who weeps blood in the James Bond adventure *Casino Royale*. That same year, Mikkelsen starred in *After the Wedding*, a Danish drama about a man who's unexpectedly reunited with an old love. The film didn't find a huge American audience, but those who did catch it loved it—including Fuller.

Years later, Mikkelsen was on Fuller's mind as he wrote the *Hannibal* pilot. The actor had an elegance and gracefulness—and a serpentine physicality—that would reflect Lecter's sense of freedom. And, like Lecter, Mikkelsen was European—a fact that would keep the character at a slight remove from the others. "He is the other, and he is different," Fuller said.

Mikkelsen, however, initially wasn't sure that he wanted to play a character as well-worn as Lecter. "I was like, 'Oh, God, Anthony Hopkins. That's just a no-go,'" the actor said. "He did it to perfection." After some nudging, he met with Fuller, who proceeded to pitch him several years' worth of ideas for *Hannibal*. "I was supposed to be there fifteen minutes, and he went on for three hours," Mikkelsen said. "I've met a few very extreme, very radical people in this business—but nothing like that. His dream and his vision were very hard to understand. But it was very compelling."

During their initial talks, Mikkelsen gave Fuller his spin on Lecter: "This character is a bit like Lucifer," he said. "He sees the beauty in the world and in humanity—but is also punitive to those who don't." Mikkelsen was also drawn to Lecter's lack of boundaries—a trait he seemed to envy. In previous roles, he noted, "[I] would often hear myself say, 'My character wouldn't do that.' That was not the case for Hannibal. He could do anything, as long as it was benefiting him in the end."

After talking to Mikkelsen, Fuller was sure that he'd found his Lecter. Some of his bosses at NBC weren't quite as convinced. "They wanted someone effusive and comedic, and has that level of charm to them to counter all of the evil," Fuller recalled. The network floated names such as John Cusack, Hugh Grant, and Paul Bettany, all of whom passed. Even then, the network was reluctant to commit to Mikkelsen. "I remember one [executive] saying, "He's kind of creepy!" Fuller recalled. "And I'm like, 'He's *Hannibal Lecter*!'"

After a long debate, NBC eventually acquiesced and allowed Fuller to hire Mikkelsen. The actor would be paired on *Hannibal* with Hugh Dancy, an English stage and screen star who'd already been cast as the troubled Will Graham (and who'd auditioned to play Lecter in *Hannibal Rising*). Dancy had spent the early 2000s starring in confectionery rom-coms (*Ella Enchanted*) and grounded indie dramas (*Martha Marcy May Marlene*). Compact and intense, he'd be playing a version of Graham that was different from the casually swaggering alpha versions seen in *Manhunter* and *Red Dragon*. Fuller had taken inspiration from Harris's descriptions of the character in his novel *Red Dragon*, in which Graham is portrayed as awkward and antisocial when focused on a case. "[Graham] could see and hear better afraid," Harris wrote. "He could not speak as concisely, and fear sometimes makes him rude."

In order to make such a standoffish character appealing to an audience, "you have to have somebody who has an innate likeability, otherwise they're just going to come off like an asshole," Fuller said. "And Hugh has that." Dancy prepared for the role by avoiding watching *Manhunter* and *Red Dragon* and instead taking his cues from Harris's novel. "There was some suggestion that maybe Will is on the spectrum," Dancy said of the character. "But my understanding of Will from *Red Dragon* was that he's, in a sense, on the opposite end of the spectrum: He's *too* porous. He's shut down because he receives too much information from people, and it's painful—as opposed to not being able to read them. And that all came from Thomas Harris."

Dancy, Mikkelsen, and the rest of the cast and crew—including the imperious Laurence Fishburne, who'd play FBI boss Jack Crawford—assembled on the *Hannibal* set in Toronto in the summer of 2012. Though the show's initial season would consist of just thirteen episodes, a little more than half of what other network TV dramas were allotted, that would be more than enough to demonstrate *Hannibal*'s otherworldly ingenuity. It was a series that aimed to be unlike anything else on TV, network or otherwise: moody and bloody, sexy and strange, with an outsized aesthetic that made some sequences all but float from the screen.

Such ambitions were evident from *Hannibal*'s pilot, "Apéritif," which opens with Graham investigating a fresh murder scene, trying to rewind the killer's actions in his mind. As blood trickles off the walls in reverse and retreats from the floorboards, Graham goes back in time in his mind and imagines *himself* committing the murders. It's a demonstration of the hardwired empathy that will haunt him throughout the series. Even when Graham's off the clock, he has nightmarish visions of crime victims disappearing, dying, or being stuck in some hallucinatory limbo. "My thoughts are often not tasty," he says—a line adapted from Harris's *Red Dragon*.

Graham's unsavory mindset prompts Crawford to pair him with Lecter, who doesn't appear until about halfway through the *Hannibal* pilot, introduced while eating a finely prepared meal. Mikkelsen plays Lecter as a nattily dressed tiger shark, making no big moves or dramatic declarations; his eyes are as hard to read as they are to ignore. When one of his whinier therapy patients casually tosses aside a dirty tissue, Lecter's disdain passes quickly but damningly across his face. It's clear that this is a guy who won't tolerate bad manners or boring people.

Lecter's eventually paired with Graham to help out as the FBI pursues the vicious Minnesota Shrike. Over time, the two become chattier and friendlier, eventually developing what Mikkelsen described as "a bromance." But after Graham fatally guns down the Minnesota Shrike, he begins spinning out of control, wondering if he might have enjoyed pulling the trigger a little *too* much. "Is Will a Natural Born CSI or a Natural Born Killer himself?" asked one critic. "Even he's not sure."

Lecter believes he knows the answer. Through a series of elaborate lies and schemes, he slowly, slyly cajoles Graham into acknowledging his unexplored dark side: "Lecter: I'm worried about you, Will. You empathize so completely with the killers Jack Crawford has your mind wrapped around, that you lose yourself to them. What if you lose time and hurt yourself? Or someone else? I don't want you to wake up and see a totem of your own making."

Of course, Lecter really *does* want Graham to wake up and see himself as a fellow murderer. In *Hannibal*, Graham is both Lecter's patient and his plaything—a living test subject the doctor can manipulate on a whim, observing the results in real time. For Lecter, teasing out Graham's killer instincts isn't an act of aggression; it's a display of affection. "I want to be his friend," Mikkelsen said of his character. "It can be lonely in the world when you're Hannibal."

• • •

Hannibal premiered on NBC on April 4, 2013, to largely admiring reviews. "Finely acted, visually scrumptious, and deliciously subversive," noted *Entertainment Weekly*'s Jeff Jensen. "Bon appétit, horror freaks." Meanwhile, in *USA Today*, Robert Bianco urged viewers to get over their skepticism about what might seem like a mindless cash grab. "It's a prequel to a movie about a cannibalistic serial killer—which for a broadcast series counts as three strikes in just one sentence," he wrote. "[But] *Hannibal* seldom seems to be operating on shock value alone; like its namesake anti-hero, something else is always going on behind the eyes."

Not all critics were as happily surprised: *Hannibal* was dismissed by both *The New York Times* ("fatally slow and pretentious") and the *Los Angeles Times* ("no fun at all"). Decades earlier, getting the brush-off from two of the country's most prominent newspapers would have been nearly fatal for a new show. But *Hannibal* was born just as the cultural conversation was moving to social media. On platforms such as Tumblr and Twitter, viewers eagerly analyzed, evangelized, and debated the latest episode of their favorite shows—sometimes before the end credits had begun rolling. A few weeks into *Hannibal*'s first season, an NBC employee pulled Fuller aside and told him that the show had a growing army of enthusiasts, who called themselves "Fannibals." Some were horror lovers cheering on the show's macabre nature. Others were like the show's titular quasi heroes: outsiders with unorthodox tastes, looking to forge connections with others. "These are savvy audience members who enjoy the same things," Fuller says. "And they're having conversations that may start with *Hannibal*, but that lead to so many other interactions."

For some Fannibals, their online boosting amounted to a rescue mission. Throughout the spring and summer of 2013, *Hannibal*'s ratings remained dangerously low. When the season finale aired, barely 2 million viewers tuned in. Those who *did* watch were treated to a daring cliffhanger: By the end of the episode, Lecter has managed to frame Graham for a series of murders, landing the profiler in the Baltimore State Hospital for the Criminally Insane—where Lecter can keep an eye on him. The season finale concludes with Graham staring at Lecter from behind the bars of his cell—a direct nod to *The Silence of the Lambs*.

For any other show, that would have been a hard-to-swallow send-off. But by that point, it had become clear that *anything* was possible on *Hannibal*. The first season had been full of acute plot twists, ever-shifting character loyalties, and plenty of scarily imaginative crime scenes: One *Hannibal* murderer—a man dying of cancer—uses his victims' bodies to create fleshy wings so that he'll have "angels" to look after him. Another slayer, desperate to get Lecter's attention, painstakingly converts a man's vocal chords into cello strings.

As nauseating as those kills were, they had a hallucinatory quality that distinguished Fuller's show from the *CSI*s and *SVU*s of the world. The many murderers of *Hannibal* (including Lecter himself) took painstaking care in the choice and presentation of their victims. They were making a statement with each new kill—and so was Fuller. He wanted to avoid the all-too-realistic homicides and sexual assaults that populated so many other prime-time crime series. "It's hard for me to make that entertainment," he said. "Whereas if you flay somebody's back and turn 'em into an angel—*that's* entertaining. It's outside of reality."

Despite *Hannibal*'s troubling numbers, NBC renewed the show for a sophomore season, which premiered in early 2014. The next batch of episodes wouldn't do much for the show's ratings. But *Hannibal* would become even more ambitious, especially in its depictions of violence. In one new storyline, nude corpses are fastened together in a giant circle so that from above, they resemble a massive upturned eye. In another episode, a body is cut up into a half-dozen pieces, which are framed behind slices of glass—like a Damien Hirst exhibit at a morgue. There's even a plot featuring the vile Mason Verger, who suffers a similar fate to that in the *Hannibal* novel, mutilating his own face while under the care of Lecter (and while under the influence of some serious drugs).

Fuller managed to get *Hannibal*'s gore on the air with little interference from NBC's censors. "They wanted the show to be what it was," he says. "I would call preemptively and say, 'Okay, we need to have a character cut off his face and feed it to dogs—and be sort of cheerful while he's doing it. How do we get that done?' And they'd say, 'Make the blood black. Keep it in shadows.'"

The network also allowed Fuller to get away with some wild on-screen sex in *Hannibal*'s second season, including a hallucinatory five-way love-making scene involving Lecter and Graham. The show's beguiling (and occasionally baffling) visual style likely alienated viewers looking for a few quick kills and a spare Chianti joke or two. But Fuller was unapologetic about *Hannibal*'s lofty aspirations. Every director hired for the show, he said, got the same lecture: "We are not making television. We are making a pretentious art film from the 80s."

For many Fannibals, the real draw of the series wasn't the show's rhapsodic violence; it was the increasingly heated relationship between Lecter and Graham. The profiler has realized the doctor's true nature, and throughout season two, the two men try to outwit, entrap, and kill each other, their connection powered by a mix of ferocity and curiosity. After Graham kills an assassin sent by Lecter, the profiler comes to a realization: Deep down inside him, there's a slayer. "I've never felt as alive as I did when I was killing him," he admits to Lecter. It was a harsh truth, similar to the one Hopkins had confessed just a few years earlier: "We feel murderous things in our lives, and anyone who denies it is a liar."

By the time *Hannibal*'s second season reached its climax, Lecter and Graham's hazily defined relationship had become a source of rampant speculation: Do they want to destroy each other? Fuck each other? And is there really a difference? Finally, after months of one-upmanship and double crosses, Lecter realizes that Graham has tried to set him up and stabs the profiler in the chest. Their bond, whatever it was, has been broken. And after the men come together in a quick and bloody embrace, Lecter makes it clear that he doesn't appreciate being rejected:

LECTER: I have let you know me, see me. I gave you a rare gift—
but you didn't want it.
GRAHAM: Didn't I?

What Mikkelsen had initially described as a bromance had evolved into something much more rich and complicated—in the words of one *Hannibal* character, the two men came off less like colleagues and more like "murder husbands." For Fuller, digging into the union between Lecter and Graham, with all of its tension and tenderness, was part of the appeal of making *Hannibal*. "It's interesting to me as a gay man to look at straight male relationships because there's a level of intimacy that's something I don't entirely understand and experience," he said after the show's second season aired. "It felt like, 'Oh, this is an interesting essay on male intimacy without components of sexuality.'"

To many Fannibals, though, *Hannibal* was decidedly queer—and so was Hannibal. Not long after the show's debut, fan fiction and artwork depicting Lecter and Graham as a couple began circulating online, some of it far racier than anything found on NBC. But viewers didn't have to swim in *Hannibal*'s subtext to glimpse the mutual attraction at its core. Even the most casual *Hannibal* viewer could tell: Those two guys were *awfully* close.

Yet no matter where viewers landed on Lecter and Graham's respective desires, it was the characters' snug relationship that became *Hannibal*'s central horror—for reasons that had nothing to do with sex or sexuality. Over the decades, Harris had granted Lecter all manner of superpowers: He could smell a freshly applied Band-Aid from a far distance and overpower an armed police officer in mere seconds. Yet none of his skills are as insidious as his ability to break into another person's mind and weaponize the cravings and secrets hidden within. On *Hannibal*, Lecter burrows so deeply into Graham's psyche that he renders him confused, agitated, and deeply paranoid. It's terrifying to watch. Because if Lecter could get to somebody as savvy and self-protective as Will Graham, he could get to anybody—even *you*. (Unless, of course, that's something you'd be into.)

Fuller had initially planned out enough storylines to keep *Hannibal* on the air for at least seven seasons. He even hoped to eventually land the rights to *The Silence of the Lambs*, so that all of Harris's characters could be thrown together on-screen. But in the summer of 2015, just weeks after the show's third-season premiere, *Hannibal* was canceled by NBC. The series' viewership had never improved. And unlike some ratings underdogs, *Hannibal* lacked the kind of awards tractions that could keep a struggling show on the air. "Every season, you hope, going in, that more people will discover the show," Fuller said right before *Hannibal*'s end was announced. "But it is a niche show."

Certainly, any casual viewer tuning in to *Hannibal*'s last episodes would have been more than a little lost. The season found Fuller mining Harris's novels with even greater fervor than before: The action begins with Lecter dodging the law in Florence (an adaptation of Harris's *Hannibal* novel). The show then follows Graham in Lithuania, as he learns of Lecter's past (a spin on *Hannibal Rising*). And the season's second half is devoted to Graham's search for Francis Dolarhyde, aka the Tooth Fairy (a character first introduced, of course, in *Red Dragon*). For Harris's devout readers, watching his various villains bleed into and onto one another was a delight; few screen adaptations have treated an author's work with as much freewheeling reverence as Fuller's *Hannibal*. For less invested viewers, though, the series had no doubt become impenetrable. When the show's thirty-ninth and final episode aired in August 2015, a little more than a million people watched.

Those who did tune in for Lecter and Graham's grand showdown were treated to an opulent adieu. The episode, titled "The Wrath of the Lamb," concludes with the two men killing the Tooth Fairy outside Lecter's luxe cliffside home. Both are badly injured during the fight, and as they struggle to stand upright, they hold each other in a blood-soaked embrace, their faces closer than ever before. The men are now partners in crime. And unlike Clarice Starling in Harris's *Hannibal* novel—whom Lecter had to drug and manipulate into joining the dark side—Will Graham in Fuller's *Hannibal* actually *is* a killer at heart; he just needs to follow the doctor's orders to realize it:

LECTER: See? This is all I ever wanted for you, Will. For both of us.

GRAHAM: It's beautiful.

With that, Graham pulls their bodies closer together—and then throws both himself and Lecter off the edge of a cliff. Whether Graham's doing so to snuff out his own murderous instincts, or to prove his deadly loyalty to his "murder husband," it's clear that Lecter was right about Graham all along: Deep down, both men are killers.

Whether they were something *more*, though, would be left to viewers' imaginations. "We actually did a couple of takes of the very last scene where we were looking at each other, and it was a little too obvious—it was almost a kiss," Mikkelsen said. "Me and Hugh were like, 'Why not?'" Ultimately, though, Fuller and the actors decided that any sort of consummation would rob the show of its central mystery. Every relationship is strange and unknowable—both to those living within it and to those watching from the outside. Why should Graham and Lecter's union be any different? "We never wanted it to be a physical thing," Mikkelsen noted. "It was something much bigger."

So was *Hannibal*, a television series that transcended its medium, its source material, even its creator's expectations. "I always knew it was a love story," Fuller says. "But I didn't know the parameters—that it would be through these characters who thought love was not on the table for them." And while the series was never a ratings success, it accomplished something remarkable in its brief run: *Hannibal* saved Hannibal. The show took a character in danger of becoming an also-ran slasher and restored his potency and allure—all while making him more dangerous than ever.

Many of the *Hannibal* faithful, including Fuller himself, still hold out hope that at some point, the show will return to the air. "If there's ever an opportunity for the rights to get reconfigured and settled out," he says, "we could do that story anytime." *Hannibal*'s series finale was coy about Lecter's fate: Despite his tumble over the cliff with Graham, a subsequent coda implies that the doctor has survived and will live to bite another day. How could he not? By the end of *Hannibal*, Lecter has dodged serial killers, crooked cops, and man-eating pigs. It's not that he's immortal—it's just that he finds human existence so fascinating, so worthy of continued study, that he simply will not *allow* himself to die. And Lecter has just enough self-regard to grasp what his many admirers have long known: that the world's more interesting with him in it.

EPILOGUE: AFTERLIFE

Donald Trump's mentions of Lecter became less frequent in the final months of his 2024 presidential campaign. But he still found time to celebrate Hannibal the Cannibal. At some stops, Trump would point to an audience member and warn them that Lecter wanted to have them for dinner. And in July 2024, more than 25 million viewers watched as Trump, his right ear bandaged after a recent assassination attempt, again complimented "the late, great Hannibal Lecter" as he accepted the Republican nomination in Milwaukee, Wisconsin. That night, Trump even managed to say *The Silence of the Lambs* correctly.

In a strange way, Lecter and Trump had worked out their *own* informal quid pro quo: Lecter provided Trump with a go-to bogeyman to invoke, while Trump gave Lecter a pop-cultural prominence he hadn't experienced since *Hannibal* was on the air a decade earlier. In 2024, it seemed as though Lecter was everywhere. *Saturday Night Live* opened an episode with a sketch in which Trump wheeled out a masked and vicious-looking Lecter in midspeech. ("I keep calling him 'the late and great,'" noted *SNL*'s Trump, played by James Austin Johnson, "even though he's not dead, he's not great, and he's not real.") And at the 2024 Democratic National Convention in Chicago, former president Bill Clinton marveled at Trump's "endless tributes" to Lecter. "President Obama once gave me the great honor of saying I was the explainer in chief," he said. "Folks, I thought and thought about it, and I don't know what to say."

Trump and Lecter became so intertwined that in the spring of 2025, just a few months after his inauguration, Trump took a moment to acknowledge a man who'd played a small but highly visible role in his return to office: "The great Hannibal Lecter. He was a very important force."

Trump clearly wasn't going to end his relationship with Lecter any time soon. In the summer of 2025, during a White House speech about a new budget bill, the president once again sang the cannibalistic serial killer's praises: "The late, great Hannibal Lecter," Trump said. "Do you know who that is?"

He needn't have asked. By the time Trump began his second term, Lecter was more recognizable than ever. He may take long hiatuses. And he may be replaced from time to time by new nightmares. But Hannibal the Cannibal is always hovering in the background, much as in the final scene of *The Silence of the Lambs*, in which the ludicrously disguised Lecter casually disappears into a throng of pedestrians. And while it's been years since Lecter appeared on the bestseller lists or on the screen his handiwork is constantly being sought out.

Harris's books remain popular, with tens of thousands of copies being sold each year. Decades after its release, *Red Dragon* is widely considered a perfect page-turner, one that's equal parts terrifying and enchanting; it's perhaps the breeziest novel ever written about a corpse-defiling madman. When James Ellroy declared *Red Dragon* to be "the best pure thriller I've ever read," he was echoing the sentiment of many of his fellow dark-hearted writers, many of whom are still chasing *Dragon*'s tail. Meanwhile, the rich and riveting *The Silence of the Lambs* is now seen as a pop-lit masterwork, appearing on fiction-writing syllabuses alongside the works of Edgar Allan Poe, Arthur Conan Doyle, and Agatha Christie. Both *The Silence of the Lambs* and *Black Sunday* were taught at Illinois State University in the 1990s by the novelist David Foster Wallace, who annotated his dog-eared copy of *The Silence of the Lambs* with countless marginalia and unanswered questions such as "What does [Lecter's] polydactyly symbolize?"

The *Hannibal* novel doesn't command quite the same level of respect. But it remains a subject of fascination among admirers and detractors, some of whom revisit the book every few years, relishing its elite ghoulishness and forgiving its unpleasant detours. "I still go back and reread parts of *Hannibal* with pleasure," notes the novelist and biographer Alec

Nevala-Lee, a longtime admirer of Harris's work. "And I don't even mind the audacity of the brain-eating stuff." (The ending, though, still irks him: "It's unforgivable—it just goes too far.") As for *Hannibal Rising*? That novel has yet to find much posthumous acclaim, and is still seen by many as the series' most skippable entry. But horror readers are famously open-minded and prone to rediscovery. In the years to come, even *Hannibal Rising* might find its own champions.

The Lecter movies, meanwhile, continue to find new audiences. *The Silence of the Lambs* is still revered and ripped off to this day, a fixture on the all-time best-of lists on sites such as Letterboxd and the Internet Movie Database. While browsing the Criterion Closet in 2025, surrounded by discs featuring hundreds of must-see films, the actor and filmmaker Ben Affleck reached for *The Silence of the Lambs*. "There's stuff in this movie that's just been borrowed by a thousand other movies," he said. "Just an example of how you make a really great pop, scary, wonderful film that's smart and terrifying and engaging."

Michael Mann's once underseen *Manhunter* is also now an established classic, with packed repertory screenings taking place around the world (tickets for one Los Angeles showing in 2023 sold out within minutes). Even the movies *Hannibal*, *Red Dragon*, and *Hannibal Rising* have found vocal acolytes, who make their cases for the lesser-appreciated Lecter adventures via podcasts, YouTube videos, and elsewhere online.

And though Harris's work seems like a strange fit for TV—a Starling-centered CBS drama titled *Clarice* came and went in 2021—NBC's *Hannibal* found an afterlife in the streaming era. The show enjoyed newfound visibility when it was aired on Netflix, siring new legions of Fannibals and prompting more demands for a fourth season. Viewers had finally caught up on a series that was always a bit ahead of its time, drawn to Mikkelsen's twenty-first-century spin on the character: a deadly dandy with an omnivorous emotional appetite.

But you don't have to rewatch *Manhunter* or NBC's *Hannibal* or re-read Harris's novels to feel Lecter's presence. His influence can be felt throughout popular culture. Box-office hits such as *Longlegs* and the *Saw* films feature cunning murderers who are all nods to Lecter (who would no doubt nod back approvingly). And the breathless cat-and-mousing found in network television crime procedurals such as *CSI: Crime Scene Investigation* and *Criminal Minds*—with their brainy maniacs and forlorn forensics experts—are indebted not only to Harris's books but also to the stylish high-tech techniques found in *Manhunter*. Few movie series have been as influential, visually and thematically, as the Hannibal films—and no series has spawned so many copycat killers. As Athena Varounis, the former FBI agent, once told Harris, "If not for you, there would be nothing on TV."

Lecter's impact isn't limited to the world of make-believe. The twenty-first century has seen an explosion in true-crime storytelling, in which horrific murders are investigated or recounted by authors, journalists, and even comedians. And whenever these crimes involve cannibalism, Lecter is bound to be mentioned. There has been a Japanese Lecter, a British Lecter, a Russian Lecter—by now so many different killers have been described as "the real-life Hannibal" that the name's almost become a franchise.

Given all that competition, and the fact that several years often pass between Lecter novels and movies, Hannibal the Cannibal *has* inevitably lost a little bit of menace. Age does something strange to even the most ghoulish creatures: Over time, they become humanized. Lecter has been around for so long that some people have lost track of what made him so scary in the first place. His chilly visage, covered by his infamous protective mask, now stares back from tattoos, greeting cards, baby onesies, and even toys. It's an unlikely arc: One minute, you're *Newsweek*'s mad-eyed embodiment of evil; the next, you're a Funko Pop. But it's better than simply fading away into the darkness of a cell.

"Lecter is like Coca-Cola or Kleenex or some other amazing brand," said the editor Ben Sevier, who worked with Harris in the 2010s. "It's come to mean more than the fictional character Tom invented."

In the spring of 2019, Thomas Harris was spotted in the wild. It had been more than a decade since he'd released a new author's photo, but Harris wasn't hard to recognize; now in his seventies, he'd maintained the same genteel smile and unreadable stare that had greeted readers from the back cover of *The Silence of the Lambs,* and he still had his beard, though it had grayed and thinned considerably. By the late 2010s, he had sold more than 50 million books. So it was inevitable that while eating lunch at a Miami restaurant near his home, he'd draw a few looky-loos. When a fan interrupted his meal and requested a picture with him, the author obliged, holding still as the woman yelled, "Everyone say Clarice!"

That Harris agreed to the impromptu photo shoot is a bit surprising, given his quest for privacy. Even more remarkable: The moment was witnessed by a reporter from *The New York Times* who was there to interview Harris about his fifth and latest novel. Titled *Cari Mora*, the book followed a Colombian refugee living in Miami, where she gets caught in the cross fire of a pair of rival gangs. It was Harris's first work since *Black Sunday* not to feature Lecter. And to promote *Cari Mora*, he had agreed to sit for a formal on-the-record interview—something he hadn't done since 1975. As Harris told the *Times'* Alexandra Alter, "You try to reinvent yourself."

In most ways, though, the author was living as he always had—grandly, yet quietly. He and his partner, Pace Barnes, still split their time between Sag Harbor and Miami Beach, where Harris often sits outside their mansion watching for dolphins or manatees, still intrigued by the ocean's subterranean menace. (As the author had once observed: "Everything is fine on the surface, and underneath, it's all this carnage.") And though Harris had acquiesced to doing a chat with *The New York Times*—and would later appear on the East Hampton public access show *Conversations*—his reemergence from seclusion would be brief. His best-selling books had afforded him wealth and luxury, but he'd found the fame that had come with it to be "more of a nuisance than anything else."

Cari Mora arrived nearly thirteen years after the release and rejection of *Hannibal Rising*. During that time, Harris had stayed busy. He usually began writing around 8:30 a.m. and continued until the early afternoon before taking his lunch (and a nap). He still occasionally wrote by hand—as he had with *Black Sunday*—and there were days when all that effort yielded little more than a single paragraph. "You have to show up at your office every day," Harris said. "If an idea comes by, you want to be there to get it in."

In recent years, such ideas had nothing to do with Lecter. Yet every once in a while, Harris missed his most fearsome companion. "The Hannibal character still occurs to me," he said, "and I wonder sometimes what it's up to."

He's out there. Lecter remains enduringly terrifying, his fearsomeness divined not from the way he indulges in his dark urges but in the way he'll expose you to your own. "Believe me, you don't want Hannibal Lecter inside your head," Jack Crawford had warned in *The Silence of the Lambs*. Yet Clarice Starling, Will Graham, and even Mason Verger had all allowed Lecter to break into their brains and sift through their secrets—secrets he had later used against them. Perhaps this is the reason why, for more than five decades, Harris preferred to be invisible: The more people know about you, the more they can hurt you.

For nearly fifty years, starting with the release of *Red Dragon* in 1981, Harris had proved that monsters don't need claws or chain saws or super-sharp teeth to do harm. The *real* monsters are equal parts charming and cunning. They look you in the eyes, listen to your fears and concerns, and figure out how to exploit your needs for their own gain—smiling all the while. And when it's over, you want to tell them even *more*. That, perhaps, is their most monstrous trait: that they don't seem monstrous at all.

By the time he was in his seventies, Harris had been asked countless times about the inspiration for Lecter and his gruesome deeds: How had such a quietly unassuming guy invented a figure as sinister, as manipulative, yet as celebrated as Hannibal the Cannibal?

When *New York Times* reporter Alter posed that query to Harris in 2019, Harris pointed out that he hadn't invented anything—that Lecter and his kind had always been out there. And they always will be. "Look around you," Harris said. "Because everything has happened."

ACKNOWLEDGMENTS

This book wouldn't have been possible if not for the efforts of several heroic librarians and researchers. Phil Hallman served as a crucial guide to Jonathan Demme's archives at the University of Michigan Library, where I was further assisted by Martha O'Hara Conway and Linda Skolarus. At Elon University in North Carolina, Randall Bowman helped me search the papers of film producer Kenneth Utt. And Peter Victor-Gasper at the New York Public Library tracked down Harris's rare 1975 interview with *Book-of-the-Month-Club News*. A ravenous reader like Hannibal Lecter would surely approve of their resourcefulness, thoroughness, and dedication to sharing knowledge.

While putting together *Hannibal Lecter: A Life*, I was also fortunate to have the help of many smart and supportive friends. Scott Brown, Chuck Klosterman, Steve Kurutz, Brett Nolan, and Phoebe Reilly all provided crucial feedback on the book's early drafts. And many other good pals offered me encouragement, leads, or all-around good cheer, including Cory Everett, Gillian Flynn, Sean Howe, Jeff Jensen, Eva Kuhle, Melissa Maerz, Chris Ryan, Mary Kaye Schilling, Alan Siegel, Dan Snierson, Ken Tucker, Ryan Walker, and Josh Wolk.

I'm also grateful to all of the interviewees and sources who shared their time, insights, and recollections as I reported the book: Art Almquist, Dawn Baillie, Diane Baker, Carole Baron, Robert Benton, Bob Bookman, Tina Brown, Shayne Buchwald, Brian Cox, Raffaella De Laurentiis, Roger Depue, John Douglas, Bryan Fuller, Carl Fullerton, Charles O. Glenn, Anthony Heald, Angela Janklow, Richard Jennings, Patricia Kirby, Kevin Krakower, Mary Ann Krauss, Michael Mann, Neal Martz, Chris McGinn, Mike Medavoy, Ray Mendez, Alec Nevala-Lee, Rick Nicita, Nicholas Pileggi, Ernie Porter, Ed Saxon, Jude Schneider, Dante Spinotti, Ted Tally,

Bill Trible, Athena Varounis, Bruce Vilanch, Peter Webber, Ronnie Wise, and Kristi Zea. I feel lucky to have been able to interview Robert Benton before his death in 2025; in addition to being a great filmmaker, he was a wonderful conversationalist.

I'd also like to thank the many journalists whose extensive reporting on Thomas Harris and Hannibal Lecter became an essential part of my research, including my fellow *Entertainment Weekly* alums Jill Bernstein, Dan Fierman, Gillian Flynn, and Chris Nashawaty.

I wrote *Hannibal Lecter: A Life* at the Muse Rooms in Burbank, California, where owner Nancy Sexton always made sure I had plenty of space, lots of quiet, and endless coffee. And my work on the book was made possible in part by a generous grant from the Hubert I. Cohen Fellowship at the University of Michigan Library.

My editor, Sean Manning, was a nonstop source of ideas, support, and gently nudging questions throughout the course of this project; he is a true collaborator, and *Hannibal Lecter: A Life* wouldn't have been possible without him. At Simon & Schuster, Mia Robertson ensured that I stayed on task without getting overwhelmed, while Associate Director of Copyediting Jonathan Evans and copyeditor Lynn Anderson corrected and redirected my sometimes glitchy prose. I thank them profusely, as well as the book's proofreaders: Jessie McNiel, Janice Lee, and Chelsey Drysdale.

My agent, Jud Laghi, has long been a sturdy (and very patient) advisor, friend, and all-around sounding board. I'm grateful, as always, for his wise counsel and support.

I also want to thank Allen and Claudia Clark, Rich Williams, and Jeff Williams and Fran Mishriki for their limitless love, and for constantly reminding me that, when it comes to in-laws, I lucked out.

My daughters, Tegan and Bridget, brighten my day and broaden my horizons in ways they don't even realize. And I feel forever grateful to have my wife, Jenny, in my corner and by my side. Their kindness and affection kept me going throughout the writing of this book.

My mother, Kay Raftery, instilled in me a love of movies and books, as well as a dedication to deadlines. She has been a constant cheerleader.

My father, Bill Raftery, and my brother, Chris Raftery, passed away in the years before this book began, but they gave me decades worth of encouragement. I miss them dearly.

One last note: Before starting work on *Hannibal Lecter: A Life*, I reached out to representatives of Thomas Harris, in the hopes of speaking with him about his life and career. He declined my requests, and while that made my work all the more challenging, I respect any artist who manages to preserve one of the twenty-first century's most rarified assets: a sense of mystery.

PROLOGUE

xi "Hannibal Lecter!": Right Side Broadcasting Network, *2023 11 02 FULL SPEECH President Trump Houston Texas*, YouTube, November 2, 2023, https://www.you tube.com/watch?v=-f246Mq8W-4.

xi "lovely": Michael Luciano, "Trump Says He Keeps Talking About Hannibal Lecter Because 'These Are Real Stories,'" Mediaite, July 24, 2024, https://www .mediaite.com/media/tv/trump-says-he-keeps-talking-about-hannibal-lecter -because-these-are-real-stories.

xi "legendary": "Trump Rally from Durham, New Hampshire 12/16/23 Transcript," Rev, December 16, 2023, https://www.rev.com/transcripts/trump-rally-from-dur ham-new-hampshire-12-16-23-transcript.

xi "Silence of the Lamb": Luciano, "Trump Says He Keeps Talking About Hannibal Lecter Because 'These Are Real Stories.'"

xi "Congratulations": "Speech: Donald Trump Holds a Political Rally in Wildwood, New Jersey—May 11, 2024," Roll Call, https://rollcall.com/factbase/trump/tran script/donald-trump-speech-political-rally-wildwood-new-jersey-may-11-2024.

xi "very good": "Speech: Donald Trump Holds a Political Rally in Wildwood, New Jersey - May 11, 2024."

xii "the great fictional monster": Stephen King, "Hannibal the Cannibal," *New York Times*, June 13, 1999, https://archive.nytimes.com/www.nytimes.com/books/99 /06/13/reviews/990613.13kingct.html.

xii "nice gentleman": "Speech: Donald Trump Addresses the Republican Jewish Coalition in Las Vegas - October 28, 2023," Roll Call, https://rollcall.com/factbase /trump/transcript/donald-trump-speech-gop-jewish-coalition-las-vegas-octo ber-28-2023.

xii "Hannibal Lecter, how great": "Speech: Donald Trump Holds a Campaign Event in Cedar Rapids, Iowa—October 7, 2023," Roll Call, https://rollcall.com/factbase /trump/transcript/donald-trump-speech-campaign-event-cedar-rapids-iowa -october-7-2023.

xii "I think he's just trying": Marianne LeVine and Clara Ence Morse, "Why Trump Keeps Talking About Fictional Serial Killer Hannibal Lecter," *Washington Post*, August 14, 2024, https://www.washingtonpost.com/politics/2024/08/14/why -trump-keeps-talking-about-fictional-serial-killer-hannibal-lecter.

xii "They're emptying out": "Read the Transcript of Donald J. Trump's Convention

Speech," *New York Times*, July 19, 2024, https://www.nytimes.com/2024/07/19/us /politics/trump-rnc-speech-transcript.html.

xiii "Ta": Thomas Harris, *The Silence of the Lambs* (St. Martin's Press, 1989), 293.

xiii "Discourtesy": Harris, *The Silence of the Lambs*, 25.

xiii "Lecter looks only": Harris, *The Silence of the Lambs*, 130.

xiii "What does [Lecter]": Thomas Harris, *Hannibal* (Dell, 2000), 101–02.

xiii "I like chaos": Laura Silver, "Trump Said He Likes 'Chaos' and Joked Melania Might Be Next to Leave the White House at a Charity Dinner," BuzzFeed News, March 4, 2018, https://www.buzzfeednews.com/article/laurasilver/trump-said-he -likes-chaos-and-joked-melania-might-be-next.

xiii "Lecter is so nakedly": Author interview, June 14, 2024.

xiii "Nobody knows": Andrew Feinberg, "Trump Says 'Nobody Knows What I'm Going to Do' About Iran as He Warns 'the Next Week Will Be Big,'" *Independent*, June 18, 2025, https://www.the-independent.com/news/world/americas/us-poli tics/trump-iran-news-war-press-conference-b2772450.html.

xiv "I'm shocked": Dominic Patten, "Anthony Hopkins on Roman Emperors, Trump's Hannibal Lecter Obsession, & Taking It All Too Seriously," Deadline, July 16, 2024, https://deadline.com/2024/07/anthony-hopkins-trump-hannibal -lecter-1236009206.

xv "WARNING": Josh Jones, "David Foster Wallace's 1994 Syllabus: How to Teach Serious Literature with Lightweight Books," Open Culture, February 25, 2013, https://www.openculture.com/2013/02/david_foster_wallaces_1994_syllabus .html.

CHAPTER 1

4 "salted and cured": "Michigan Officers Link Gruesome Find of Heads with Turner Murder," *Greenwood Commonwealth*, January 14, 1935.

4 "cannibal slayer": "Cannibal Killer Admits Carving Woman Victim," *Decatur Daily Review*, January 17, 1935.

4 "an insatiable desire": "Mississippi Leads," *Vicksburg Post*, March 8, 1935.

4 "get the bones": "Cannibal Killer Admits Carving Woman Victim," *Decatur Daily Review*, January 17, 1935.

4 "I could tell yous": "Cannibalism Seen as Killing Motive," *Evening Star*, January 15, 1935.

4 "What is to be": "Coyner Is Fatalist," *Greenwood Commonwealth*, February 4, 1935.

4 "Everything we do": "Claim Suspected Murderer of White Man and Woman Is Sadist," *California Eagle*, January 25, 1935.

4 "I just had an impulse": "Cannibal Killer Admits Carving Woman Victim," *Decatur Daily Review*, January 17, 1935.

4 "just to see": "Coyner Asks Cremation for His Body Following Execution Next Tuesday," *Daily Clarion-Ledger*, March 2, 1935.

5 "He just seemed": Author interview, March 12, 2024.

5   "He was someone": Author interview, March 12, 2024.

5   "There's a tradition": LTV East Hampton, *Conversations - Thomas Harris - 07.09.2019*, YouTube, July 9, 2019, https://www.youtube.com/watch?v=XlH-cD_0kCM.

6   "In casual conversation": Email to author, March 13, 2024.

6   "I got sort of interested": LTV East Hampton, *Conversations*.

6   "a sort of gravity": LTV East Hampton, *Conversations*.

7   "He collected everything": Mike Cochran and Jeff Guinn, "Mystery Man," *Fort Worth Star-Telegram*, July 2, 1999.

7   "at its worst": LTV East Hampton, *Conversations*.

7   "You write about": LTV East Hampton, *Conversations*.

CHAPTER 2

8   "You drive through it": Author interview, March 12, 2024.

8   "I earned my lunch": LTV East Hampton, *Conversations - Thomas Harris - 07.09.2019*, YouTube, July 9, 2019, https://www.youtube.com/watch?v=XlH-cD_0kCM.

8   "I said, 'Uh, hey, look'": LTV East Hampton, *Conversations*.

9   "If we help you": LTV East Hampton, *Conversations*.

9   "a dim little light": LTV East Hampton, *Conversations*.

9   "The water had better": LTV East Hampton, *Conversations*.

9   "I just work": Phoebe Hoban, "The Silence of the Writer," *New York*, April 15, 1991, https://books.google.com/books?id=aukCAAAAMBAJ&pg=PA48&source=gbs_toc_r&cad=2#v=onepage&q&f=false, 49.

9   "Good luck getting information": Meg Laughlin, "Silence of the Author," *Tulsa World*, August 15, 1991.

9   "Do not use": Laughlin, "Silence of the Author."

10 "plain as an old shoe": Don O'Briant, "Despite Success, 'Lambs' Author Still a Silent Type," *Waco Tribune-Herald*, February 24, 1991.

10 "Ernest Hemingway bent": O'Briant, "Despite Success, 'Lambs' Author Still a Silent Type."

10 "read all day": O'Briant, "Despite Success, 'Lambs' Author Still a Silent Type."

10 "If you've read his books": Bob Minzesheimer, "Hungry Fans Eat Up 'Hannibal,'" *USA Today*, June 9, 1999, https://usatoday30.usatoday.com/life/enter/books/book128.htm.

10 "Dr. Lecter likes his fun": Thomas Harris, *The Silence of the Lambs* (St. Martin's Press, 1989), 255.

11 "the history of Native Americans": "Polly Harris Obituary," *Clarion-Ledger*, https://www.legacy.com/us/obituaries/clarionledger/name/polly-harris-obituary?id=21949684.

11 "It took two hours": Linda Kuehl, "A Conversation with Tom Harris," *Book-of-the-Month-Club News*, March 1975.

12 "smarter, more quick-witted": Laughlin, "Silence of the Author."

12   "By the time we reach": Thomas Harris, "An Ideal English Class Syllabus for 9th Graders," *Mouth2Mouth*, Spring 1994, https://web.archive.org/web/20110 629120256/http://sites.google.com/site/lektalekton/Home/an-ideal-english -class-syllabus-for-9th-graders.

12   "the Code": Thomas Harris, *Black Sunday* (Dell, 1990), 60.

12   "When you are a child": Harris, *Black Sunday*, 60.

12   "He was a very quiet kid": O'Briant, "Despite Success, 'Lambs' Author Still a Silent Type."

12   "As a small boy": Thomas Harris, "Author's Note," *The Silence of the Lambs*, rev. ed. (St. Martin's Griffin, 2013).

12   "He did not want": O'Briant, "Despite Success, 'Lambs' Author Still a Silent Type."

13   "My companions": Alexandra Alter, "Hannibal Lecter's Creator Cooks Up Something New (No Fava Beans or Chianti)," *New York Times*, May 18, 2019, https:// www.nytimes.com/2019/05/18/books/thomas-harris-new-book.html.

13   "Thomas wore out": Panny Mayfield, "Top Movie Thriller Authored by Coahoma County's Thomas Harris," *Clarksdale Press Register*, March 2, 1991.

13   "They were never": Laughlin, "Silence of the Author."

13   "I wish": Harris, "An Ideal English Class Syllabus for 9th Graders."

13   "It was just dull": Kuehl, "A Conversation with Tom Harris."

13   "In high school": Laughlin, "Silence of the Author."

14   "One of the things": Laughlin, "Silence of the Author."

14   "But Tom got revenge": Laughlin, "Silence of the Author."

14   "One of the most harrowing": Thomas Harris, "250cc Touring," *Cycle World*, January 1964.

14   "skinny 250cc workhorses": Harris, "250cc Touring."

14   "dog-tired": Harris, "250cc Touring."

15   "He was already pretty set": O'Briant, "Despite Success, 'Lambs' Author Still a Silent Type."

15   "a sparkling musical revue": Tom Harris, "JACFB Revue Scores Opening Night Success," *Waco Times-Herald*, December 2, 1961.

15   "I thought the lid": Tom Harris, "Little Conversation in Ole Miss Hangouts," *Waco News-Tribune*, October 4, 1962.

15   "The students ate": Harris, "Little Conversation in Ole Miss Hangouts."

16   "The wages": LTV East Hampton, *Conversations*.

16   "He was game": Hoban, "The Silence of the Writer," 50.

16   "Sometimes he got": O'Briant, "Despite Success, 'Lambs' Author Still a Silent Type."

16   "He was not a talkative member": Mike Cochran and Jeff Guinn, "Mystery Man," *Fort Worth Star-Telegram*, July 2, 1999.

16   "best bunch of newspaper employees": "Make Me a Newspaper, Today!," *Waco Tribune-Herald*, October 10, 1965.

17   "every magazine rack": "Taft Mothers Launch Drive on Lurid Sex Books," *North Star*, February 20, 1958.

17   "Hanging by the feet": "House of Horror Stuns," *Life*, December 2, 1957.

18   "nonfiction novel": George Plimpton, "The Story Behind a Nonfiction Novel," *New York Times*, January 16, 1966, https://archive.nytimes.com/www.nytimes.com/books/97/12/28/home/capote-interview.html?r=1.

18   "The human heart": Plimpton, "The Story Behind a Nonfiction Novel."

18   "They paid": LTV East Hampton, *Conversations*.

19   "a prep school": Tom Harris, "Sisters in Slaughter," *Argosy*, July 1964.

19   "the headquarters": Harris, "Sisters in Slaughter."

19   "When she looks": Harris, "Sisters in Slaughter."

19   "When the investigators": Harris, "Sisters in Slaughter."

19   "robbed, rolled and dropped": Harris, "Sisters in Slaughter."

19   "an appetite to examine": Chris Nashawaty, "The Hunger," *Entertainment Weekly*, May 7, 1999.

19   "the eyes": Tom Harris, "Texan Against the Wall," *Argosy*, March 1965.

20   "I was twenty-three": Harris, "Author's Note."

20   "a small, lithe man": Harris, "Author's Note."

20   "This man was very": LTV East Hampton, *Conversations*.

20   "Do you have sunglasses": Harris, "Author's Note."

20   "Early torment": Harris, "Author's Note."

20   "He looked up": Harris, "Author's Note."

20   *"Hombre!"*: Harris, "Author's Note."

20   "The doctor is a murderer": Harris, "Author's Note."

21   "friends on": "Young Surgeon Slays Man, Dismembers Body," *Paris News*, October 12, 1959.

21   "neatly carved": "Package Murder Traced to Doc," *Brownsville Herald*, October 18, 1959.

21   "He is not insane": Harris, "Author's Note."

CHAPTER 3

22   "Clyde Barrow started out stupid": Thomas Harris, "The Murderous Rampage of Bonnie and Clyde," *Argosy*, January 1968.

22   "You could compete": LTV East Hampton, *Conversations - Thomas Harris - 07.09.2019*, YouTube, July 9, 2019, https://www.youtube.com/watch?v=XlH-cD_0kCM.

22   "In six months": Mike Cochran and Jeff Guinn, "Mystery Man," *Fort Worth Star-Telegram*, July 2, 1999.

23   "The first year": LTV East Hampton, *Conversations*.

23   "It was cops": LTV East Hampton, *Conversations*.

23   "There was a lot": LTV East Hampton, *Conversations*.

23   "Most of the stories": Author interview, March 25, 2024.

23   "I can't tell you": Phoebe Hoban, "The Silence of the Writer," *New York*, April 15, 1991, https://books.google.com/books?id=aukCAAAAMBAJ&pg=PA48&source=gbs_toc_r&cad=2#v=onepage&q&f=false.

23   "He understood precision": Meg Laughlin, "Silence of the Author," *Tulsa World*, August 15, 1991.

23   "He is just naturally shy": Cochran and Guinn, "Mystery Man."

23   "I had to put up": Linda Kuehl, "A Conversation with Tom Harris," *Book-of-the-Month Club News*, March 1975.

24   "We were prisoners": Kuehl, "A Conversation with Tom Harris."

24   "What about blowing up": Kuehl, "A Conversation with Tom Harris."

24   "People would never believe": Allen Oren, "'Black Sunday' Is Blend of Today's Hot News," *Charlotte Observer*, April 1, 1977.

24   "We were going": Kuehl, "A Conversation with Tom Harris."

25   "They let me fly": LTV East Hampton, *Conversations*.

25   "I can't write it ": Chris Nashawaty, "The Hunger," *Entertainment Weekly*, May 7, 1999.

26   "The idea was": Bob Minzesheimer, "Hungry Fans Eat Up 'Hannibal,'" *USA Today*, June 9, 1999, https://usatoday30.usatoday.com/life/enter/books/book128.htm.

26   "I felt like a man": Kuehl, "A Conversation with Tom Harris."

26   "We passed it around": LTV East Hampton, *Conversations*.

26   "Dahlia had helped": Thomas Harris, *Black Sunday* (Dell, 1990), 3.

26   "The stadium spread": Harris, *Black Sunday*, 121.

27   "a garden hose": Harris, *Black Sunday*, 113.

27   "Silver": Harris, *Black Sunday*, 58.

27   "What's the hottest": Robin Adams Sloan, "Gossip," *Pacific Daily News*, January 20, 1975.

27   "Could it really happen?": Harris, *Black Sunday*, inside cover.

27   "Given Mr. Harris's ability": Christopher Lehmann-Haupt, "Steelers, Vikings and Arabs," *New York Times*, January 9, 1975, https://www.nytimes.com/1975/01/09/archives/books-of-the-times-steelers-vikings-and-arabs-psychopath-of-a-pilot.html.

27   "In the final analysis": Cochran and Guinn, "Mystery Man."

27   "I don't think": LTV East Hampton, *Conversations*.

28   *"Black Sunday"*: Clifton Fadiman, "Report by Clifton Fadiman," *Book-of-the-Month Club News*, March 1975.

28   "I'm free of the news": Kuehl, "A Conversation with Tom Harris."

29   "After he sold": Cochran and Guinn, "Mystery Man."

29   "I always did know": Kuehl, "A Conversation with Tom Harris."

29   "My feathers aren't dried yet": Kuehl, "A Conversation with Tom Harris."

29   "fast-paced": Kuehl, "A Conversation with Tom Harris."

CHAPTER 4

30   "I will be more responsive": "Gray to Run FBI with Difference," *Mexico Ledger*, May 5, 1972.

31   "Human behavior": Richard L. Ault, Jr., and James T. Reese, "A Psychological Assessment of Crime: Profiling," *FBI Law Enforcement Bulletin*, March 1980.

31   "back room": John Douglas, *Mindhunter: Inside the FBI's Elite Serial Crime Unit* (Pocket Books, 1996), 81.

31   "In dramatic terms": Robert K. Ressler and Tom Shachtman, *Whoever Fights Monsters: My Twenty Years Hunting Serial Killers for the FBI* (St. Martin's Press, 1992), 29.

32   "signature": Douglas, *Mindhunter*, 252.

32   "what the perpetrator": Douglas, *Mindhunter*, 252.

32   "There'd be a lecture": Author interview, February 13, 2024.

32   "road schools": Douglas, *Mindhunter*, 97.

32   "find out what": Douglas, *Mindhunter*, 99.

32   "[I] just wondered": "Boy, 15, Wondered 'How It Would Feel to Shoot Grandma,'" *Corpus Christi Caller-Times*, August 29, 1964.

32   "serial-murder capital": Douglas, *Mindhunter*, 101.

33   "[Ressler] and I worried": Douglas, *Mindhunter*, 104.

33   "I'm sorry to sound": Ressler and Shachtman, *Whoever Fights Monsters*, 86.

33   "Many of these guys": Douglas, *Mindhunter*, 110.

33   "We had to tell them": Author interview, February 13, 2024.

33   "manipulative genius": Ressler and Shachtman, *Whoever Fights Monsters*, 56.

34   "I'm not a real big guy": Ressler and Shachtman, *Whoever Fights Monsters*.

34   "old-style crime": Andy Warhol, *The Andy Warhol Diaries*, ed. Pat Hackett (Warner Books, 1989), 62.

35   "the all-American boy": George Carpozi Jr., "The Ted Bundy Slayings: The All-American Terror," *Philadelphia Inquirer*, August 29, 1979.

35   "The Behavioral Science Unit": Author interview, April 3, 2024.

35   "little-known FBI unit": Patricia Leeds, "They Study the Strangest of Slayings," *Chicago Tribune*, February 15, 1980.

35   "worthless bullshit": Douglas, *Mindhunter*, 80.

36   "a clearing house": Douglas, *Mindhunter*.

36   "Do you remember": Linda Kuehl, "A Conversation with Tom Harris," *Book-of-the-Month Club News*, March 1975.

36   "I thought that doing": "Black Sunday—1st Edition/1st Printing," Books Tell You Why, https://web.archive.org/web/20240518101406/https://bookstellyouwhy.cdn .bibliopolis.com/pictures/19826_2.jpg.

37   "a great agitation": *Red Dragon* production notes, Cinema.com, https://cinema .com/articles/1355/red-dragon-about-the-production.phtml.

37   "They make profiling seem": Ressler and Shachtman, *Whoever Fights Monsters*, 239.

37   "After the Olympics": Author interview, April 3, 2024.

38   "He was interested": Author interview, January 27, 2025.

38   "He just let me": Meg Laughlin, "Silence of the Author," *Tulsa World*, August 15, 1991.

38   "Harris was like": Ressler and Shachtman, *Whoever Fights Monsters*, 240.

38   "Seldom will the lust murderer": Robert R. Hazelwood and John E. Douglas, "The Lust Murderer," *FBI Law Enforcement Bulletin*, April 1980.

38   "Who would do": Ault and Reese, "A Psychological Assessment of Crime: Profiling."

CHAPTER 5

40   "Black Sunday was pretty good": Linton Weeks, "Delta Days," *Washington Post*, September 18, 1999, https://www.washingtonpost.com/archive/entertainment/books/1999/09/19/delta-days/41d1f106-3253-46a8-99f1-470797d7b958.

40   "Southern, worldly": Weeks, "Delta Days."

40   "pure pretension": Weeks, "Delta Days."

40   "The Mississippi Delta": Weeks, "Delta Days."

41   "Your drawing is so good": "Good Student," *Clarksdale Press Register*, November 15, 1978.

41   "When I looked back": Thomas Harris, "Foreword to a Fatal Interview," *Red Dragon*, rev. ed. (Berkley Books, 2000).

41   "At the time": Thomas Harris, "Foreword to a Fatal Interview."

42   "uncomfortable gift": Thomas Harris, *Red Dragon* (Dell, 1990), 152.

42   "There were no effective": Harris, *Red Dragon*, 15.

42   "When you are writing": Harris, "Foreword to a Fatal Interview."

42   "some trepidation": Harris, "Foreword to a Fatal Interview."

43   "Graham felt that Lecter": Harris, *Red Dragon*, 63.

43   "Do you know how": Harris, *Red Dragon*, 67.

43   "spilling into the margin": Harris, "Foreword to a Fatal Interview."

43   "superfluous static": Harris, "Foreword to a Fatal Interview."

44   "I was not comfortable": Harris, "Foreword to a Fatal Interview."

44   "Who do you suppose": Thomas Harris, "Author's Note," *The Silence of the Lambs*, rev. ed. (St. Martin's Griffin, 2013).

44   "I won't say": LTV East Hampton, *Conversations - Thomas Harris - 07.09.2019*, YouTube, July 9, 2019, https://www.youtube.com/watch?v=XlH-cD_0kCM.

44   "a peculiar understanding": Harris, "Author's Note."

44   "small, lithe man": Harris, *Red Dragon*, 63.

45   "He did it": Harris, *Red Dragon*, 53.

45   "She managed to save": Harris, *Red Dragon*, 60.

45   "the first and worst sign": Harris, *Red Dragon*, 53.

46   "When in the winter": Harris, "Author's Note."

46   "each sentence": Weeks, "Delta Days."

46   "After this one": Weeks, "Delta Days."

46   "two hundred bucks": Weeks, "Delta Days."

47   "We don't invent our natures": Harris, *Red Dragon*, 270.

47   "I want to help you": Harris, *Red Dragon*, 270–71.

47   "I don't think": Harris, *Red Dragon*, 61.

49   "blood-drop trajectories": Harris, *Red Dragon*, 13–14.

50   "These mink socks tickle!": Liz Smith, "Don't Stop Here, the Best Is Yet . . . ," *Daily News*, April 30, 1981.

50   "probably the best": Stephen King, "The Cannibal and the Cop," *Washington Post*, October 31, 1981, https://www.washingtonpost.com/archive/entertainment/books/1981/11/01/the-cannibal-and-the-cop/54022626-8c6b-4aa6-b4ba-d52e3a9438e6.

50   "There's too much fingerprinting": Bart Everett, "When the Moon Is Full Another Family May Die," *Los Angeles Times Book Review*, December 6, 1981.

50   "the most repulsive": David Traxel, "The Bookshelf," *Philadelphia Inquirer*, December 6, 1981.

51   "Coffee and cold drinks": *Clarksdale Press Register*, March 3, 1982.

51   "These frightening days": Christopher Lehmann-Haupt, "Books of the Times," *New York Times*, November 10, 1981, https://www.nytimes.com/1981/11/10/books/books-of-the-times-086752.html.

51   "cold, hard look": Robert Merritt, "Thriller 'Red Dragon' Is Relentlessly Chilling," *Richmond Times-Dispatch*, December 27, 1981.

52   "The best popular fiction": King, "The Cannibal and the Cop."

52   "I thought *Red Dragon*": Author interview, April 3, 2024.

52   "potential monster[s]": Barry Paris, "Villain's Cleft Palate Spurs Protest to Author," *Pittsburgh Post-Gazette*, March 21, 1983.

52   "Nowhere in *Red Dragon*": Paris, "Villain's Cleft Palate Spurs Protest to Author."

52   "scared the shit out of me": James Ellroy, "Introduction," *L.A. Noir* (Mysterious Press, 1998).

53   "a rat hole": Harris, *Red Dragon*, 346.

53   "We live": Harris, *Red Dragon*, 349.

53   "I wish you": Harris, *Red Dragon*, 349.

53   "My God": Joel Achenbach, "Hack Writer," *Washington Post*, June 21, 1999, https://www.washingtonpost.com/archive/lifestyle/1999/06/21/hack-writer/7d57d83a-e630-4b85-b8a4-dee31b821000.

CHAPTER 6

54   "Hemingway said that": LTV East Hampton, *Conversations - Thomas Harris - 07.09.2019*, YouTube, July 9, 2019, https://www.youtube.com/watch?v=XlH-cD_0kCM.

55   "He had heard": Thomas Harris, *Red Dragon* (Dell, 1990), 149.

55   "six large figures": Liz Smith, "How Goldie Handled Having More than One," *Daily News* June 2, 1981.

55   "Will, is a pig's ass pork?": Walon Green, *Red Dragon* screenplay, September 1983, https://archive.org/details/red-dragon-walon-green, 29.

55   "Remember when I cut you": Green, *Red Dragon* screenplay, 32.

55   "his hand": Green, *Red Dragon* screenplay, 50.

56   "I got sick of it": David Breskin, "David Lynch," https://davidbreskin.com/books/inner-views/david-lynch-3.

56   "I don't know how many times": "Public Enemies Director Michael Mann Shares His Favorite Chicago Memories," *Time Out*, April 27, 2011, https://www.timeout.com/film/public-enemies-director-michael-mann-shares-his-favorite-chicago-memories.

56   "I just became": Phil Perrillo, "Jericho Mile at 45: Michael Mann on the Making of His Landmark TV Movie," Television Academy, March 18, 2024, https://www

.televisionacademy.com/features/news/online-originals/michael-mann-jericho
-mile-45th-anniversary-interview.

57   "We had 13 stabbings": Ken Tucker, "The Michael Mann Interview Part 1: 'Miami Vice,' 'The Jericho Mile,' 'Luck,' and More," *Entertainment Weekly*, January 21, 2012, https://ew.com/article/2012/01/21/michael-mann-interview-luck-hbo.

57   "I work to very": Gregg Kilday, "Thief's Michael Mann Is a Caan Artist," *Nanaimo Daily News*, April 22, 1981.

57   "It was the best": Candice Russell, "Mann Hunter of Perfection," *South Florida Sun Sentinel*, August 15, 1986.

57   "a single bone": William Farr, "Suspect Waits Decision on Acid Death Retrial," *Los Angeles Times*, December 17, 1973.

58   "psych-type poetry": Author interview, June 20, 2024.

58   "He had the ability": Author interview, June 20, 2024.

58   "I couldn't find any traction": Author interview, June 20, 2024.

58   "What Dolarhyde wants": Author interview, June 20, 2024.

58   "He commits heinous crimes": Author interview, June 20, 2024.

58   "Regardless of how much": *Manhunter* (Collector's Edition), Shout! Factory Blu-ray, 2016.

59   "For me, the most exciting": Bill Cosford, "Films Excite Creator of 'Miami Vice,'" *Tampa Tribune*, September 3, 1986.

59   "If you have a very": Author interview, April 3, 2024.

59   "universal opprobrium": Michael Sragow, "Michael Mann's Second Thoughts and New 'Vices,'" *San Francisco Examiner*, August 18, 1986.

59   "the man who gave": James Rampton, "From Titus to Hannibal," *Independent*, March 3, 1989.

60   "the three C's": Douglas Eby, "Dino De Laurentiis: The Last of the Old-Time Movie Moguls," *Cinefantastique*, February 2001.

60   "Dino was entertaining": Author interview, June 27, 2025.

60   "He's lethal": *Dino De Laurentiis: The Last Movie Mogul*, BBC, 2001.

60   "the next Robert De Niro!": Liz Smith, "'Final Cut' Is Last Word on 'Heaven's Gate' Fiasco," *Austin American-Statesman*, July 17, 1985.

61   "*nobody* knew who I was": *Manhunter* (Collector's Edition) Blu-ray.

61   "He wanted to create": cold144, *William Petersen Interview for Manhunter 1986*, YouTube, January 22, 2009, https://www.youtube.com/watch?v=awrdXN6Eboo.

61   "He was a good student": Author interview, April 3, 2024.

61   "I was asking them": "TF Classics: Manhunter," *Total Film*, March 2011, https://www.gamesradar.com/tf-classic-manhunter.

61   "Michael said": *Manhunter* (Collector's Edition) Blu-ray.

62   "a bunch of weirdo parts": Vadim Rizov, "'He's like Napoleon'": Tom Noonan on Making Michael Mann's *Manhunter*," *Filmmaker*, January 14, 2015, https://filmmakermagazine.com/89010-hes-like-napoleon-tom-noonan-on-making-michael-manns-manhunter.

62   "*Jeez, I don't want*": withoutyourhead, *Tom Noonan of Manhunter interview*

- *Without Your Head Horror Podcast*, YouTube, July 19, 2015, https://www.you tube.com/watch?v=sxSGbzzTx6s.

62   "I was really": Rizov, "'He's like Napoleon.'"

62   "I didn't do anything": Rizov, "'He's like Napoleon.'"

62   "this feeling of power": *Manhunter* (Collector's Edition) Blu-ray.

62   "[I said], 'It'd be great": Rizov, "'He's like Napoleon.'"

63   "a pro football type": Neil Genzlinger, "Brian Dennehy, Tony Award–Winning Actor, Dies at 81," *New York Times*, April 16, 2020, https://www.nytimes.com /2020/04/16/movies/brian-dennehy-dead.html.

63   "He campaigned for it": Craig and Friends, *Michael Mann MANHUNTER Q&A with Jim Hemphill, BEYOND FEST 09.28.23 at the Aero Theatre*, YouTube, September 20, 2023, https://www.youtube.com/watch?v=It_5JPAj86Y.

63   "I'm going to prove": Craig and Friends, *Michael Mann MANHUNTER Q&A*.

CHAPTER 7

64   "That was where": Robin Thornber, "In Praise of Work," *Guardian*, September 15, 1987.

64   "tour de force": Frank Rich, "Stage: 'Rat in the Skull,' From Britain," *The New York Times*, May 22, 1985, https://www.nytimes.com/1985/05/22/theater/stage -rat-in-the-skull-from-britain.html.

64   "something of an overnight": Leslie Bennetts, "An Actor Blooms in a Terrorist Tale," *New York Times*, June 18, 1985, https://www.nytimes.com/1985/06/18/the ater/an-actor-blooms-in-a-terrorist-tale.html.

64   "It was kind of": Author interview, June 14, 2024.

65   "The character became": Author interview, June 20, 2024.

65   "It was my bid": Author interview, June 14, 2024.

65   "I've got a theory": *Manhunter* (Collector's Edition), Shout! Factory Blu-ray, 2016.

65   "I was obsessed": Author interview, June 14, 2024.

65   "[lived] in a world": Ruth Reynolds, "Peter Manuel Picked Up 47 Times on Charges Including Mass Murder," *Knoxville Journal*, November 7, 1958.

65   "He conducted his own defense": Author interview, June 14, 2024.

66   "had no sense": *Manhunter* (Collector's Edition) Blu-ray.

66   "threatens to outstrip": Carolyn Banks, "Ted Bundy: Talking About Murder," *Stuart News*, May 1, 1983.

66   "Bundy could have": Author interview, June 14, 2024.

67   "Thank the Lord": Robert Lindsey, "Man Held in Coast Deaths After Capture by Citizens," *New York Times*, September 1, 1985, https://www.nytimes.com/1985/09 /01/us/man-held-in-coast-deaths-after-capture-by-citizens.html.

67   "The film was": Lane Crockett, "A Success on Stage, Petersen Is Now Scoring in Films," *San Bernardino County Sun*, August 1, 1986.

67   "a little tiny imperfection": Vadim Rizov, "'He's like Napoleon'": Tom Noonan

on Making Michael Mann's *Manhunter*," *Filmmaker*, January 14, 2015, https://
filmmakermagazine.com/89010-hes-like-napoleon-tom-noonan-on-making
-michael-manns-manhunter.

67   "I learned over time": Rizov, "'He's like Napoleon.'"

67   "I often compare him": *Manhunter* (Collector's Edition) Blu-ray.

68   "I got into": Author interview, June 20, 2024.

68   "a chop-socky": Craig and Friends, *Michael Mann MANHUNTER Q&A with Jim Hemphill, BEYOND FEST 09.28.23 at the Aero Theatre*, YouTube, September 20, 2023, https://www.youtube.com/watch?v=It_5JPAj86Y.

68   "One of my favorites": Michael Sragow, "Michael Mann's Second Thoughts and New 'Vices,'" *San Francisco Examiner*, August 18, 1986.

68   "federal manhunters": Thomas Harris, *Red Dragon* (Dell, 1990), 92.

68   "time is luck": Harris, *Red Dragon*, 163.

68   "If he could shoot": *Manhunter* (Collector's Edition) Blu-ray.

69   "We just reconstituted": *Manhunter* (Collector's Edition) Blu-ray.

69   "They never let anybody in": Candice Russell, "Mann Hunter of Perfection," *South Florida Sun Sentinel*, August 15, 1986.

69   "My aim was": Author interview, April 19, 2024.

69   "He told me": Author interview, April 19, 2024.

69   "Michael said": Author interview, April 19, 2024.

70   "Lecter's personality": Author interview, June 20, 2024.

71   "I played it broader": *Manhunter* (Collector's Edition) Blu-ray.

72   "I traveled on": *Manhunter* (Collector's Edition) Blu-ray.

72   "Noonan just ran": James Rampton, "From Titus to Hannibal," *Independent*, March 3, 1989.

73   "It was at a very spooky place": *Manhunter* (Collector's Edition) Blu-ray.

73   "Everybody was way inside": Author interview, June 20, 2024.

73   "All of a sudden": *Manhunter* (Collector's Edition) Blu-ray.

74   "I never met Billy": *Manhunter* (Collector's Edition) Blu-ray.

74   "The whole thing": *Manhunter* (Collector's Edition) Blu-ray.

74   "just so that": *Manhunter* (Collector's Edition) Blu-ray.

74   "I was going": Sragow, "Michael Mann's Second Thoughts and New 'Vices.'"

74   "Basically, I sued him": Author interview, June 20, 2024.

74   "He responded": Author interview, June 20, 2024.

74   "To this day": *Manhunter* (Collector's Edition) Blu-ray.

75   "He didn't want": *Manhunter* (Collector's Edition) Blu-ray.

75   "*Manhunter* is": Sragow, "Michael Mann's Second Thoughts and New 'Vices.'"

76   "Kathie Lee was": *Manhunter* (Collector's Edition) Blu-ray.

76   "a police procedural": Richard Corliss, "Cinema: No Slumming in Summertime," *Time*, August 25, 1986, https://time.com/archive/6706953/cinema-no-slumming
-in-summertime.

76   "The main trouble": Walter Goodman, "Screen: 'Manhunter,'" *New York Times*, August 15, 1986, https://www.nytimes.com/1986/08/15/movies/screen-manhun
ter.html.

76 "klunker of a hero": Sheila Benson, "Movie Review: Just Temporarily in the Clutches of 'Manhunter,'" *Los Angeles Times*, August 15, 1986, https://www.latimes.com/archives/la-xpm-1986-08-15-ca-3956-story.html.

76 "the most galvanizing": andyfilm, *At the Movies Classics (Reed & Harris) - 8/15/86—Stand by Me, Manhunter, The Fly*, YouTube, January 5, 2003, https://www.youtube.com/watch?v=kLLMNusPr_E.

76 "You want to look": Gene Siskel, "Siskel's Flicks Picks," *Chicago Tribune*, October 10, 1986.

77 "It was designed": "Films Excite Creator of 'Miami Vice,'" *Tampa Tribune*, September 3, 1986.

77 "brainy, powerful, focused": Benson, "Movie Review."

77 "based on the novel": Print advertisement, *Clarksdale Press Register*, September 12, 1986.

77 "local boy made good": Ray Mosby, "Local Author's Book on Screen," *Clarksdale Press Register*, September 13, 1986.

77 "He didn't like it much": Chris Nashawaty, "The Hunger," *Entertainment Weekly*, May 7, 1999.

CHAPTER 8

81 "Her name was Joann": Author interview, April 2, 2024.

81 "The Coke went flying": Author interview, April 2, 2024.

81 "Why?": Author interview, April 2, 2024.

81 "The mayor": Author interview, April 2, 2024.

82 "I was pretty depressed": Author interview, April 2, 2024.

82 "I'm glad I'll be gone": James Feron, "Fashion, if Not Tradition, Ready for Women Cadets at West Point," *New York Times*, November 21, 1975, https://www.nytimes.com/1975/11/21/archives/fashion-if-not-tradition-ready-for-women-cadets-at-west-point.html.

82 "they were under pressure": Author interview, April 2, 2024.

83 "a bunch of lumberjacks": Author interview, April 2, 2024.

83 "I couldn't spell": Author interview, June 24, 2025.

83 "I don't cook": Author interview, April 2, 2024.

83 "the sixteen longest weeks": Author interview, April 2, 2024.

83 "I ran up": Author interview, April 2, 2024.

84 "I said, 'I'm not going to talk'": Author interview, April 2, 2024.

84 "I'm thinking to myself": Author interview, April 2, 2024.

84 "The appropriate thing": Author interview, April 2, 2024.

84 "He had a soft voice": Author interview, April 2, 2024.

84 "The men had never worked": Author interview, April 2, 2024.

85 "The FBI building": LTV East Hampton, *Conversations - Thomas Harris - 07.09.2019*, YouTube, July 9, 2019, https://www.youtube.com/watch?v=XlH-cD_0kCM.

85 "antilullaby tape": James F. Clarity and Warren Weaver Jr., "Briefing: Starling

Wars," *New York Times*, December 1, 1984, https://www.nytimes.com/1984/12/01 /us/briefing-starling-wars.html.

85 "good ole [boy]": Liz Smith, "Hurt Feels So Good as Proud Papa," *South Bend Tribune*, January 28, 1983.

86 "This is not a guy": Phoebe Hoban, "The Silence of the Writer," *New York*, April 15, 1991, https://books.google.com/books?id=aukCAAAAMBAJ&pg=PA48&source =gbs_toc_r&cad=2#v=onepage&q&f=false.

86 "She was a distinct character": LTV East Hampton, *Conversations*.

86 "Will's face looks": Thomas Harris, *The Silence of the Lambs* (St. Martin's Press, 1989), 6.

86 "She knew what happens": Harris, *The Silence of the Lambs*, 4.

87 "Women still have to prove": "Washington Talk: 14 Years of Women as Federal Agents," *New York Times*, September 26, 1986, https://www.nytimes.com/1986/09 /26/us/washington-talk-14-years-of-women-as-federal-agents.html.

87 "very nice": Author interview, October 31, 2024.

87 "I thought": Author interview, October 31, 2024.

88 "What's a nice girl": Roger Twigg, "Young Woman Gives Up Guilford Good Life for Rigors of Police Work," *Baltimore Sun*, September 13, 1976.

88 "You're right there": Author interview, October 31, 2024.

88 "We all made fun": Author interview, October 31, 2024.

88 "A lot of the men": Author interview, October 31, 2024.

88 "Ressler would tell him": Author interview, October 31, 2024.

89 "I was five feet eight": Author interview, October 31, 2024.

89 "He was trying to determine": "The Silence of the Lambs," *The Real Story*, TV episode, 2002.

89 "I think the impression": "The Silence of the Lambs," *The Real Story*.

89 "outstanding": Thomas Harris, fax to Jonathan Demme, July 11, 1989, courtesy of University of Michigan Library (Special Collections Library).

CHAPTER 9

90 "I'd show slides": Author interview, February 13, 2024.

90 "I knew the way": John Douglas, *Mindhunter: Inside the FBI's Elite Serial Crime Unit* (Pocket Books, 1996), 1.

91 "I was there": Author interview, February 13, 2024.

91 "We probably scared": Author interview, February 13, 2024.

91 "not exactly the kind": Author interview, February 13, 2024.

92 "He doesn't even": George Thwaites, "What's Happened to Hannibal?," *Daily Telegraph*, December 6, 1997.

93 "Sometimes you really": Alexandra Alter, "Hannibal Lecter's Creator Cooks Up Something New (No Fava Beans or Chianti)," *New York Times*, May 18, 2019, https://www.nytimes.com/2019/05/18/books/thomas-harris-new-book.html.

93 "I know Tommy": Joel Achenbach, "Hack Writer," *Washington Post*, June 21,

1999, https://www.washingtonpost.com/archive/lifestyle/1999/06/21/hack-writer/7d57d83a-e630-4b85-b8a4-dee31b821000.

93 "He's always thinking": Phoebe Hoban, "The Silence of the Writer," *New York*, April 15, 1991, https://books.google.com/books?id=aukCAAAAMBAJ&pg=PA48&source=gbs_toc_r&cad=2#v=onepage&q&f=false.

94 "Looks like a straw": Thomas Harris, *The Silence of the Lambs* (St. Martin's Press, 1989), 173–74.

94 "quantify": Harris, *The Silence of the Lambs*, 24.

94 "It takes an orderly," Harris, *The Silence of the Lambs*, 11.

95 "entertain himself," Harris, *The Silence of the Lambs*, 172.

95 "I've been in this room": Harris, *The Silence of the Lambs*, 62.

95 "If Lecter talks to you": Harris, *The Silence of the Lambs*, 6.

95 "comforting chug": Harris, *The Silence of the Lambs*, 293.

95 "Am I evil?": Harris, *The Silence of the Lambs*, 21–22.

96 "Nothing happened to me": Harris, *The Silence of the Lambs*, 21.

96 "Do you think": Harris, *The Silence of the Lambs*, 230.

97 "You know what": Harris, *The Silence of the Lambs*, 6.

97 "FBI, you're safe": Harris, *The Silence of the Lambs*, 343.

97 "seemed to have exploded": Harris, *The Silence of the Lambs*, 243.

97 "Lecter's gone platinum": Harris, *The Silence of the Lambs*, 356.

97 "I have no plans": Harris, *The Silence of the Lambs*, 366.

98 "She sleeps deeply": Harris, *The Silence of the Lambs*, 367.

98 "a stab of happiness": Thomas Harris, "Author's Note," *The Silence of the Lambs*, rev. ed. (St. Martin's Griffin, 2013).

CHAPTER 10

99 *"Hannibal Lecter is back!"*: F. Paul Wilson, "'Silence of Lambs' Laced with Horror," *Asbury Park Press*, September 4, 1988.

99 "I never push him": Robert W. Welkos and Paul Lieberman, "Preparing to Feast on 'Hannibal,'" *Los Angeles Times*, April 2, 1999, https://www.latimes.com/archives/la-xpm-1999-apr-02-ca-23352-story.html.

100 "He just won't do interviews": O'Briant, "Despite Success, 'Lambs' Author Still a Silent Type."

100 "It isn't easy": Christopher Lehmann-Haupt, "The Return of Hannibal the Cannibal," *New York Times*, August 15, 1988.

101 "a tour de force": Lehmann-Haupt, "The Return of Hannibal the Cannibal."

101 "The car springs groaned": Thomas Harris, *The Silence of the Lambs* (St. Martin's Press, 1989), 52.

101 "It's marvelous": Harris, *The Silence of the Lambs*, inside cover.

101 "Lecter emerges": Print ad, *New York Times Book Review*, August 28, 1988.

102 "The closer Harris": Wilson, "'Silence of Lambs' Laced with Horror."

102 "my kind of man": Print ad, *Guardian*, April 28, 1989.

102 "He remains at large": Harry Levins, "Super Thriller Features Two Serial Killers," *St. Louis Post-Dispatch*, September 6, 1988.

102 "I was so proud": Author interview, April 2, 2024.

102 "It said, 'Dear Clarice'": Author interview, October 31, 2024.

103 "If this one isn't": Gene Williams, "Suspense Writer Deals in Chill Factors," *Cleveland Plain Dealer*, August 24, 1988.

CHAPTER 11

104 "There was absolutely": Author interview, February 7, 2024.

104 "It was the typical": Author interview, February 7, 2024.

105 "Big mistake": Jill Bernstein, "Eat Drink Man Woman," *Premiere*, February 2001.

105 "I really believed": Author interview, June 27, 2025.

105 "I've wanted to try": Charles Fleming, "Hackman Suffers 'Mississippi' Burn-Out," *Sunday News*, February 12, 1989.

106 "I was furious": Author interview, March 19, 2024.

106 "I had dinner": Author interview, March 19, 2024.

106 "I figured somebody": Author interview, March 19, 2024.

107 "Luckily, I did": Author interview, March 19, 2024.

107 "We see this memory": Ted Tally, *The Silence of the Lambs* screenplay outline, February 10, 1989, courtesy of University of Michigan Library (Special Collections Library).

107 "He did say": Mike Fleming, Jr., "Jonathan Demme and Untold 'Silence of fhe Lambs' Tales: Hannibal, Clarice, Tally, Hackman, and a Discarded Scary Ending," Deadline, April 26, 2017, https://deadline.com/2017/04/the-silence-of-the-lambs-25th-anniversary-untold-tales-jonathan-demme-ted-tally-hannibal-lecter-clarice-starling-1201703981.

108 "She called her father": Fleming, "Jonathan Demme and Untold 'Silence of the Lambs' Tales."

108 "I didn't have the energy": Stephen Schaefer, "On Screen and in Service: Gene Hackman Goes Military in 'Package,'" *Record*, August 25, 1989.

CHAPTER 12

109 "How'd you like": Michael Henry and Hubert Niogret, "Interview with Jonathan Demme," *Positif*, January 1989.

109 "I kind of fell": Austin Film Festival, *On Story: 414 Jonathan Demme and Paul Thomas Anderson: A Conversation*, YouTube, March 23, 2015, https://www.youtube.com/watch?v=RXT0WOUceak.

110 "Characters who are": Henry and Niogret, "Interview with Jonathan Demme."

110 "He was undefined": Author interview, February 27, 2024.

110 "There are dark parts": Author interview, February 15, 2024.

111 "a visual guy": Author interview, February 15, 2024.

111 "It wasn't the kind": Amy Taubin, "Demme's Monde," *Village Voice*, February 19, 1991.

111 "We wanted to make": Author interview, February 20, 2024.

111 "Ever since my days": Gavin Smith, "Identity Check," *Film Comment*, January–February, 1991.

111 "I'm pulling for women": Nikke Finke, "A Hollywood Education," *Los Angeles Times*, February 10, 1991.

111 "This country has": *The Silence of the Lambs* Blu-ray, Criterion Collection, 2018.

111 "Serial killers exist": Fred Schruers, "A Kind of Redemption," *Premiere*, March 1991.

112 "These aren't very funny": Jonathan Demme, press conference transcript, January 25, 1991, courtesy of University of Michigan Library (Special Collections Library).

112 "a little alarmed": Author interview, March 19, 2024.

112 "At the end": Rachel Syme, "Michelle Pfeiffer Chooses Carefully," *New Yorker*, January 31, 2021, https://www.newyorker.com/culture/the-new-yorker-interview /michelle-pfeiffer-chooses-carefully.

112 "dangerous": FYI, *Why We Turned Down Silence of the Lambs | Michelle Pfeiffer & Meg Ryan*, YouTube, September 19, 2017, https://www.youtube.com/watch?v =mNbpa_-Qiyo.

112 "I said, 'This is the one'": Austin Film Festival, *On Story*.

113 "You know": Gwynne Watkins, "How Jodie Foster Fought for 'Silence of the Lambs' Role," Yahoo! Movies, April 1, 2015, https://web.archive.org/web/2019 1210055140/https://www.yahoo.com/entertainment/how-jodie-foster-fought -for-silence-of-the-lambs-115219601237.html.

113 "The story of": Print ad, *Detroit Free Press*, February 15, 1974.

113 "To me": Schruers, "A Kind of Redemption."

113 "I thought": Judy Klemesrud, "Jodie Foster's Rise from Disney to Depravity," *New York Times*, March 7, 1976, https://www.nytimes.com/1976/03/07/archives /jodie-fosters-rise-from-disney-to-depravity.html.

113 "I was 12 years old": Christopher Hooton, "Jodie Foster Details How 'Uncomfortable' It Was Playing a Prostitute Aged 12 in Taxi Driver," *Independent*, May 20, 2016, https://www.the-independent.com/arts-entertainment/films/news/jodie -foster-details-how-uncomfortable-it-was-playing-a-prostitute-aged-12-in-taxi -driver-a7040016.html.

114 "Every acting part": Julia Cameron, "Burden of the Gift," *American Film*, November–December 1991.

114 "Jodie!": John J. Goldman, "'I'm Scared,' Jodie Foster Says of Link to Hinckley," *Los Angeles Times*, April 2, 1981.

114 "I got her!": Jodie Foster, "Why Me?," *Esquire*, December 1982.

114 "Oh, yeah": Eleanor Ringel, "New Film Showcases 'Grown-Up' Jodie Foster," *Santa Cruz Sentinel*, October 17, 1988.

115 "I got very bruised": Sonia Taitz, "Jodie Foster: Tough Hero," *New York Times*, October 16, 1988, https://www.nytimes.com/1988/10/16/arts/jodie-foster-tough -hero.html.

115 "that year before": C. Carr, "Jodie Foster: Can She Conquer Tinseltown?," *Mirabella*, February 1991.

115 "I'd never met her": Author interview, March 19, 2024.

115 "There's nothing better": Author interview, February 15, 2024.

115 "I wouldn't believe": Austin Film Festival, *On Story*.

115 "I was worried," Marc Maron, "Jodie Foster," *WTF with Marc Maron* (podcast), February 15, 2021, https://www.wtfpod.com/podcast/episode-1201-jodie-foster.

115 "There are all these movies": Austin Film Festival, *On Story*.

116 *"I'm going to use"*: Austin Film Festival, *On Story*.

116 "I thought about": Austin Film Festival, *On Story*.

116 "Let's say, 'lima beans'": Ed Saxon, story notes for *The Silence of the Lambs*, August 4, 1989, courtesy of University of Michigan Library (Special Collections Library).

116 "Jonathan was a guy": Author interview, June 25, 2025.

116 "I thought": Author interview, April 9, 2024.

117 "That's the ending": Author interview, March 19, 2024.

117 "They said": Author interview, February 7, 2024.

CHAPTER 13

118 "You have to play": Jeff Hayward, "Delighted to Eat You!," *South Wales Echo*, May 16, 1991.

118 "Our education": Dana Kennedy, "Hopkins Happy Playing Madman," *Los Angeles Times*, January 30, 1991, https://www.latimes.com/archives/la-xpm-1991-01 -30-ca-466-story.html.

118 "I remember": Meredith Berkman, "Playing Hannibal Lecter," *Entertainment Weekly*, March 29, 1991, https://ew.com/article/1991/03/29/playing-hannibal-lecter.

119 "I wanted to become": Lawrence Grobel, "Playboy Interview: Anthony Hopkins," *Playboy*, March 1994, https://web.archive.org/web/20240311192439/https://www .oocities.org/hopkinsfanatic/playboy1.htm.

119 "I used to feel": Kennedy, "Hopkins Happy Playing Madman."

119 "That part": Quentin Falk, *Anthony Hopkins: The Authorized Biography* (Interlink Books, 1994), 171–72.

120 "My favorite character": Barry Koltnow, "Hopkins Dishes Out a Third Helping of Hannibal," *News and Record*, October 4, 2002.

120 "I somehow knew": Falk, *Anthony Hopkins*, 173–74.

120 "would just take you": Tananarive Due, "Dr. Lecter, My Name Is Clarice Starling," *Vanity Fair*, February 23, 2021, https://www.vanityfair.com/hollywood/2021/02 /dr-lecter-my-name-is-clarice-starling.

120 "It sounds like": Jim Emerson, "Hopkins Called on Nightmare to Play Demented Dr. Lecter," *Tallahassee Democrat*, February 25, 1991.

120 "Every male": *The Silence of the Lambs* Criterion Blu-ray.

120   "I didn't get": Gavin Smith, "Identity Check," *Film Comment*, January–February, 1991.

121   "There's just something": Jonathan Demme, press conference transcript, January 25, 1991.

121   "trapped in": Due, "Dr. Lecter."

121   "I'd like to think": Demme, press conference transcript, January 25, 1991.

121   "I said, 'I don't understand'": Author interview, June 30, 2025.

121   "in such a manner": Anthony Hopkins, agreement for *The Silence of the Lambs*, December 22, 1989, courtesy of University of Michigan Library (Special Collections Library).

121   "Table reads are weird": Author interview, February 20, 2024.

122   "If you stare": Due, "Dr. Lecter."

122   "a cockamammy American accent": Falk, *Anthony Hopkins*, 174.

122   "I knew I had got": Falk, *Anthony Hopkins*, 174.

CHAPTER 14

124   *"I don't need"*: Jim Emerson, "Hopkins Called on Nightmare to Play Demented Dr. Lecter," *Tallahassee Democrat*, February 25, 1991.

124   "As soon as": Jonathan Demme, press conference transcript, January 25, 1991.

124   "They are helpful": Demme, press conference transcript, January 25, 1991.

125   "Some of the institutions": Fred Schruers, "A Kind of Redemption," *Premiere*, March 1991.

125   "In all responsibility": Schruers, "A Kind of Redemption."

125   "We most definitely": Milt Ahlerich, letter to Ed Saxon, September 18, 1989, courtesy of University of Michigan Library (Special Collections Library).

125   "We may be": Milt Ahlerich, letter to Ed Saxon, September 18, 1989.

125   "a PG rather than": Milt Ahlerich, letter to Ed Saxon, November 3, 1989, courtesy of University of Michigan Library (Special Collections Library).

126   "show the American public": Milt Ahlerich, letter to Ed Saxon, September 18, 1989, courtesy of University of Michigan Library (Special Collections Library).

126   "I was appalled": Author interview, September 23, 2024.

126   "I said to Jonathan": Author interview, September 23, 2024.

126   "It was very tight quarters": Author interview, September 23, 2024.

127   "When I heard": Author interview, February 13, 2024.

127   "I opened everything up": Author interview, February 13, 2024.

127   "He's incarcerated": Ed Saxon, notes from Quantico visit, undated, courtesy of University of Michigan Library (Special Collections Library).

127   "I don't have": Demme, press conference transcript, January 25, 1991,

128   "After I'd been there": *The Silence of the Lambs* Criterion Blu-ray.

128   "I just wanted": *The Silence of the Lambs* Criterion Blu-ray.

128   "It is not the kind": Frank Walker, "Inside the Mind of the World's Most Chilling Killers," *Sydney Morning Herald*, April 28, 1991.

128   "dressing way down": Schruers, "A Kind of Redemption."

129 "We're classmates": Sari Horwitz, "Over 18 Weeks, an Arduous Path to the Badge," *Washington Post*, August 17, 2008, https://www.washingtonpost.com/archive /politics/2006/08/17/over-18-weeks-an-arduous-path-to-the-badge/2cddb850 -8588-420f-b723-d53f5706a7d5.

129 "So, guys": Author interview, April 2, 2024.

129 "She would never tell": Author interview, March 13, 2024.

130 "Everything about the Bureau": Author interview, March 13, 2024.

130 "I always tried": Author interview, March 13, 2024.

130 "a positive recruitment tool": Author interview, March 13, 2024.

130 "We spent months": Email to author, June 9, 2025.

130 "They wanted me": Author interview, March 13, 2024.

130 "treated like a prize": Author interview, March 13, 2024.

131 "because he'd be likely": Adrian Wootton, "Jonathan Demme (II)," *Guardian*, October 10, 1998, https://www.theguardian.com/film/1998/oct/10/1.

131 "Don't take this": Wootton, "Jonathan Demme (II)."

131 "in the hands": Wootton, "Jonathan Demme (II)."

131 "sort of down": LTV East Hampton, *Conversations - Thomas Harris - 07.09.2019*, YouTube, July 9, 2019, https://www.youtube.com/watch?v=XlH-cD_0kCM.

131 "Good luck": Harris, fax to Demme, July 11, 1989, courtesy of University of Michigan Library (Special Collections Library).

CHAPTER 15

133 "I figured they'd put": Author interview, September 23, 2024.

134 "They put plexiglass": Author interview, September 23, 2024.

134 "Everyone else": Author interview, September 23, 2024.

134 "I don't think": Dan Persons, "The Silence of the Lambs," *Cinefantastique*, February, 1992.

135 "It's like Bogart": Richard Ouzounian, "Mad Hopkins, Again," *Toronto Star*, September 26, 2005.

135 "Jonathan said": *The Silence of the Lambs* Criterion Blu-ray.

135 "I know what scares people": Tananarive Due, "Dr. Lecter, My Name Is Clarice Starling," *Vanity Fair*, February 23, 2021, https://www.vanityfair.com/hollywood /2021/02/dr-lecter-my-name-is-clarice-starling.

135 "I want them": *The Silence of the Lambs* Criterion Blu-ray.

136 "Jonathan didn't know me": Shane A. Bassett, "Interview: Costume Designer Colleen Atwood Talks 'Into the Woods,' 'Big Eyes,' & Career," The Young Folks, December 17, 2014, https://www.theyoungfolks.com/film/45314/interview-colleen-atwood-into-the-woods-big-eyes.

136 "super precise": Kevin Polowy, "Colleen Atwood on Creating Iconic 'Edward Scissorhands' Costume, Finding Hannibal Lecter's Flesh-Colored Mask and More," Yahoo! Entertainment, October 27, 2023, https://www.yahoo.com/enter tainment/article/colleen-atwood-costume-designe-edward-scissorhands -silence-of-the-lambs-pain-hustlers-interview-004500823.html.

136 "It was as effective": Thomas Harris, *The Silence of the Lambs* (St. Martin's Press, 1989), 171.

136 "So, you want me": Ed Cubberly, "The Story Behind the Mask," https://edcub berly.com/hannibal.html.

137 "to make it look mean": Cubberly, "The Story Behind the Mask."

137 "It was appalling": Author interview, March 27, 2024.

138 "As fit": Michael Feeney Callan, *The Unauthorized Biography of Anthony Hopkins* (Charles Scribner's Sons, 1994), 309.

138 "Aren't you": Barbara Vancheri and Christopher Rawson, "Busy in Film and on Stage, Anthony Hopkins Looks for Calmer Life," *Pittsburgh Post-Gazette*, January 27, 1990.

138 "You finish your job": Vancheri and Rawson, "Busy in Film and on Stage."

139 "I was kind of": Author interview, April 12, 2024.

139 "He leaned in": Author interview, April 12, 2024.

140 "two people": Mike Fleming, Jr., "Jonathan Demme and Untold 'Silence of the Lambs' Tales: Hannibal, Clarice, Tally, Hackman, and a Discarded Scary Ending," Deadline, April 26, 2017, https://deadline.com/2017/04/the-silence-of-the-lambs -25th-anniversary-untold-tales-jonathan-demme-ted-tally-hannibal-lecter-clarice -starling-1201703981.

140 "He would do": Due, "Dr. Lecter."

140 "When you literally": Terry Gross, "Celebrating Movie Icons: Jodie Foster," NPR, August 27, 2024, https://www.whro.org/2024-08-27/celebrating-movie-icons -jodie-foster.

140 "totally depressed": Author interview, June 25, 2025.

140 "a giant birdcage": *The Silence of the Lambs* Criterion Blu-ray.

141 "It's almost a shock": *The Silence of the Lambs* Criterion Blu-ray.

141 "After all that passivity": *The Silence of the Lambs* Criterion Blu-ray.

141 "brief snapshot from hell": Ted Tally, *The Silence of the Lambs* screenplay, fourth draft, October 6, 1989, 81.

142 "We wanted to show": *The Silence of the Lambs* Criterion Blu-ray.

142 "He brought that voice out": Gross, "Celebrating Movie Icons: Jodie Foster."

142 "I was scared": Ramin Setoodeh, "Jodie Foster and Anthony Hopkins Reunite for 'Silence of the Lambs' 30th Anniversary," *Variety*, January 19, 2021, https://va riety.com/2021/film/news/jodie-foster-anthony-hopkins-silence-of-the-lambs -30th-anniversary-1234887496.

142 "I was eating": The Graham Norton Show, *Jodie Foster's TERRIFIED of Anthony Hopkins!*, YouTube, October 9, 2023, https://www.youtube.com/watch?v=y_kbB kYtdSs.

CHAPTER 16

143 "white male": Thomas Harris, *The Silence of the Lambs* (St. Martin's Press, 1989), 135.

143 "rocking hillbilly Jew": Patrick Z. McGavin, "Ted Levine Is Not a Bad Guy,"

Chicago Reader, February 28, 1991, https://chicagoreader.com/news/ted-levine -is-not-a-bad-guy.

144 "Billy thinks he wants": Harris, *The Silence of the Lambs*, 163.

144 "I drove myself nuts": McGavin, "Ted Levine Is Not a Bad Guy."

144 "Something that is": McGavin, "Ted Levine Is Not a Bad Guy."

144 "He's not a transexual": Harris, *The Silence of the Lambs*, 169.

144 "Male sexuality": *The Silence of the Lambs* Criterion Blu-ray.

144 "an old glitter rocker": McGavin, "Ted Levine Is Not a Bad Guy."

145 "He walks up to me": Author interview, April 23, 2024.

145 "The research is always": Author interview, June 19, 2024.

145 "He was fearful": Author interview, June 19, 2024.

146 "It looked almost too beautiful": Dan Persons, "Makeup Effects Behind-the-Scenes," *Cinefantastique*, February, 1992.

146 "They didn't know": Author interview, April 23, 2024.

146 "We tried to get": Author interview, June 19, 2024.

146 "This country was built": Author interview, September 23, 2024.

147 "I got a call": Author interview, March 11, 2024.

147 "If at any point": Author interview, March 11, 2024.

147 "Jonathan comes over": Author interview, March 11, 2024.

147 "Everything was a joke": Mark Goodman, "Cops, Killers & Cannibals," *People*, April 1, 1991.

148 "They installed a refrigerator": Michael Sauter, "Brooke Smith," *Premiere*, February 1991.

148 "I was doing": Matt Gourley, "Silence of the Lambs with Brooke Smith," *I Was There Too* (podcast), December 4, 2018, https://www.earwolf.com/episode/si lence-of-the-lambs-with-brooke-smith.

148 "We had to take care": Rachel Handler, "Brooke Smith Answers Every Question We Have About *The Silence of the Lambs*," Vulture, November 5, 2020, https:// www.vulture.com/2020/11/brooke-smith-answers-every-silence-of-the-lambs -question.html.

149 "made this psychotic monster": Will Harris, "Ted Levine on *Monk*, Skinny Jeans, and Buffalo Bill," AV Club, January 10, 2014, https://www.avclub.com /ted-levine-on-monk-skinny-jeans-and-buffalo-bill-1798265448., January 10, 2014, https://www.avclub.com/ted-levine-on-monk-skinny-jeans-and-buffalo-bill -1798265448.

150 "I put a flap": Author interview, February 21, 2024.

150 "You can't just bring": Author interview, February 21, 2024.

150 "We were going to have": Author interview, February 20, 2024.

151 "Your flock is still": Ted Tally, *The Silence of the Lambs* alternate ending draft, November 4, 1989, 120, courtesy of University of Michigan Library (Special Collections Library).

151 "We hate Chilton": Author interview, March 19, 2024.

152 "I was like": Mike Fleming, Jr., "Jonathan Demme and Untold 'Silence of fhe

Lambs' Tales: Hannibal, Clarice, Tally, Hackman, and a Discarded Scary Ending," Deadline, April 26, 2017, https://deadline.com/2017/04/the-silence-of-the-lambs -25th-anniversary-untold-tales-jonathan-demme-ted-tally-hannibal-lecter-clarice -starling-1201703981.

152   "Tom, I need to talk": Adrian Wootton, "Jonathan Demme (II)," *Guardian*, October 10, 1998, https://www.theguardian.com/film/1998/oct/10/1.

152   "I tell you what": Wootton, "Jonathan Demme (II)."

152   "I wanted him": *The Silence of the Lambs* Criterion Blu-ray.

152   "We were told": Author interview, April 12, 2024.

CHAPTER 17

153   "Some [moviegoers] indicated": The National Research Group, *The Silence of the Lambs* recruited audience survey, September 7, 1990, courtesy of University of Michigan Library (Special Collections Library).

154   "He didn't want it": Author interview, March 29, 2024.

154   "I used to go": Author interview, June 30, 2025.

154   "There's a simplicity": Email to author, June 27, 2025.

155   "It was my attempt": Email to author, June 27, 2025.

155   "The goal was": Author interview, June 30, 2025.

155   "Hello. I'm Hannibal Lecter": Hannibal Lecter ShoWest memo, January 15, 1990, courtesy of University of Michigan Library (Special Collections Library).

156   "This is the bowels": Elisabeth Weis, "Creating Sound for Demme," FilmSound .org, https://www.filmsound.org/synctanks/demme.htm.

156   "We worked it": Mike Fleming, Jr., "Jonathan Demme and Untold 'Silence of fhe Lambs' Tales: Hannibal, Clarice, Tally, Hackman, and a Discarded Scary Ending," Deadline, April 26, 2017, https://deadline.com/2017/04/the-silence-of -the-lambs-25th-anniversary-untold-tales-jonathan-demme-ted-tally-hannibal -lecter-clarice-starling-1201703981.

156   "They tell me": Thomas Harris, fax to Jonathan Demme, September 12, 1990, courtesy of University of Michigan Library (Special Collections Library).

156   "Everybody was saying": Author interview, April 12, 2024.

156   "Our school was in": Author interview, June 24, 2025.

157   "She said": Author interview, June 24, 2025.

157   "What movie are you seeing?": Art Almquist, "Cultural Analysis of Jonathan Demme's 'The Silence of the Lambs,'" master of arts thesis, Scholarworks at University of Montana, https://scholarworks.umt.edu/cgi/viewcontent.cgi?arti cle=2971&context=etd, 2–3.

157   "a big guy": Author interview, June 24, 2025.

158   "I haven't heard anything": Meredith Berkman, "Playing Hannibal Lecter," *Entertainment Weekly*, March 29, 1991, https://ew.com/article/1991/03/29/play ing-hannibal-lecter.

158   "pop film making": Vincent Canby, "Review/Film; Methods of Madness in

'Silence of the Lambs,'" *New York Times*, February 14, 1991, https://www.nytimes .com/1991/02/14/movies/review-film-methods-of-madness-in-silence-of-the -lambs.html.

158 "stunning": Sheila Benson, "A Stunning 'Silence,'" *Los Angeles Times*, February 13, 1991.

158 "way overplayed": andyfilm, *Siskel & Ebert Classics - 2/8/91 - Silence of the Lambs, Sleeping with the Enemy*, YouTube, April 25, 1991, https://www.youtube.com /watch?v=VoUx6YwsPo4.

158 "It worked for me!": andyfilm, *Siskel & Ebert Classics - 2/8/91 - Silence of the Lambs, Sleeping with the Enemy*.

159 "the scariest man in movies": *Entertainment Weekly*, March 29, 1991.

159 "I was in Memorial Sloan Kettering": Author interview, March 27, 2024.

159 "They've lost three": Berkman, "Playing Hannibal Lecter."

159 "These are people": Berkman, "Playing Hannibal Lecter."

159 "I'm not easily scared": Panny Mayfield, "Top Movie Thriller Authored by Coa-homa County's Thomas Harris," *Clarksdale Press Register*, March 2, 1991.

160 "[Lecter] was so even-tempered": Mike Cochran and Jeff Guinn, "Mystery Man," *Fort Worth Star-Telegram*, July 2, 1999.

160 "Hannibal the Cannibal": Bill Carter, "'The Curse of Hannibal Lecter' Is Old Film in 'Lamb's' Clothing," *Lexington Herald-Leader*, May 3, 1991.

161 "true to the film": Stanley Desantis, fax to Orion Pictures, March 29, 1991, cour-tesy of University of Michigan Library (Special Collections Library).

161 "On my way in": "Remarks by the President in Address at FBI National Academy Commencement Ceremony," White House transcript, May 30, 1991, courtesy of University of Michigan Library (Special Collections Library).

161 "So there is": Thomas Harris, Letter to Barbara Bush, December 13, 1990, cour-tesy of University of Michigan Library (Special Collections Library).

161 "Does he have to": Thomas Harris, fax to Morton Janklow, June 1991, courtesy of University of Michigan Library (Special Collections Library).

161 "Splendid!": Thomas Harris, fax to Jonathan Demme and Ed Saxon, February 1991, courtesy of University of Michigan Library (Special Collections Library).

162 "I have two reasons": Thomas Harris, fax to Jonathan Demme, February 21, 1991, courtesy of University of Michigan Library (Special Collections Library).

162 "He and Pace are having": Phoebe Hoban, "The Silence of the Writer," *New York*, April 15, 1991, https://books.google.com/books?id=aukCAAAAMBAJ&pg =PA48&source=gbs_toc_r&cad=2#v=onepage&q&f=false.

162 "The first time I went": Athena Varounis, letter to Jonathan Demme, Ed Saxon, and Kenneth Utt, March 28, 1991.

162 "I was like 'Holy moly'": Author interview, March 13, 2024.

162 "The FBI people": Walter B. Stowe, Jr., letter to Jonathan Demme, February 15, 1991, courtesy of University of Michigan Library (Special Collections Library).

162 "Lecter fascinated me": Email to author, June 24, 2025.

163 "They'd say": Author interview, June 24, 2025.

163 "oohed and aahed": Peter Plagens et al., "Violence in Our Culture," *Newsweek*, April 1, 1991.

163 "I cannot believe": Alex Witchel, "O.K., Says Anthony Hopkins, More Mr. Nice Guy," *New York Times*, December 19, 1991, https://www.nytimes.com/1993/12/19/movies/ok-says-anthony-hopkins-more-mr-nice-guy.html.

163 "I'm shaking": Transcript of Anthony Hopkins's March 18, 1991, appearance on *Mark & Brian*, courtesy of University of Michigan Library (Special Collections Library).

164 "I always used to feel": "Stargazing," *Kansas City Star*, July 25, 1991.

164 "I just pulled over": Meredith Berkman, "Playing Hannibal Lecter," *Entertainment Weekly*, March 29, 1991, https://ew.com/article/1991/03/29/playing-hannibal-lecter.

CHAPTER 18

165 "Yes, the picture": Stephen Farber, "Why Do Critics Love These Repellent Movies?," *Los Angeles Times*, March 17, 1991.

165 "an appalling accretion": Peter Plagens et al., "Violence in Our Culture," *Newsweek*, April 1, 1991.

166 "I hated": Melanie McFarland, "Theatrical Serial Killers Compel Viewers in Scary Ways," *Tampa Tribune*, November 11, 1997.

166 "I don't think": Rhonda Bell, "Ex–FBI Man Says Real Violence Fueled by Media," *Patriot-News*, February 21, 1994.

166 "not inconsistent with cannibalism": Associated Press, "17 Slayings Tied to Milwaukee Man," *New York Times*, July 26, 1991, https://www.nytimes.com/1991/07/26/us/17-slayings-tied-to-milwaukee-man.html.

167 "a Real-Life": *People*, August 12, 1991.

167 "burst from flat-screen fiction": "Sick Jokes," *New York Times*, August 6, 1991, https://www.nytimes.com/1991/08/06/opinion/sick-jokes.html.

167 "I worry a lot": Joan Lenherr, "From the Silents to 'Silence,' Killers Thrill and Fear Fascinates," *Wausau Daily Herald*, October 27, 1991.

168 "sick pornography of butchery": Elaine Dutka, "'Silence' Fuels a Loud and Angry Debate," *Los Angeles Times*, March 20, 1991, https://www.latimes.com/archives/la-xpm-1991-03-20-ca-482-story.html.

168 "Why do we": Maureen Downey, "Women's Groups Say Violence as Entertainment Is a Mistake," *Waco Tribune-Herald*, May 12, 1991.

168 "Don't go outside": Downey, "Women's Groups Say Violence as Entertainment Is a Mistake."

168 "anti-violence": Jonathan Demme, press conference transcript, January 25, 1991.

168 "We don't want": Fred Schruers, "A Kind of Redemption," *Premiere*, March 1991.

168 "They couldn't have made": Ryan Murphy, "Boycott Urged on Film; Stereotyping Is Alleged," *Miami Herald*, February 15, 1991.

169 "They were watching": Author interview, March 14, 2024.

169 "portrayed as gay": Demme, press conference transcript, January 25, 1991.

169   "endowed with all": Stephen Harvey, "Writers on the 'Lambs,'" *Village Voice*, February 15, 1991.

169   "opened my eyes": Jonathan Demme, "The Lambs, Demme, and 'The Advocate,'" *Guide*, April 1991.

170   "mincing homosexual": *The Silence of the Lambs* Criterion Blu-ray.

170   "I thought": Author interview, March 19, 2024.

171   "A dazzling film": William Goldman, "The Big Picture: Pushing the Envelope," *New York*, March 30, 1992.

171   "We were looking": Author interview, March 29, 2024.

172   "We're telling them": Robert W. Welkos and Eric Malnic, "Gay Activists Rally on Streets Outside Music Center," *Los Angeles Times*, March 31, 1992.

172   "as disruptive as possible": Carla Hall, "'Instinct' Battle Plan: Gay Groups Prepare Assault, Eye Oscars," *Washington Post*, March 19, 1992, https://www.washington post.com/archive/lifestyle/1992/03/19/instinct-battle-plan-gay-groups-prepare -assault-eye-oscars/1248943d-94bb-48c9-9835-dbfd4bae47e0.

172   "The show was": Author interview, March 29, 2024.

173   "They were all panicked": Author interview, March 27, 2024.

173   "We worried": Author interview, March 19, 2024.

173   "I'm having some": Oscars, *Billy Crystal's Hannibal Lecter Entrance: 1992 Oscars*, YouTube, November 24, 2010, https://www.youtube.com/watch?v=a9cER vUX6sE.

173   "Look inside my pot": Oscars, *Billy Crystal's Opening Monologue: 1992 Oscars*, YouTube, November 28, 2011, https://www.youtube.com/watch?v=UCAi1744S a0&t=13s.

173   "graciously [lending] me": Oscars, *The Silence of the Lambs Wins Adapted Screenplay: 1992 Oscars*, YouTube, October 31, 2013, https://www.youtube.com /watch?v=9ZgaDDCspTI.

174   "That was the only": Author interview, March 27, 2024.

174   "My God": Oscars, *Anthony Hopkins Wins Best Actor | 64th Oscars (1992)*, You-Tube, January 4, 2010, https://www.youtube.com/watch?v=ftUGtsdSXeU.

174   "I had put": Quentin Falk, *Anthony Hopkins: The Authorized Biography* (Interlink Books, 1994), 181.

174   "It's going to be": Mike Fleming, Jr., "Jonathan Demme and Untold 'Silence of the Lambs' Tales: Hannibal, Clarice, Tally, Hackman, and a Discarded Scary Ending," Deadline, April 26, 2017, https://deadline.com/2017/04/the-silence-of -the-lambs-25th-anniversary-untold-tales-jonathan-demme-ted-tally-hannibal -lecter-clarice-starling-1201703981.

174   "The reason": Oscars, *Jodie Foster Wins Best Actress | 64th Oscars (1992)*, You-Tube, August 25, 2010, https://www.youtube.com/watch?v=CYikmz2AI24.

174   "extraordinarily moral": Oscars, *Jonathan Demme Wins Best Directing: 1992 Oscars*, YouTube, April 26, 2013, https://www.youtube.com/watch?v=1YS2ovtUveQ.

174   "cannibal indigestion": Oscars, *The Silence of the Lambs Wins Best Picture: 1992 Oscars*, YouTube, November 24, 2010, https://www.youtube.com/watch ?v=28ZkmJJ8320.

174   "'Lamb'-slide": "It's a 'Lamb'-slide," *Staten Island Advance*, March 31, 1992.

175   "Dear Jonathan": Steven Spielberg, letter to Jonathan Demme, March 31, 1992, courtesy of University of Michigan Library (Special Collections Library).

175   "The dialogue": Alexandra Alter, "Hannibal Lecter's Creator Cooks Up Something New (No Fava Beans or Chianti)," *New York Times*, May 18, 2019, https://www.nytimes.com/2019/05/18/books/thomas-harris-new-book.html.

175   "great movie": Phoebe Hoban, "The Silence of the Writer," *New York*, April 15, 1991, https://books.google.com/books?id=aukCAAAAMBAJ&pg=PA48&source=gbs _toc_r&cad=2#v=onepage&q&f=false.

CHAPTER 19

179   "I'd like to know": Jim Emerson, "His Performance Is a Fine Madness," *Philadelphia Inquirer*, March 3, 1991.

179   "We have seen": Arnold Braeske, "Hopkins Is Hungering to Reprise Dr. Lecter," *Star-Ledger*, February 26, 1992.

179   "change a single": Joel Achenbach, "Hack Writer," *Washington Post*, June 21, 1999, https://www.washingtonpost.com/archive/lifestyle/1999/06/21/hack-writer /7d57d83a-e630-4b85-b8a4-dee31b821000.

179   "hot, hot, hot": Trip Gabriel, "Call My Agent!," *New York Times*, February 19, 1989, https://www.nytimes.com/1989/02/19/magazine/call-my-agent.html.

180   "The numbers kept getting": Gabriel, "Call My Agent!"

180   "His books come": Bill Goldstein, "Top Dollar for Top-Dog Authors," *Newsday*, December 11, 1988.

180   "Those were the days": Author interview, February 21, 2024.

180   "Why is it taking": "Walter Scott's Personality Parade," *Parade*, May 21, 1995.

180   "We can't begin": "Walter Scott's Personality Parade"

181   "everyone wanted to know": Author interview, February 21, 2024.

181   "Sorry you would participate": Philip Potempa, "Brian Dennehy Still Haunted by Killer John Wayne Gacy Role," *Times*, February 28, 2010.

181   "A big-screen onslaught": Pat H. Broeske, "Serial Killers Claim Movies as Their Prey," *New York Times*, https://www.nytimes.com/1992/12/13/movies/film-serial -killers-claim-movies-as-their-prey.html.

182   "Hannibal Lecter lite": Jeffrey Westhoff, "'Copycat' Lives Up to Its Name," *Northwest Herald*, October 27, 1995.

182   "You have no right": Brian Mockenhaupt, "The Curious Case of David Fincher," *Esquire*, March 2007, https://www.esquire.com/news-politics/a2155/esq0307 fincher.

183   "quaint": Carrie Rickey, "Gus Van Sant's Remake of 'Psycho' Is More of a Rehash of Slash," *The Philadelphia Inquirer*, December 5, 1998.

183   "This is": Richard Guilliatt and Bernard Zuel, "Making a Killing," *Sydney Morning Herald*, July 9, 1994.

184   "We want as much": Laurie Taylor, "We All Want Criminals Now," *Independent*, December 4, 1994.

184   "Everyone has": John Marchese, "Exceeding Odd," *New York Times*, March 14, 1993, https://www.nytimes.com/1993/03/14/style/out-there-philadelphia-exceeding-odd.html.

184   "You can't glorify": Barbara Anderson, "Sing Along with Charlie," *Reno Gazette-Journal*, December 9, 1993.

184   "Manson's come to symbolize": "Creepy, Repulsive—Fascinating," *Honolulu Star-Bulletin*, May 9, 1994.

184   "No matter who": Jim Sullivan, "25 Years After Murders, Manson Still Mesmerizes," *Boston Globe*, August 9, 1994.

185   "Go a little insane": Marchese, "Exceeding Odd."

185   "We just want": "Groups Find Serial Killer Fascinating," *Quad City Times*, January 29, 1992.

185   "Killers are the hottest": Bernard Weinraub, "How a Movie Satire Turned into Reality," *New York Times*, August 14, 1994, https://www.nytimes.com/1994/08/16/movies/how-a-movie-satire-turned-into-reality.html.

185   "The world is violent": Stephen Schiff, "The Last Wild Man," *New Yorker*, August 8, 1994, https://www.newyorker.com/magazine/1994/08/08/the-last-wild-man.

186   "The most pacifistic": Peter M. Nichols, "With Video, 'Cut!' Needn't Be the Director's Final Word," *New York Times*, April 14, 1996, https://www.nytimes.com/1996/04/14/arts/film-with-video-cut-needn-t-be-the-director-s-final-word.html.

186   "debased, condemned": Joyce Carol Oates, "I Had No Other Thrill or Happiness," *New York Review*, March 24, 1994, https://www.nybooks.com/articles/1994/03/24/i-had-no-other-thrill-or-happiness.

187   "Kiss my ass": Lindsey Tanner, "Gacy Grunts Once Before He Dies," *Lancaster New Era*, May 10, 1994.

CHAPTER 20

188   "Ain't that something!": Letter to author, April 21, 2024.

188   "the bearded guy": John Barry, "The Silence of Thomas Harris," *Miami Herald*, Mary 31, 1993.

188   "Yes": Barry, "The Silence of Thomas Harris."

188   "a blessing": Athena Varounis, notes from February 1992 visit with Harris.

189   "It's brought": Varounis, notes from February 1992 visit with Harris.

189   "He refused to say much": Nicholas Farrell, "The Lamb and the Slaughter," *Sunday Telegraph*, April 24, 1994.

189   "I never saw him": Meg Laughlin, "Silence of the Author," *Tulsa World*, August 15, 1991.

189   "He's a hoot": Alexandra Alter, "Hannibal Lecter's Creator Cooks Up Something New (No Fava Beans or Chianti)," *New York Times*, May 18, 2019, https://www.nytimes.com/2019/05/18/books/thomas-harris-new-book.html.

190   "Harris lost contact with us": Author interview.

190   "The men would be": Letter to author, April 21, 2024.

190 "Let me tell you": Nikke Finke, "A Tough Act to Swallow," *Guardian*, June 7, 1999, https://www.theguardian.com/culture/1999/jun/08/artsfeatures.thomasharris.

190 "I was thinking": Author interview, May 8, 2024.

191 "What I expected": Author interview, May 8, 2024.

191 "A world odd enough": Thomas Harris, "An Ideal English Class Syllabus for 9th Graders," *Mouth2Mouth*, Spring 1994, https://web.archive.org/web/201106 29120256/http://sites.google.com/site/lektalekton/Home/an-ideal-english -class-syllabus-for-9th-graders.

191 "Tom tormented himself": Author interview, February 7, 2024.

191 "In a way": Author interview, August 16, 2024.

192 "He always takes": "Info Needed on Silence of the Lambs Sequel," rec.arts.mys-tery, Usenet, October 17, 1997, https://groups.google.com/g/rec.arts.mystery/c/40 n11UKjsjw/m/6cDQ5neBT3QJ?pli=1.

192 "There was a gush": Joyce Carol Oates, "Zombie," *New Yorker*, October 16, 1994, https://www.newyorker.com/magazine/1994/10/24/zombie.

193 "Tom would talk": Author interview, February 21, 2024.

193 "Are you busy?": Dinitia Smith, "Long After 'Lambs,' Dr. Lecter Is Returning," *New York Times*, March 30, 1999, https://www.nytimes.com/1999/03/30/books /long-after-lambs-dr-lecter-is-returning.html.

193 "I practically got": Author interview, February 21, 2024.

193 "I dreaded doing *Hannibal*": Thomas Harris, "Foreword to a Fatal Interview," *Red Dragon*, rev. ed. (Berkley Books, 2000).

CHAPTER 21

194 "a rising star": Thomas Harris, *Hannibal* (Dell, 2000), 57.

195 "You are a warrior": Harris, *Hannibal*, 37.

195 "He has found": Harris, *Hannibal*, 153.

196 "In cyberspace at least": Harris, *Hannibal*, 53–54.

196 "Noseless and lipless": Harris, *Hannibal*, 65.

196 "hard-core fun": Harris, *Hannibal*, 451.

196 "capable of lifting": Harris, *Hannibal*, 246.

196 "rebreathing the farts": Harris, *Hannibal*, 281.

196 "Like many others": Harris, *Hannibal*, 282.

197 "You can't reduce me": Thomas Harris, *The Silence of the Lambs* (St. Martin's Press, 1989), 21.

197 "Dr. Lecter wants time": Harris, *Hannibal*, 490.

197 "Size for size": Harris, *Hannibal*, 415.

198 "His face": Harris, *Hannibal*, 255.

198 "as though he savored": *Hannibal*, 323.

198 "Did you ever think": Harris, *Hannibal*, 211.

198 "Out of the eater": Judges 14:14, New International Version, https://biblehub .com/judges/14-14.htm.

198   "People said": Author interview, February 21, 2024.

199   "Everyone would read": Author interview, February 21, 2024.

199   "No interviews": Joel Achenbach, "Hack Writer," *Washington Post*, June 21, 1999, https://www.washingtonpost.com/archive/lifestyle/1999/06/21/hack-writer/7d57d83a-e630-4b85-b8a4-dee31b821000.

199   "He was very gracious": Achenbach, "Hack Writer."

200   "It's just going": Jayne Freer, "Customers Hungry for Hannibal," *Evening Herald*, June 11, 1999.

200   "The readers who": Stephen King, "Hannibal the Cannibal," *New York Times*, June 13, 1999, https://archive.nytimes.com/www.nytimes.com/books/99/06/13/reviews/990613.13kingct.html.

200   "vast, pungent": Owen Gleiberman, "Hannibal," *Entertainment Weekly*, June 25, 1999, https://ew.com/article/1999/06/25/hannibal-4.

200   "a Grand Guignol romp": Annie Gottlieb, "Free-Range Rude," *Nation*, July 1, 1999, https://www.thenation.com/article/archive/free-range-rude.

200   "deliciously frightening": Daniel Handler, "Deliciously Frightening," *Newsday*, June 14, 1999.

201   "on all levels," Martin Amis, "Snobbo Sadist," *Talk*, September 1999.

201   "Martin loved books": Email to author, April 22, 2024.

201   "I got through": Amis, "Snobbo Sadist."

201   "a bloody dish": Harris, *Hannibal*, 477.

201   "reeks of snuff": Tom Long, "Readers Have Strong Appetite for More Hannibal," *St. Cloud Times*, June 13, 1999.

201   "Yuck": Bob Minzesheimer, "Disturbing 'Hannibal' Frolics in Gory Muck," *Courier-Post*, June 13, 1999.

201   "Does anyone else": "Hannibal" and the Movies (No Spoilers)," rec.arts.movies.current-films Usenet post, June 15, 1999, https://groups.google.com/g/rec.arts.movies.current-films/c/URaQU8Hp17c/m/5tdxJiYguB0J.

201   "smelled no fear": Harris, *Hannibal*, 477.

202   "Wiggle, wiggle, Mason": Harris, *Hannibal*, 484.

202   "Clarice, I'm going": Harris, *Hannibal*, 509.

202   "cornpone country pussy": Harris, *Hannibal*, 300.

202   "All we ask": Harris, *Hannibal*, 531.

202   "Their relationship": Harris, *Hannibal*, 543.

203   "I thought": Author interview, June 24, 2025.

203   "Simply no excuse": David Forsmark, "'Hannibal' Cannibalized by Creator,' *Flint Journal*, June 20, 1999.

203   "The ultimate discourtesy": Jabari Asim, "Hannibal Lecter Meets His Match," *Washington Post*, June 9, 1999, https://www.washingtonpost.com/archive/lifestyle/1999/06/10/hannibal-lecter-meets-his-match/a4d7dfb3-6816-44f8-b170-194fb538d777.

203   "completely unbelievable": "Hannibal—The Ending," rec.arts.movies.current-films Usenet post, September 11, 1999, https://groups.google.com/g/rec.arts.movies.current-films/c/Ll-TsDZKmxU/m/us-DdHZll04J.

203   "I didn't like it": Author interview, April 2, 2024.

203   "For the sake": Daniel Fierman, "The Gory Details," *Entertainment Weekly*, February 9, 2001.

204   "[I] feared for Starling": Thomas Harris, "Foreword to a Fatal Interview" *Red Dragon*, rev. ed. (Berkley Books, 2000).

204   "Now that ceaseless exposure": Harris, *Hannibal*, 144.

204   "He told me once": Harris, *Hannibal*, 99.

CHAPTER 22

205   "It definitely influenced": Author interview, March 19, 2024.

205   "It absolutely broke my heart": Ty Burr, "Filmmaker Breaks His 'Silence,'" *Boston Globe*, October 20, 2002.

205   "It wasn't a sequel": Author interview, February 20, 2024.

206   "We would have had": Author interview, March 19, 2024.

206   "I had to tell Tom": Ty Burr, "Filmmaker Breaks His 'Silence,'" *Boston Globe*, October 20, 2002.

206   "When the Pope-a die": Jill Bernstein, "Eat Drink Man Woman," *Premiere*, February 2001.

206   "foregone conclusion": "The Silence of the Lambs," *Inside Story*, TV episode, 2010.

206   "Dino, I don't want": Bernstein, "Eat Drink Man Woman."

207   "Oh, no": "*Hannibal*: Screenplay by David Mamet," September 8, 1999, https://web.archive.org/web/20071011153342/http://www.dailyscript.com/scripts/hannibal_unproduced.html.

207   "the James Bond": Ryan Faughnder, "The Traditional Indie Film System Is Hurting. This Executive Says He's Built a Winning Formula," *Los Angeles Times*, April 21, 2025, https://www.latimes.com/entertainment-arts/business/newsletter/2025-04-01/the-traditional-indie-film-system-is-broken-this-company-is-trying-to-work-around-it-the-wide-shot.

207   "I just couldn't buy that": Mike Fleming, Jr., "Ridley Scott On 'The Martian' and Why 'Star Wars' and '2001' Sent Him to Space with 'Alien:' Toronto Q&A," Deadline, September 12, 2015, https://deadline.com/2015/09/ridley-scott-the-martian-star-wars-2001-alien-blade-runner-prometheus-toronto-film-festival-1201522484.

208   "I grieved about that": LTV East Hampton, *Conversations - Thomas Harris - 07.09.2019*, YouTube, July 9, 2019, https://www.youtube.com/watch?v=XlH-cD_0kCM.

208   "I don't really": Bernstein, "Eat Drink Man Woman."

208   "After four days": Bernstein, "Eat Drink Man Woman."

208   "bizarre": Daniel Fierman, "The Gory Details," *Entertainment Weekly*, February 9, 2001.

208   "I have a big": Drew Weisholtz, "Martha Stewart Reveals the Unexpected Reason She Broke Up with Anthony Hopkins," *Today*, January 20, 2022, https://www

.today.com/popculture/movies/martha-stewart-told-ellen-degeneres-broke
-anthony-hopkins-rcna12862.

209 "Judy Foster": Bernstein, "Eat Drink Man Woman."

209 "The only thing": Daniel Fierman, "Killer Instinct," *Entertainment Weekly*, March 17, 2000.

209 "I stand to make": "'Hannibal' Role Proves Too Much for Jodie Foster," *Gazette*, November 9, 1999.

209 "trample": "The Total Film Interview—Jodie Foster," Total Film, December 2005, https://www.gamesradar.com/the-total-film-interview-jodie-foster.

209 "Give my love": Bernstein, "Eat Drink Man Woman"

209 "They haven't contacted": Daniel Fierman, "Lamb Chops," *Entertainment Weekly*, January 14, 2000.

210 "This movie": *Hannibal* production notes, https://web.archive.org/web/2006 0709020253/https://www.cinema.com/articles/44/hannibal-production-notes .phtml.

210 "It's a bit": Jess Cagle, "The Bite Stuff," *Time*, February 6, 2001, https://time.com /archive/6953009/the-bite-stuff.

210 "Julianne Moore is": Fierman, "Killer Instinct."

210 "This will add nothing": Rory Carroll, "Florentines Try to Silence Hannibal," *Guardian*, May 11, 2000.

210 "I'm very competitive": Associated Press, "A Matter of Taste," *Calgary Herald*, May 5, 2000.

211 "The reaction to Lecter": Fierman, "The Gory Details."

211 "I thought": Bernstein, "Eat Drink Man Woman."

212 "It made me gag": Fierman, "The Gory Details."

213 "Hannibal! Face eater!": Fierman, "The Gory Details."

213 "I hope things": Jonathan Demme, letter to Thomas Harris, August 8, 2000, courtesy of University of Michigan Library (Special Collections Library).

214 "That was a little weird": Claudia Puig, "'Hannibal' Can't Scare Off Kids with Parents," *USA Today*, February 12, 2001.

214 "A lot can happen": Kenneth Turan, "A Cannibalized Tale," *Los Angeles Times*, February 9, 2001.

214 "I saw *Hannibal*": "The Total Film Interview—Jodie Foster."

214 "I liked Lecter": Glenn Lovell, "Will the Public Buy the 'New' Hannibal Lecter?," *Messenger-Inquirer*, February 9, 2001.

215 "When Lecter has": Elvis Mitchell, "Whetting That Large Appetite for Second Helpings," *New York Times*, February 9, 2001, https://www.nytimes.com/2001 /02/09/movies/film-review-whetting-that-large-appetite-for-second-helpings. html.

215 "He's as big a star": Patrick Goldstein, "The Master Showman in Winter," *Los Angeles Times*, January 23, 2001.

215 "It's like Batman": David Germain, "'Hannibal' Chews Up Record Books," *Lansing State Journal*, February 13, 2001.

CHAPTER 23

216   "Everybody asks me": Gillian Flynn, "First Blood," *Entertainment Weekly*, October 11, 2002.

217   "After *Silence of the Lambs*": Ann Oldenburg, "Marquee Names Serve Up Another Helping of Hannibal," *USA Today*, October 4, 2002, https://usatoday30.usatoday.com/life/movies/2002-10-03-red-dragon-cover_x.htm.

217   "I told my agent": Oldenburg, "Marquee Names Serve Up Another Helping of Hannibal."

217   "We open in": Jim Slotek, "Hannibal Goes Back for Thirds," *Winnipeg Sun*, September 29, 2003.

217   "I don't think": Slotek, "Hannibal Goes Back for Thirds."

218   "You have more leverage": Conan O'Brien, *Why Anthony Hopkins Is Done with Hannibal Lecter | Late Night with Conan O'Brien*, YouTube, January 23, 2023, https://www.youtube.com/watch?v=gplM_zsVm5M.

218   "I'd done the cutesy stuff": Franz Lidz, "The Scenery, Though, He Won't Chew," *New York Times*, September 29, 2002, https://www.nytimes.com/2002/09/29/movies/film-the-scenery-though-he-won-t-chew.html.

218   "more menace": Megan Turner, "Chew on This! Hopkins Is Back for a Third Helping of Hannibal," *New York Post*, September 30, 2002, https://nypost.com/2002/09/30/chew-on-this-hopkins-is-back-for-a-3rd-helping-as-hannibal.

218   "Tom Harris was the first": Amy Longsdorf, "Caged Fury," *Record*, September 29, 2002.

219   "I would send him": Author interview, March 19, 2024.

219   "We never heard back": Flynn, "First Blood."

219   "I'm true to myself": Alex Godfrey, "Brett Ratner: 'If It Wasn't for Eddie Murphy, Rush Hour Wouldn't Exist,'" *Guardian*, October 29, 2011, https://www.theguardian.com/film/2011/oct/29/brett-ratner-tower-heist-interview.

220   *"I'm not a dark guy"*: *Red Dragon* (Director's Edition) DVD, Universal Studios Home Video, 2003.

220   "Nobody knows that film": Flynn, "First Blood."

220   "He *said* that?": Flynn, "First Blood."

220   "I was hearing the voices": "Red Dragon," *Charlie Rose*, October 1, 2002, https://charlierose.com/videos/10627.

220   "We give you some money": *Red Dragon* (Director's Edition) DVD, 2003.

220   "Every morning": Author interview, October 16, 2024.

221   "I don't think Edward Norton": Flynn, "First Blood."

221   "He saw me": Author interview, April 12, 2024.

221   "fucking great": Flynn, "First Blood."

221   "fucking awesome": Flynn, "First Blood."

222   "I got yelled at": Flynn, "First Blood."

222   "I was always bickering": Oldenburg, "Marquee Names Serve Up Another Helping of Hannibal."

222　"Why?": *Red Dragon* (Director's Edition) DVD, 2003.

222　"My eyes tend": Flynn, "First Blood."

222　"Demme and Ridley": Author interview, February 27, 2024.

222　"When in my whole life": Oldenburg, "Marquee Names Serve Up Another Help-ing of Hannibal."

223　"a Charles Manson anger": Douglas J. Rowe, "Anthony Hopkins Comes Back for a Third Course," *Courier-News*, October 5, 2002.

223　"We came in": Slotek, "Hannibal Goes Back for Thirds."

223　"It was a weird scene": Oldenburg, "Marquee Names Serve Up Another Helping of Hannibal."

224　"the Elvis of screen villains": Slotek, "Hannibal Goes Back for Thirds."

224　"He said": Flynn, "First Blood."

224　"darkly seductive": Richard Corliss, "Here Be Monsters," *Time*, September 30, 2002, https://web.archive.org/web/20110204060802/https://time.com/time/mag azine/article/0,9171,1101021007-356086,00.html.

224　"sure, stylish": Roger Ebert, "Red Dragon," RogerEbert.com, October 4, 2002, https://www.rogerebert.com/reviews/red-dragon-2002.

224　"By now": Lisa Schwarzbaum, "Lecter Circuit," *Entertainment Weekly*, October 11, 2002, https://web.archive.org/web/20080303070517/https://ew.com/ew/article /0,,357204,00.html.

225　"Lecter is such": Elvis Mitchell, "Taking a Bite Out of Crime," *New York Times*, October 4, 2002, https://www.nytimes.com/2002/10/04/movies/film-review-tak ing-a-bite-out-of-crime.html.

225　"Look, I wanna": Slotek, "Hannibal Goes Back for Thirds."

225　"I like the idea": Oldenburg, "Marquee Names Serve Up Another Helping of Han-nibal."

225　"Nobody will entice me": Flynn, "First Blood."

225　"Made the mistake": Daniel Holloway, "Anthony Hopkins Regrets Making 'Han-nibal,' 'Red Dragon,'" The Wrap, January 8, 2016, https://www.thewrap.com /anthony-hopkins-regrets-making-hannibal-red-dragon.

225　"What does this": Friday Night with Jonathan Ross, *Anthony Hopkins Pretends to Be Hannibal Lecter in Public! | Friday Night with Jonathan Ross*, YouTube, Oc-tober 31, 2020, https://www.youtube.com/watch?v=P-yVqgaSjQ0.

CHAPTER 24

229　"I would be crazy": Jim Slotek, "Hannibal Goes Back for Thirds," *Winnipeg Sun*, September 29, 2003.

229　"Dino would say": Slotek, "Hannibal Goes Back for Thirds."

230　"Aw, gee *whiz*": Ty Burr, "Filmmaker Breaks His 'Silence,'" *Boston Globe*, October 20, 2002.

230　"I don't want": Daniel Fierman, "Hannibal Lecter Meets His End," *Entertain-ment Weekly*, February 16, 2007, https://ew.com/article/2007/02/16/hannibal -lecter-meets-his-end.

230 "Maybe we should do": *Hannibal Rising* production notes, https://madein atlantis.com/movies_central/2007/hannibal_rising.htm#google_vignette.

230 "I say to Thomas": Fierman, "Hannibal Lecter Meets His End."

231 "Nothing happened to me": Thomas Harris, *The Silence of the Lambs* (St. Martin's Press, 1989), 21.

232 "friendly blackmail": Fierman, "Hannibal Lecter."

232 "[De Laurentiis] could have done": Alexandra Alter, "Hannibal Lecter's Creator Cooks Up Something New (No Fava Beans or Chianti)," *New York Times*, May 18, 2019, https://www.nytimes.com/2019/05/18/books/thomas-harris-new-book .html.

232 "Both Freddy and Jason": Elvis Mitchell, "Ol' Razor Fingers vs. Ol' Hockey Face," *New York Times*, August 15, 2003, https://www.nytimes.com/2003/08/15/movies /film-review-ol-razor-fingers-vs-ol-hockey-face.html.

233 "The nation and the world": Author interview, May 1, 2025.

233 "People were paying": Author interview, May 1, 2025.

234 "He lived in this": Author interview, May 1, 2025.

234 "When we came back": Author interview, May 1, 2025.

234 "I couldn't remember": Author interview, May 1, 2025.

234 "Leave me alone": Aileen Jacobson, "Talk About Cannibalized Stories," *Newsday*, February 5, 2007.

235 "At one point": Author interview, April 17, 2024.

235 "He had a magic": Author interview, April 17, 2024.

235 "It's not that shocking": ArtisanNewsService, *THE NEW HANNIBAL LECTER ATTENDS AUTOPSY CLASS*, YouTube, May 3, 2007, https://www.youtube.com /watch?v=jWbZgdMf510.

236 "I remember sitting": Author interview, April 17, 2024.

236 "he just sat in there": Author interview, April 17, 2024.

236 "Millions of readers": Associated Press, "New Hannibal Lecter Novel Due Next Fall," *Today*, October 28, 2004, https://www.today.com/popculture/new-han nibal-lecter-novel-due-next-fall-wbna6355035.

237 "Although this isn't": Terrence Rafferty, "First Course," *New York Times*, December 31, 2006, https://www.nytimes.com/2006/12/31/books/review/Rafferty 4.t.html.

237 "You know that": Deirdre Donahue, "'Hannibal' Prequel Doesn't Go Down Well," *USA Today*, December 7, 2006.

237 "Her eyes cleared": Thomas Harris, *Hannibal Rising* (New York: Dell Books, 2007), 160.

238 "ham-handed and choppy" John Keenan, "Less Evil 'Hannibal' Also Less Hypnotic," *Omaha World-Herald*, December 31, 2006.

238 "effete and European": David Hiltbrand, "How He Got That Appetite," *Philadelphia Inquirer*, December 13, 2006.

238 "a novel a parodist": David Sexton, "The Making of a Monster," *Evening Standard*, December 11, 2006.

238 "I know that some": Michael Ordoña, "They Created a (Proto) Monster," *Los*

Angeles Times, February 9, 2007, https://www.latimes.com/archives/la-xpm-2007 -feb-09-et-hannibal9-story.html.

238 "It's surely the most hated": Author interview, April 17, 2024.

238 "should only exist": Jeannette Catsoulis, "How He Arrived at the Acquired Taste," New York Times, February 9, 2007, https://www.nytimes.com/2007/02/09 /movies/09hann.html.

238 "It's surely": Author interview, April 17, 2024.

238 "Rationalize Lecter's brand": John Anderson, "Hannibal's Raw Beginnings," *Newsday*, February 9, 2007.

238 "There are a lot": Author interview, April 17, 2024.

239 "It was disappointing": Fierman, "Hannibal Lecter."

239 "The audience had had enough": Alter, "Hannibal Lecter's Creator."

239 "I did that for myself": Alter, "Hannibal Lecter's Creator."

CHAPTER 25

243 "It's part of who I am": James Brady, "In Step with Anthony Hopkins," *Parade*, October 8, 2007.

243 "I have no idea": Associated Press, "Hopkins Was Leary of a 3rd Course of Hanni-bal," *Columbus Ledger-Enquirer*, October 6, 2002.

244 "We feel murderous things": "Rogues Gallery," *Entertainment Weekly*, April 3, 2009.

245 "I kind of saw": kevinpollaktalkshow, *KPCS: Bryan Fuller #177*, YouTube, July 29, 2013, https://www.youtube.com/watch?v=ydGPnSgekfA.

245 "There were a lot": Author interview, May 1, 2025.

245 "I live in active terror": Dan Hyman, "The Cheerful Mind Behind *Hannibal*'s Deeply Disturbing, Gruesome Fantasia," Vulture, June 3, 2015, https://www .vulture.com/2015/06/bryan-fuller-the-cheerful-mind-behind-hannibals-grue some-fantasia.html.

246 "Do you think": Abbie Bernstein, "Exclusive Interview: HANNIBAL News on Season 1, Season 2 and Beyond from Showrunner Bryan Fuller," AssignmentX, June 13, 2013, https://www.assignmentx.com/2013/exclusive-interview-hannibal -news-on-season-1-season-2-and-beyond-from-showrunner-bryan-fuller.

246 "People interpret": Author interview, May 1, 2025.

246 "I love *The Silence of the Lambs*": Jennifer M. Wood, "Bryan Fuller on *Pushing Daisies, Dead Like Me*, and Being Cancelled," *Esquire*, March 19, 2015, https:// www.esquire.com/entertainment/tv/interviews/a33774/bryan-fuller-interview.

247 "Everybody in the world": AfterBuzz TV, *Hannibal | Interview with Martha De Laurentiis -- June 20th, 2013 | AfterBuzz TV AfterShow*, YouTube, June 20, 2013, https://www.youtube.com/watch?v=scsMDZ5g9AY.

247 "He said": AfterBuzz TV, *Hannibal*.

247 "he's got to be hypersane": AfterBuzz TV, *Hannibal After Show Season 1 Inter-view with Bryan Fuller -- June 19th, 2013" | AfterBuzz TV*, YouTube, June 20, 2013, https://www.youtube.com/watch?v=h-3UKJqr4a0.

247 "I always felt": Christina Radish, "Bryan Fuller Talks HANNIBAL, the Overall

Series Plan, the RED DRAGON Storyline, and More," Collider, May 13, 2013, https://collider.com/bryan-fuller-hannibal-interview.

248 "Thomas set the bar": AfterBuzz TV, *Hannibal | Interview with Martha De Laurentiis*.

249 "I've always described": ATX TV, *ATX Festival Q&A: Hannibal (2015)*, YouTube, July 18, 2015, https://www.youtube.com/watch?v=uZahQakPPAg.

249 "I would have loved": Author interview, May 1, 2025.

249 "When I sat down": Melanie Votaw, "Exclusive Interview: Hannibal Creator Bryan Fuller on Dream Sequences, David Lynch, and FBI Consultants," Reel Life with Jane, April 8, 2013, https://www.reellifewithjane.com/2013/04/exclusive-interview-hannibal-creator-bryan-fuller-on-dream-sequences-david-lynch-fbi-consultants.

250 "Everybody's fucked up": AfterBuzz TV, *Hannibal | Interview with Martha De Laurentiis*.

250 "Networks are hemorrhaging viewers": Radish, "Bryan Fuller Talks HANNIBAL."

251 "There were no actors": Hunchback Media, *Mads Mikkelsen (short documentary) 2018*, YouTube, September 13, 2018, https://www.youtube.com/watch?v=lOsv_dShDjo.

251 "I was a working-class little boy": Gia Kourlas, "His Dancing Days Were Over. Then Came 'Another Round,'" *New York Times*, January 12, 2021, https://www.nytimes.com/2021/01/12/arts/dance/mads-mikkelsen-another-round.html.

251 "Everything was just like": E. Alex Jung, "In Conversation: Mads Mikkelsen," Vulture, April 20, 2021, https://www.vulture.com/article/mads-mikkelsen-in-conversation.html.

251 "pure rock n' roll": Hunchback Media, *Mads Mikkelsen (short documentary)*.

252 "He is the other": Radish, "Bryan Fuller Talks HANNIBAL."

252 "I was like": Jung, "In Conversation: Mads Mikkelsen."

252 "I was supposed": Infamous GOATS Podcast, *MADS MIKKELSEN & HUGH DANCY | FULL C2E2 PANEL*, YouTube, May 27, 2024, https://www.youtube.com/watch?v=UesqwSUlO_I.

252 "This character is a bit": Radish, "Bryan Fuller Talks HANNIBAL."

252 "[I] would often": Infamous GOATS Podcast, *MADS MIKKELSEN & HUGH DANCY | FULL C2E2 PANEL*.

252 "They wanted someone effusive": Brian Hiatt, "Inside the Past and Possible Future of 'Hannibal,' Now on Netflix," *Rolling Stone*, October 30, 2020, https://web.archive.org/web/20220622000429/https://www.rollingstone.com/tv-movies/tv-movie-features/hannibal-season-four-netflix-bryan-fuller-interview-1022121.

252 "I remember one": Hiatt, "Inside the Past and Possible Future of 'Hannibal.'"

253 "[Graham] could see": Thomas Harris, *Red Dragon* (Dell, 1990), 10.

253 "you have to have": Radish, "Bryan Fuller Talks HANNIBAL."

253 "There was some suggestion": Infamous GOATS Podcast, *MADS MIKKELSEN & HUGH DANCY | FULL C2E2 PANEL*.

254 "a bromance": AfterBuzz TV, *Hannibal After Show Season 1 Interview with Bryan Fuller*.

254 "Is Will a Natural Born CSI": Jeff Jensen, 'Hannibal' TV Review: Mads Mikkelsen Mesmerizes," *Entertainment Weekly*, April 4, 2013, https://web.archive.org/web /20170509201521/https://ew.com/article/2013/04/04/review-hannibal.

254 "I want to be his friend": *Hannibal: Season Two*, DVD, 2014.

255 "Finely acted": Jensen, "'Hannibal' TV Review."

255 "It's a prequel": Robert Bianco, "'Hannibal' Serves Up Visceral Surprises," *USA Today*, April 3, 2013, https://www.usatoday.com/story/life/tv/2013/04/03/bianco -hannibal-review-april-4/2047241.

255 "fatally slow and pretentious": Mike Hale, "A Serial Killer Now Prepared for TV Dinners," *New York Times*, April 3, 2013, https://www.nytimes.com/2013/04/04 /arts/television/mads-mikkelsen-in-hannibal-on-nbc.html.

255 "no fun at all": Mary McNamara, "No Appetite for This 'Hannibal,'" *Los Angeles Times*, April 4, 2013.

255 "These are savvy": Author interview, May 1, 2025.

256 "It's hard for me": *Hannibal: Season Two* DVD.

256 "They wanted the show": Author interview, May 1, 2025.

257 "We are not making television": Eric Thurm, "Hannibal Showrunner: 'We Are Not Making Television. We Are Making a Pretentious Art Film from the 80s,'" *Guardian*, https://www.theguardian.com/tv-and-radio/2015/jun/03/hannibal-tv -showrunner-bryan-fuller.

258 "It's interesting to me": Ross Scarano, "Bryan Fuller Knows You're Reading into 'Hannibal's' Homoeroticism, and He Thinks It's Hilarious," Complex, September 16, 2024, https://www.complex.com/pop-culture/a/ross-scarano/bryan-fuller -hannibal-interview-slash-fiction.

259 "Every season": James Hibberd, "'Hannibal' Showrunner on His Master Plan," *Entertainment Weekly*, June 2, 2015, https://ew.com/article/2015/06/02/hanni bal-interview-bryan-fuller.

260 "We actually did": Jung, "In Conversation: Mads Mikkelsen."

260 "We never wanted": Jung, "In Conversation: Mads Mikkelsen."

260 "I always knew": Author interview, May 1, 2025.

260 "If there's ever an opportunity": Author interview, May 1, 2025.

EPILOGUE

261 "the late, great Hannibal Lecter": "Read the Transcript of Donald J. Trump's Convention Speech," *New York Times*, July 19, 2024, https://www.nytimes.com /2024/07/19/us/politics/trump-rnc-speech-transcript.html.

261 "I keep calling him": Saturday Night Live, *Summer of Trump Cold Open - SNL*, YouTube, May 18, 2024, https://www.youtube.com/watch?v=R3N6Iqp8QIk.

261 "endless tributes": "Bill Clinton Speaks at 2024 Democratic National Convention," Rev, https://www.rev.com/transcripts/bill-clinton-speaks-at-2024-demo cratic-national-convention.

261 "The great Hannibal Lecter": Michael Luciano, "Trump Reminisces About the 'Great Hannibal Lecter' as Being 'a Very Important Force,'" Mediaite, April 8, 2025,

https://www.mediaite.com/politics/trump/trump-reminisces-about-the-great
-hannibal-lecter-as-being-a-very-important-force.

262　"The late, great Hannibal Lecter.": Liam O'Dell, "Trump Finally Explains Why
He Can't Stop Talking About Hannibal Lecter," MSN, June 27, 2025, https://
www.msn.com/en-us/news/politics/trump-finally-explains-why-he-can-t-stop
-talking-about-hannibal-lecter/ar-AA1HxF6o.

262　"the best pure thriller": Nathaniel Rich, "James Ellroy, The Art of Fiction No. 201,"
Paris Review, Fall 2009, https://web.archive.org/web/20101103233405/https://
www.theparisreview.org/interviews/5948/the-art-of-fiction-no-201-james
-ellroy.

262　"What does [Lecter's] polydactyly symbolize?": Josh Jones, "David Foster Wallace's 1994 Syllabus: How to Teach Serious Literature with Lightweight Books,"
Open Culture, February 25, 2013, https://www.openculture.com/2013/02/david
_foster_wallaces_1994_syllabus.html.

262　"I still go back": Author interview, May 3, 2024.

263　"There's stuff in this movie": CRITERION, *Ben Affleck's Closet Picks*, YouTube,
April 28, 2025, https://www.youtube.com/watch?v=3TJ2BlReus0.

264　"If not for you": Author interview, April 2, 2024.

264　"Lecter is like Coca-Cola": Alexandra Alter, "Hannibal Lecter's Creator Cooks
Up Something New (No Fava Beans or Chianti)," *New York Times*, May 18, 2019,
https://www.nytimes.com/2019/05/18/books/thomas-harris-new-book.html.

265　"Everyone say Clarice!": Alter, "Hannibal Lecter's Creator."

265　"You try to reinvent yourself": Alter, "Hannibal Lecter's Creator."

265　"more of a nuisance": Alter, "Hannibal Lecter's Creator."

265　"You have to show up": Alter, "Hannibal Lecter's Creator."

266　"The Hannibal character": Alter, "Hannibal Lecter's Creator."

266　"Look around you": Alter, "Hannibal Lecter's Creator."

ABOUT THE AUTHOR

Brian Raftery's work has appeared in such publications as *The New York Times, Wired, GQ,* and *The Ringer.* He's the author of *Best. Movie. Year. Ever.: How 1999 Blew Up the Big Screen,* and the host of multiple podcasts for the Ringer, including the acclaimed *Gene & Roger.* He lives in Burbank, California, with his wife and daughters, and will never eat meat again.